A PARENT'S GUIDE TO EXPLORING FUN PLACES IN OHIO WITH CHILDREN. . .YEAR ROUND!

Kids Love Publications
7438 Sawmill Road, PMB 500
Columbus, OH 43235

Dedicated to the Families
of Ohio

For the latest updates corresponding to the pages in this book visit
our website:

www.kidslovepublications.com

Although the authors have exhaustively researched all sources to
ensure accuracy and completeness of the information contained in
this book, we assume no responsibility for errors, inaccuracies,
omissions or any other inconsistency herein. Any slights against
any entries or organizations are unintentional.

ISBN# 09663457-4-6

KIDS ♥ OHIO ™   Kids Love Publications

MISSION STATEMENT

At first glance, you may think that this is a book that just lists hundreds of places to travel. While it is true that we've invested thousands of hours of exhaustive research (*and drove nearly 3000 miles in Ohio*) to prepare this travel resource...just listing places to travel is <u>not</u> the mission statement of these projects.

As children, Michele and I were able to travel extensively throughout the United States. We consider these family times some of the greatest memories we cherish today. We, quite frankly, felt that most children had this opportunity to travel with their family as we did. However, as we became adults and started our own family, we found that this wasn't necessarily the case. We continually heard friends express several concerns when deciding how to spend "quality" and "quantity" family time. 1) What to do? 2) Where to do it? 3) How much will it cost? 4) How do I know that my kids will enjoy it?

Interestingly enough, as we compare our experiences with our families when we were kids, many of our fondest memories were not made at an expensive attraction, but rather when it was least expected.

It is our belief and mission statement that if you as a family will study and <u>use</u> the contained information <u>to create family memories</u>, these memories will grow a stronger, tighter family. Our ultimate mission statement is, that your children will develop a love and a passion for quality family experiences that they can pass to another generation of family travelers.

We thank you for purchasing this book, and we hope to see you on the road (*and hearing your travel stories!*) God bless your journeys and happy exploring!

George, Michele, Jenny and Daniel

INTRODUCTION

HOW TO USE THIS BOOK

If you are excited about discovering Ohio, this is the book for you and your family! We've spent over a thousand hours doing all the scouting, collecting and compiling (*and most often visiting!*) so that you could spend less time searching and more time having fun.

Here are a few hints to make your adventures run smoothly:

- ❑ Consider the **child's age** before deciding to take a visit.
- ❑ Know **directions** and parking. Call ahead (or visit the company's website) if you have questions *and* bring this book. Also, don't forget your camera! *(please honor rules regarding use).*
- ❑ **Estimate the duration** of the trip. Bring small surprises (favorite juice boxes) and travel books and toys.
- ❑ Call ahead for **reservations** or details, if necessary.
- ❑ Most listings are **closed major holidays** unless noted.
- ❑ Make a **family "treasure chest"**. Decorate a big box or use an old popcorn tin. Store memorabilia from a fun outing, journals, pictures, brochures and souvenirs. Once a year, look through the "treasure chest" and reminisce.
- ❑ Plan **picnics** along the way. Many Historical Society sites and state parks are scattered throughout Ohio. Allow time for a rural/scenic route to take advantage of these free picnic facilities.
- ❑ Some activities, especially tours, require **groups** of 10 or more. To participate, you may either ask to be part of another tour group or get a group together yourself (neighbors, friends, school organizations). If you arrange a group outing, most places offer discounts.

❑ For the latest updates corresponding to the pages in this book, visit our website: **www.kidslovepublications.com**.

❑ Each chapter represents an area of the state (*see map below*). Each listing is further identified by city, zip code, and place/event name. **The front index lists places by Activity Heading (i.e. Ohio History, Tours, Outdoors, Museums, etc.), the back index is alphabetical.**

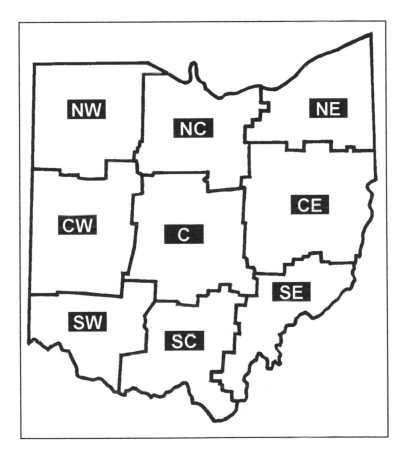

Acknowledgements

We are most thankful to be blessed with our parents, Barbara Darrall and George and Catherine Zavatsky who helped us every way they could – researching, typesetting, proofing and babysitting. More importantly, they were great sounding boards and offered loving, unconditional support.

Our own young kids, Jenny and Daniel, were delightful and fun children during all of our trips across the state.

We both sincerely thank each other – our partnership has created a great "marriage of minds" with lots of exciting moments and laughs woven throughout. Above all, we praise the Lord for His many answered prayers and special blessings throughout the completion of this project.

We think Ohio is a wonderful, friendly area of the country with more activities than you could imagine! Our sincere wish is that this book will help everyone "fall in love" with Ohio!

In a Hundred Years...

It will not matter, The size of my bank account...
The kind of house that I lived in, the kind of car
that I drove... But what will matter is...
That the world may be different
Because I was important in the life of a child.
author unknown

"Where to go?, What to do?, and How much will it cost?", are all questions that they have heard throughout the years from friends and family. These questions became the inspiration that motivated them to research, write and publish the "Kids Love" travel series.

This adventure of writing and publishing family travel books has taken them on a journey of experiences that they never could have imagined. They have appeared as guests on over 50 radio and television shows, had featured articles in statewide newspapers and magazines, spoken to thousands of people at schools and conventions, and write monthly columns in many publications talking about "family friendly" places to travel.

George Zavatsky (*formerly of Steubenville*) and Michele (Darrall) Zavatsky (*formerly of Cleveland*) were raised in Ohio and have lived in many different cities throughout the state. They currently reside in a suburb of Columbus, Ohio. They are both graduates of The Ohio State University (where they met) and have been happily married since 1987. Along with writing and publishing a series of best-selling kids' travel books, each of them also owns and operates a courier business and an internet marketing company. Besides the wonderful adventure of marriage, they place great importance on being loving parents to Jenny and Daniel.

GENERAL INFORMATION

Call the services of interest. Request to be added to their mailing lists.

- ❑ Ohio Division Of Travel & Tourism (800) BUCKEYE http://ohiotourism.com
- ❑ Welcome Centers, www.dot.state.oh.us
- ❑ **C** - Columbus Metro Parks (614) 891-0700
- ❑ **C** - Columbus Recreation & Parks (614) 645-3300
- ❑ **CE** - Canton Park District (330) 489-3015
- ❑ **CW** - Dayton/Five Rivers Metroparks (937) 275-Park
- ❑ **CW** - Greene County Parks (937) 376-7440
- ❑ **NC** - Medina County Parks (330) 722-9364
- ❑ **NC** - Port Clinton Parks & Rec (419) 732-2206
- ❑ **NC** - Sandusky County Parks (419) 334-4495
- ❑ **NE** - Ashtabula County Metroparks (800) 3-Drop-In
- ❑ **NE** - Cleveland Discount Card (800) 321-1004
- ❑ **NE** - Cleveland Metroparks (216) 351-6300
- ❑ **NE** - Lake Metroparks (800) 669-9226
- ❑ **NE** - Summit City MetroParks (330) 867-5511
- ❑ **NW** - Lima City Parks & Rec (419) 221-5195
- ❑ **NW** - Lima/Johnny Appleseed Metroparks (419) 221-1232
- ❑ **NW** - Toledo Area Metroparks (419) 535-3050
- ❑ **SW** - Butler County Metroparks (513) 867-5835
- ❑ **SW** - Cincinnati Parks Department (513) 352-4080
- ❑ **SW** - Cincinnati Recreation Department (513) 352-4001
- ❑ **SW** - Great Cincinnati Getaways (800) Cincy-USA
- ❑ **SW** - Hamilton County Park District (513) 521-Park

GREAT STATE OUTDOORS INFORMATION

- greatoutdoors.com
- National Camping Information
  www.gocampingamerica.com
- Ohio Boating (800) 446-3140
- Ohio Campground Owner's Association (614) 764-0279
- Ohio Camping (800) 376-4847
- Ohio Dept. of Natural Resources (614) 265-6565 or
  www.dnr.state.oh.us/odnr
- Ohio Resident Free Fishing Days - 1st long weekend
  (Friday - Sunday) in June.
- Ohio State Parks (614) 466-0652, http://opraonline.org
- Ohio State Parks Calendar of Events (614) 265-7000
- Rent-A -Camp State Park Programs   A unique program
  for beginning or infrequent campers to enjoy the
  experience of camping without purchasing the equipment.
  The basic cost is around $17 per night. You will arrive at
  your campsite to find a 10 x 12-foot sleeping tent already
  set up complete with a dining canopy. Inside are two cots,
  sleeping pads, cooler, propane stove, lantern, broom,
  dustpan and welcome mat! Outside, you will find a fire
  ring and picnic table. This way of camping allows you to
  pack up and go without packing up a lot of gear. The
  campsites are limited, so make you plans early and call to
  make your reservation.
- State Park Lodges & Resorts (800) 282-7275

Check out these businesses / services in your area for tour ideas:

AIRPORTS

All children love to visit the airport! Why not take a tour and understand all the jobs it takes to run an airport. Tour the terminal, baggage claim, gates and security / currency exchange. Maybe you'll even get to board a plane.

ANIMAL SHELTERS

Great for the would-be pet owner. Not only will you see many cats and dogs available for adoption, but a guide will show you the clinic and explain the needs of a pet. Be prepared to have the children "fall in love" with one of the animals while they are there!

BANKS

Take a "behind the scenes" look at automated teller machines, bank vaults and drive-thru window chutes. You may want to take this tour and then open a savings account for your child.

ELECTRIC COMPANY / POWER PLANTS

Modern science has created many ways to generate electricity today, but what really goes on with the "flip of a switch". Because coal can be dirty, wear old, comfortable clothes. Coal furnaces heat water, which produces steam, that propels turbines, that drive generators, that make electricity.

FIRE STATIONS

Many Open Houses in October, Fire Prevention Month. Take a look into the life of the firefighters servicing your area and try on their gear. See where they hang out, sleep and eat. Hop aboard a real-life fire engine truck and learn fire safety too.

HOSPITALS

Some Children's Hospitals offer pre-surgery and general tours.

NEWSPAPERS

You'll be amazed at all the new technology. See monster printers and robotics. See samples in the layout department and maybe try to put together your own page. After seeing a newspaper made, most companies give you a free copy (dated that day) as your souvenir. National Newspaper Week is in October.

RESTAURANTS

DOMINO'S PIZZA

❑ Various locations

Telephone your local shop for tour status. Free. Usually ages 4+. Takes 15 – 20 minutes. Your children can be pizza bakers! While the group is instructed on ingredients and pizza secrets, they will get to make their own special pizza. After the custom made pizza bakes, your tour guide will take it out of the special oven, box it up and you get to take it home.

PIZZA HUT
❏　Many participating restaurants

Telephone the store manager. Best days are Monday, Tuesday and Wednesday mid-afternoon. Minimum of 10 people. $3.50 per person. All children love pizza – especially when they can create their own! As the children tour the kitchen, they learn how to make a pizza, bake it, and then eat it. The admission charge includes lots of creatively make pizzas, beverage and coloring book.

MCDONALD'S RESTAURANTS
❏　Participating locations

Telephone the store manager. They prefer Monday or Tuesday. Free. What child doesn't love McDonald's food? This is your child's chance to go behind the counter and look at the machines that make all the fun food. You will be shown the freezer and it's alarm, the fryer and hamburger flipping on the grills. There is a free snack at the end of the tour.

SUPERMARKETS
Kids are fascinated to go behind the scenes of the same store where Mom and Dad shop. Usually you will see them grind meat, walk into large freezer rooms, watch cakes and bread bake and receive free samples along the way. Maybe you'll even get to pet a live lobster!

TV / RADIO STATIONS
Studios, newsrooms, Fox kids clubs. Why do weathermen never wear blue clothes on TV? What makes a "DJ's" voice sound so deep and smooth?

WATER TREATMENT PLANTS

A giant science experiment! You can watch seven stages of water treatment. The favorite is usually the wall of bright buttons flashing as workers monitor the different processes.

U.S. MAIN POST OFFICES

Did you know Ben Franklin was the first Postmaster General (over 200 years ago)? Most interesting is the high-speed automated mail processing equipment. Learn how to address envelopes so they will be sent quicker (there are secrets). To make your tour more interesting, have your children write a letter to themselves and address it with colorful markers. Mail it earlier that day and they will stay interested trying to locate their letter in all the high-speed machinery.

COURT WATCHING

Call for an agenda of trials (docket info.) for the following: Common Pleas, Small Claims, Municipal, Domestic/Juvenile. See the Government Section or Community Services of your local White Pages. Did you know as citizens we have the right to enter a courtroom to observe *(except in special cases when a "Do Not Disturb" sign warns otherwise)*. Watching trials in session can be wonderful exposure to our legal system, especially for children who have studied law and government. Be sure your children have self-control before planning your visit.

CITY INDEX (Listed by City & Area)

CITY INDEX (Listed by City & Area)

Index by Activity (Area, City, Place/Event Name, Page)

Index by Activity (Area, City, Place/Event Name, Page)

Index by Activity (Area, City, Place/Event Name, Page)

Index by Activity (Area, City, Place/Event Name, Page)

Index by Activity (Area, City, Place/Event Name, Page)

Index by Activity (Area, City, Place/Event Name, Page)

Index by Activity (Area, City, Place/Event Name, Page)

TOURS (cont.)

Table of Contents

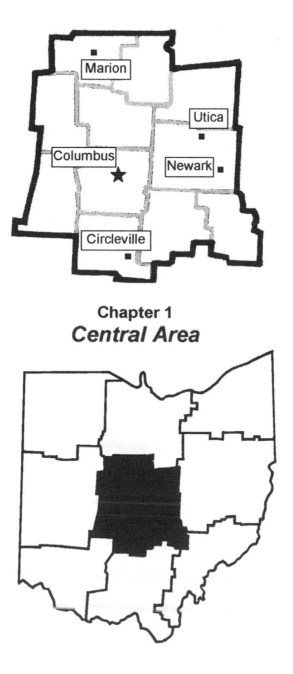

Chapter 1
Central Area

Our Favorites...

- American Whistle Corporation
- Columbus Zoo
- COSI
- Newark Earthworks
- The Ohio State University Campus
- Ohio Village
- Popcorn & Wyandot Museum
- Velvet Ice Cream – Ye Old Mill

Blow the loudest whistle in the world!
AMERICAN WHISTLE CO.

HOMESTEAD PARK

Amlin - 4675 Cosgray Road (I-270 to SR-33 to Plain City exit), 43002. *Activity:* Outdoors. *Hours:* Dawn to Dusk. Free admission. Homestead Park is a fabulous adventure for everyone. The country setting, pond, trails, shelter houses, picnic area and grill provide a great place for an all day picnic. The special feature for the children is the elaborate playground with everything from a sandpit to concrete tunnels, swings and bridges, towers and cranes. Separate from this play area is "Fort Washington", a fully equipped fort featuring seasonal wet activities. The attached squirt guns have a continuous supply of water!

SLATE RUN HISTORICAL FARM

9130 Marcy Road (in Slate Run Park on SR-674), **Ashville** 43103

- ❑ Activity: Ohio History
- ❑ Telephone: (614) 508-8000 or (614) 833-1880
- ❑ Hours: Tuesday, Wednesday, Thursday, 9:00 am – 4:00 pm, Friday and Saturday 9:00 am – 6:00 pm, Sunday 11:00 am – 6:00 pm (June – August) Wednesday – Saturday, 9.00 am – 4:00 pm, Sunday 11:00 am – 4:00 pm (September – May) Daily, Noon – 6:00 pm (Memorial and Labor Day)
- ❑ Admission: Free
- ❑ Tours: Available by appointment (special prices)

This historic farm depicts life on a working family farm of the 1880's. Visitors may join in with the barnyard and household chores. All the work is done using equipment and methods of the time (some horse-powered machinery). Some of the specially scheduled programs have been: maple syrup demonstrations and production, toy making, fishing, ice cream socials, making root beer, rope making and pretend old-fashioned school. Kids love getting involved and doing chores at Slate Run. They offer nature trails, picnic grounds, and children's play facilities at the adjoining Slate Run Metro Park.

FLINT RIDGE STATE MEMORIAL MUSEUM

7091 Brownsville Road SE (3 miles North of US-40 and SR-68)
Brownsville 43739

❑ Activity: Ohio History

❑ Telephone: (740) 787-2476, **www.ohiohistory.org/places**

❑ Hours: Wednesday - Saturday, 9:30 am - 5:00 pm. Sunday, Noon - 5:00 pm (Memorial Day - Labor Day) Weekends Only, (September and October)

❑ Admission: $3.00 Adult, $1.25 Youth (6-12)

❑ Miscellaneous: Flint Preserve open April - October, 9:30 am to Dusk for further exploration.

Indians came to see this stretch of hills for flint stone (our official gem of the State of Ohio) to use for tools and weapons. Displays show how flint is formed from silica and what objects can be made today with flint (like sparks that start flames when flint is rubbed against steel). How else can we use flint?

BARBER'S MUSEUM AND HALL OF FAME

Canal Winchester - 2 ½ South High Street, 43110. *Activity:* Museums. (614) 833-9931. The museum is open by appointment only. Free admission. See a collection of shaving mugs and old barber chairs, some over 150 years old. Reflections of other trades related to barbering (surgery, dentistry, and medicine) are also displayed because early barbers dabbled in many of these areas. You will see 6 rooms set up depicting different eras of barbering.

MID-OHIO HISTORICAL DOLL AND TOY MUSEUM

Canal Winchester - 700 Winchester Pike (off US-33 at Gender Road), 43110. *Activity:* Museums. (614) 837-5573. *Hours:* Wednesday - Saturday, 11:00 am - 5:00 pm. (Spring - mid December). *Admission:* $2.00 (6 and under FREE). *Miscellaneous:* Gift Shop, Old and New Collectibles. As you step in the door, you will see a train display in the lobby. To your left, you will go through a door into the magical world of dolls. The collection includes rare antique dolls and toys dating from the 1700's to contemporary. Barbie fans of all ages will love the extensive Barbie collection.

A.W. MARION STATE PARK

Circleville - (5 miles East of Circleville of US-22), 43113. Activity: Outdoors. 454 acres of camping, hiking trails, boating and rentals, fishing, and winter sports. (740) 869-3124. **www.dnr.state.oh.us/odnr/parks/directory/awmarin.htm**.

PICKAWAY COUNTY HISTORICAL SOCIETY – CLARKE MAY MUSEUM

Circleville - 162 West Union Street, 43113. *Activity:* Ohio History (740) 474-1495. Hours: Tuesday – Friday, 1:00 – 4:00 pm (April – October). Ohio bird's eggs and nests, Indian artifacts, and early dental office.

OHIO STATE UNIVERSITY ENTOMOLOGY DEPARTMENT

1735 Neil Avenue (SR-315 to King Avenue - North on Neil Avenue), **Columbus** 43201

❑ Activity: Animals & Farms
❑ Telephone: (614) 292-9634
   http://iris.biosci.ohio-state.edu/osuent/
❑ Admission. Free
❑ Tours: Appointment Necessary (Be sure to ask about parking arrangements – street parking may not be available). 15 or more persons, 4th grade and up. (Weekdays)

This is a great introduction to science. Learn how and why "bugs" are important to us. Even the mothers in our group found this tour interesting. Your group will see and maybe touch many interesting live insects. You can combine the tour with the Botany Department Tour.

OHIO STATEHOUSE

Broad and High Streets (10-acre square in downtown)
Columbus 43201

- ❑ Activity: Ohio History
- ❑ Telephone: (614) 728-2695 or (888) OHIO-123
  www.statehouse.state.oh.us/welcome
- ❑ Admission: Free
- ❑ Tours: Monday - Friday, 9:30 am - 3:30 pm, every 30 minutes. Saturday and Sunday 11:15am, 12:30pm, 2:00 & 3:00pm. (45 minutes long). Begins at 3rd Street entrance.

Visit the place where Abraham Lincoln made speeches in 1859 and 1861. The Statehouse is a Greek Revival building with Doric columns. Inside you'll see the rotunda with the state seal and historic paintings and documents. Why was the skylight hidden for years? If the Ohio House or Senate is in session, you'll be able to listen to the debates. Outside is home to several war memorials and statues including the new Veterans Plaza where visitors read the letters sent home from enlisted men and women. Educational displays and touch-screen kiosks (ex. Pass through all 88 counties in the Map Room). Did you know inmates from the former state penitentiary (that was located near downtown Columbus) built it?

DAVIS DISCOVERY CENTER

Columbus - Franklin Park, 1755 E. Broad Street, 43203. *Activity: The Arts.* (614) 645-SHOW (7469). The Children's Drama Company for 9 to 12-year-olds and the Park Playhouse Teen Community Theater stage productions are held at the center. At the Davis Youth Complex, classes for children ages 6 through 12 include magic, piano, ballet, acting, puppetry and more. The Davis Dance Ensemble is open to all 9 to 18-year-olds by audition. Children who are home-schooled may take advantage of theater and dance classes offered in the daytime at both locations.

FRANKLIN PARK CONSERVATORY AND BOTANICAL GARDENS

1777 East Broad Street (off I-71), **Columbus** 43203

❑ Activity: Outdoors
❑ Telephone: (614) 645-TREE, **www.fpconservatory.org**
❑ Hours: Tuesday – Sunday, 10:00 am - 5:00 pm. Monday, Wednesday & Holidays, 5:00 - 8:00 pm
❑ Admission: $5.00 Adults, $3.50 Seniors/Students, $2.00 Children (2-12).

A place where you can learn where coffee comes from or watch the careful pruning of Bonsai trees. The large 1895 glass structure resembles the style of London's Crystal Palace. Walk through a simulated tropical rain forest, a desert, a tree fern forest, a Pacific Island water garden and then on to the Himalayan Mountains. Outside is a sculpture garden.

ENGINE HOUSE NO. 5

Columbus - 121 Thurman Avenue, 43206. *Activity:* Theme Restaurants. **www.enginehouse5.savvydiner.com**.(614) 443-4877. A real 100 year old firehouse converted into a fine dining restaurant (their specialty is seafood). When celebrating birthdays, the server slides down a shiny brass fire pole complete with cake and a lit sparkler.

COLUMBUS MOTOR SPEEDWAY

Columbus - 1845 Williams Road, 43207. *Activity:* Sports. (614) 491-1047. **www.columbusspeedway.com**. Stock car racing. Kids Day (late August or September). Climb into a real race car! 7:00 pm race starts Saturdays.

GALLERY PLAYERS

Columbus - 1125 College Avenue, 43209. *Activity:* The Arts. (614) 231-2731. **www.theatreroundtable.org/gallery.html**. Oldest and largest community theatre company in Columbus performs at the Leo Yassenoff Jewish Center. Youth Theatre. (November-July)

BUCKEYE HALL OF FAME CAFÉ

Columbus - 1421 Olentangy River Road, 43210. *Activity:* Theme Restaurants. (614) 291-2233. Fun casual dining. While waiting for your food order, walk down the hallway named the Ohio State Walk of Fame (memorabilia displayed from all sports at Ohio State University including Archie Griffin's 1975 Heismann Trophy) on your way to the Arena gameroom. Floor tiles throughout the restaurant are inscribed with the names of famous Ohio State University greats.

THE OHIO STATE UNIVERSITY BUCKEYES

Columbus - Ohio State Campus facilities, 43210. *Activity:* Sports. Ticket Office: (614) 292-2624. Sports Information: (614) 292-6861. **www.ohiostatebuckeyes.com**. Big 10 College Sports. Football, Ohio Stadium. Basketball (Men's & Women's), Hockey, OSU Ice Rink, Golf & Swimming, Tennis, Volleyball – Larkins Hall.

THE OHIO STATE UNIVERSITY MAIN CAMPUS

Columbus - 1871 North High Street (Mershon Auditorium), 43210. *Activity:* Tours. (614) 292-8027. **www-afa.adm.ohio-state.edu/visitorpage10.html**. Geological Museum (dinosaur skeletons, meteorites, fossils, rocks) Orton Hall Bell Tower, Ohio Stadium - GO BUCKS!, Sports Center, Main Library, and the Oval (kids run and play). Ohio buckeye (nut) and Ohio State University souvenirs. Minimum 10 people. Reservations a must, weeks in advance.

WEXNER CENTER FOR THE ARTS

Columbus - North High Street & 15th Avenue, 43210. *Activity:* The Arts. (614) 292-3535. **www.wexarts.org**. Features contemporary visual, performance and media arts in unique building and layout. Parental guidance suggested.

COLUMBUS CREW

Columbus - Crew Stadium (near Ohio State Fairgrounds), 43211. *Activity:* Sports. (614) 221-CREW. **www.thecrew.com**. Major League Soccer (Mid April – Late September).

OHIO HISTORICAL CENTER

1982 Velma Avenue (I-71 to 17ᵗʰ Avenue Exit), **Columbus** 43211

- ❑ Activity: Ohio History
- ❑ Telephone: (614) 297-2300 or (800) 646-5184
  www.ohiohistory.org/places/ohc
- ❑ Hours: Monday - Saturday, 9:00 am - 5:00 pm. Sunday and Holidays, 10:00 am - 5:00 pm
- ❑ Admission: Adult $5.00, $1.25 Children (6-12). Includes Ohio Village. ** Half Price on Monday and Tuesday ** (Center only)
- ❑ Miscellaneous: Gift Shop, food and picnic tables

This is a museum and a whole lot more. There are exhibits and artifacts covering the history of Ohio from archaeology to natural history and the history of Ohio. There are many historical collections from early fossils and Indian tribes, original accounts from early explorers, and papers from political leaders such as General Meigs and Thomas Worthington. The building is recognized as an architectural landmark. "The Nature of Ohio" exhibit is guarded by a huge mastodon found in a swamp in Clark County. See the quirky 2-headed calf and Egyptian mummy.

OHIO STATE HIGHWAY PATROL TRAINING FACILITY

740 East 17ᵗʰ Avenue (West of I-71 and 17ᵗʰ Avenue Exit)
Columbus 43211

- ❑ Activity: Tours
- ❑ Telephone: (614) 466-4896
- ❑ Admission: Free
- ❑ Tours: Tuesday and Wednesday, 10:00 am or 2:00 pm (Approx. 45 minutes). Minimum 15 people, Maximum 40 people

A State Trooper guide will escort you through the life of a highway patrol trainee. Your children learn the history of the patrol and how Ohio has developed its programs. You will probably bump into a few trainees as you pass through the weight room, swimming pool and gymnasium. Most favorite stop on the tour is the practice firing range. Gun safety and legal use will be discussed.

OHIO VILLAGE

1982 Velma Avenue (I-71 and 17th Avenue Exit), **Columbus** 43211

- ❑   Activity: Ohio History
- ❑   Telephone: (614) 297-2300
     www.ohiohistory.org/places/ohvillag
- ❑   Hours: Wednesday - Saturday 9:00 am - 5:00 pm, Sunday, 10:00 am - 5:00 pm (April - Early December). Extended December hours. Weekends only (January - March).
- ❑   Admission: Adult $5.00, $4.00 Senior (62+), $1.25 Children (6-12) Includes Historical Center. ** Half Price on Monday and Tuesday **

S ee an 1800's village that is a must for all ages. Authentic with unpaved and dusty roads. Be sure to get some postcards stamped with the official Ohio Village postmark at the village post office. Your children will see how doctors, blacksmiths, printers and many others practiced their trades in the America of the 1860's. Baseball fans can catch the Ohio Village Muffins in a real game played according to 19th Century rules. The Ohio Village has a general store offering hand-crafted goods and 1860's reproduction items. Colonel Crawford Inn serves an assortment of tempting traditional dishes. The Ohio Historical Center is next door, so plan your day for both of these.

OHIO VILLAGE MUFFINS

Columbus – 43211. Activity: Sports. 614-297-2606. **www. ohiohistory.org/places/ohvillag/muffins.html**. 19th Century Style baseball team. Authentic uniforms and rules. Commentator assists visitors to understand the "old-fashioned" ball game. (Summer)

BIG BEAR WAREHOUSE

Columbus - 770 West Goodale Blvd (SR-315 to Goodale Exit), 43212. *Activity:* Tours. (614) 464-6750. Free admission. *Tours:* Tuesday or Wednesday (Appointment Necessary). 10:00 am. (1 hour long). 35 people maximum. 3rd grade and up. Tours include both the grocery and refrigerated areas. Some highlights for children include going into the large freezer, watching the fork lifts, seeing the train cars come in and out of the railroad room, and walking through the banana ripening room. Wear comfortable shoes.

KAHIKI RESTAURANT

Columbus - 3583 East Broad Street, 43213. *Activity:* Theme Restaurants. (614) 237-5425. Inside or out it's Polynesian with lots of tropical plants and fish. Order fun juice drinks with umbrellas as you look over their extensive children's menu. **www.kahiki.com**.

BALLETMET

Columbus - 322 Mt. Vernon Avenue, 43215. *Activity:* The Arts. (614) 229-4860. **www.balletmet.org**. Classic to contemporary ballet. Kids Culture Corps - spend time with dancers.

COLUMBUS ASSOCIATION FOR THE PERFORMING ARTS

Columbus - 55 East State Street, 43215. *Activity:* The Arts. (614) 469-0939. **www.capa.com**. CAPA operates theatres and presents touring arts and entertainment including children's concerts.

COLUMBUS BLUE JACKETS HOCKEY

Columbus - (Nationwide Arena), 43215. *Activity:* Sports. (614) 677-9000 or (800) NHL-COLS. New NHL team begins play with the 2000/1 season.

COLUMBUS CHILDREN'S THEATRE

Columbus - 504 North Park Street, 43215. *Activity:* The Arts. (614) 224-6672, Theatre activities for youth of all ages, backgrounds or cultures. **http://colschildrenstheatre.org**.

COLUMBUS CITY HALL

Columbus - 90 West Broad Street (Corner of Broad and Front Streets), 43215. *Activity:* Ohio History. (614) 645-6404. **http://ci.columbus.oh.us**. Free admission. *Tours:* Weekdays, Allow 1 hour for the tour. 30 people or less. (Appointment necessary). The tour begins with a walk through the Columbus Hall of Fame. The Hall contains pictures of outstanding Columbus natives such as James Thurber, former Miss Americas, OSU Coach Woody Hayes, OSU Heismann Trophy Winner Archie Griffin, and professional golfing legend, Jack Nicklaus. Next, the group goes inside City Council chambers where City Council meetings are held every Monday night. After that, you will visit the Mayor's office and conference room. If the Mayor is in and not too busy, he will probably peek out to say "hello". Lastly, the tour walks outside to see the bronze statue of Christopher Columbus. This statue was a gift given many years ago to the city from Genoa, Italy. Did you know that there was a secret box hidden inside the statue but it was not discovered until 1988. Guess what was inside the box?

COLUMBUS CULTURAL ARTS CENTER

Columbus - 139 West Main Street, 43215. *Activity:* The Arts. (614) 645-7047. **www.columbusrecparks.com/arts**. Family oriented workshops, demonstrations, performances, and exhibits.

COLUMBUS MUSEUM OF ART

Columbus - 480 East Broad Street, 43215. *Activity:* The Arts. (614) 221-4848. **www.columbusart.mus.oh.us**. American and European art from 1850-1950. See the life-size horse of welded steel or the works of Columbus realist George Bellows and folk artist Elijah Pierce. Saturday parent/child workshops. Café and gift shop.

COLUMBUS SYMPHONY ORCHESTRA

Columbus - 55 East State Street, 43215. *Activity:* The Arts. (614) 228-8600. **www.columbussymphony.org**. Lollypop Concerts on

Saturday mornings. Youth Orchestra. Popcorn Pops are outdoor theme concerts with games, crafts and food.

COSI

333 West Broad Street (Downtown on the river) **Columbus** 43215

❑ Activity: Museums
❑ Telephone: (614) 228-COSI or (888) 228-2674, **www.cosi.org**
❑ Hours: Sunday – Thursday, 10:00 am – 5:00 pm. Friday – Saturday, 10:00 am – 9:00 pm.
❑ Admission: $12.00 Adult, $10.00 Seniors (60+), $7.00 Children (2-12)
❑ Miscellaneous: Science 2 Go Store, Atomic Café

Children and adults of every age love COSI. The new structure is divided into learning worlds. The idea of a learning world is to make visitors feel like they are someplace else. Explore of hands-on exhibits focusing on science, technology, health and history. Take your preschool -aged children to Kid-Space. They will pet live animals (mice, chickens, turtles), paint their faces, do a puppet show, water play, ride in a boat, and just have a good active time there. Other favorite areas are Mad Science Park or older kids conquer their fears and ride the high wire cycle. Ocean Learning World features a simulated shipwreck with dive tanks. Adventure World takes you on an archeological dig and the area is full of climbing and balancing areas (tilted room). Other areas such as the I/o experience are more geared towards teens and adults who are video and computer game buffs. The simulator region is worth noting too. It has social-oriented game simulators that are not featured elsewhere in the country.

DODGE SKATE PARK

Columbus - 667 Sullivant Avenue, 43215. *Activity:* Sports. (614) 645-8151. *Hours:* Saturday and Sunday, 10:00 am – 8:00 pm. Weekdays hours vary – call for schedule (April – November). Outdoor park only. *Admission:* $10.00 membership (Columbus Parks/Rec.), $5.00 Day Pass. Dodge Skateboard Park is unique. This particular design is the only one east of the Mississippi River.

There are in-ground bowls at 3, 4, and 6 feet deep. Skateboarders must wear helmet, and suggested elbow and kneepads, wrist guards. Some equipment is available for rent. No in-line skating.

GLASS AXIS

Columbus - 280 Cozzins Street, 43215. *Activity:* The Arts. (614) 228-4011. **http://cave.net/glass-axis/**. Visit a working glass-blowing studio. Tour lasts about 1 hour. Nominal admission fee. (September –June)

GRANDPARENTS LIVING THEATRE

Columbus - 51 Jefferson Avenue, 43215. *Activity:* The Arts. (614) 228-7458. **www.glt-theatre.org**. Older actors perform theatre that is sensitive to issues of aging and speaks to audiences of all ages with a lasting impact.

KING ARTS COMPLEX

Columbus - 867 Mount Vernon Avenue, 43215. *Activity:* The Arts. (614) 252-5464. Storytelling Festival. Activities to increase awareness of African American artists, develop talents and preserve culture.

MUSIC IN THE AIR

Columbus - 549 Franklin Avenue, 43215. *Activity:* The Arts. (614) 645-7995. **www.columbusrecparks.com**. Free outdoor concerts and festivals of music, dance, poetry, theatre and Magical Musical Mornings children's programs. (May – September)

OPERA COLUMBUS

Columbus - 177 Naghten Street, 43215. *Activity:* The Arts. (614) 461-0022. **www.operacols.org**. Professional opera company produces three works each year with major guest artists in November, February and April. Dress Rehearsals the Tuesday before opening night are open for students to observe.

SANTA MARIA

Battelle Park Scioto River (Downtown – Northeast of Broad Street Bridge), **Columbus** 43215

❑   Activity: Ohio History

❑   Telephone: (614) 645-8760, **www.santamaria.org**

❑   Hours: Wednesday-Friday, 10:00 am – 3:00 pm (April – October). Weekends Noon - 5:00 pm. Early evenings in Summer

❑   Admission: $3.00 Adult, $2.50 Senior (60+), $1.50 Student (5-17)

The Columbus Santa Maria is the world's most authentic, museum quality representation of Christopher Columbus' flagship. Climb aboard and return to 1492 as costumed guides share facts about the ship and the famous voyage. Feel the challenges and hardships faced by Columbus and his crew. You better be on your best behavior or you'll have to "walk the gang plank"! Sleeping quarters available for campouts.

THURBER HOUSE

Columbus - 77 Jefferson Avenue (Downtown), 43215. *Activity:* Museums. (614) 464-1032. **www.thurberhouse.org**. *Hours:* Daily, Noon – 4:00 pm. *Admission:* $2.00 Adult , $1.50 Children (12+). *Tours:* Guided tours Sundays, 2:00 pm or by appointment. *Group Tours:* 8 – 18 (or larger), Appointment only. James Thurber, the well-known humorist and cartoonist, grew up in Columbus. The restored home is where James lived during his college years The house is featured in several of Thurber's stories. Be sure to read some of Thurber's works before you visit or purchase some of his books at the bookstore in Thurber House.

TOPIARY GARDEN

Columbus - 408 East Town Street (Deaf School Park), 43215. *Activity:* Outdoors. (614) 645-3300. The topiary (greenery shaped like people, boats, animals, etc.) garden depicts the theme "A Sunday Afternoon on the Island of La Grande Jatte". Free.

94TH AERO SQUADRON

Columbus - 5030 Sawyer Road (Port Columbus Airport), 43219. *Activity:* Theme Restaurants. (614) 237-8887. WWI French Countryside Inn décor with a view of the planes taking off and landing.

OHIO HISTORY OF FLIGHT MUSEUM

4275 Sawyer Road (at Port Columbus Airport), **Columbus** 43219

- ❑ Activity: Museums
- ❑ Telephone: (614) 231-1300, **www.ohioflight.org**
- ❑ Hours: Monday – Friday, 10:00 am – 4:00 pm. Weekends, (By Appointment)
- ❑ Admission: $3.00 Adult, $2.00 Children (5-15)
- ❑ Tours: Call for appointment

There's much to see and it is a great way to teach children the flight history of Ohio. The museum features a Curtiss Model D built on 1911-1912 in Wilbur Curtiss' attic, a 1927 WACO 9 and Foster Lane's first airplane. There's much to learn about Ohio's inventor pilots and aircraft. Most children spend a lot of time looking over the prototype of a rubber-like inflat-a-plane, sitting in a flight simulator, pushing buttons on a working model of an old airplane engine, or playing on the space shuttle and rocket outside. Before you leave, ask a guide for a look at one of their flight videos. We saw "The Thunderbirds".

POPCORN OUTLET

1500 Bethel Road (SR-315 to Bethel Road exit west), **Columbus** 43220

- ❑ Activity: Tours
- ❑ Telephone: (614) 451-7677 or (800) 396-7010 **www.falcon.nu/popcorn/tours.htm**.
- ❑ Tours: By appointment (approximately 20-30 minutes) No minimum or maximum number of people

W hat a treat to meet Al, The Popcorn Man! This wonderfully enthusiastic owner will answer every question you've ever had about popcorn. Kids love watching the video tour of the large poppers and closely watch the popped corn flow out. They have a tremendous assortment of spicy and sweet flavors to coat the popcorn. We tasted bubble gum when we were there! You won't leave without trying your favorite flavors. Kids and parents will want to bring their allowance to spend on these treats!

SHRUM MOUND

Columbus - Campbell Park, McKinley Avenue, 43222. *Activity:* Ohio History. **www.ohiohistory.org/places/shrum**. (614) 297-2630. Conical Adena Indian burial mound - 20 feet high and 100 feet in diameter. Grass covered, it has steps leading to the summit. Open daylight hours.

COLUMBUS CLIPPERS

Columbus - Cooper Stadium, 43223. *Activity:* Sports. (614) 462-5250. **www.clippersbaseball.com** Semi-professional farm team for the New York Yankees. Kids Club and Mascot "Captain Clipper". (April – Labor Day)

ANTHONY THOMAS CANDY COMPANY

1777 Arlingate Lane (I-270 to Roberts Road Exit)
Columbus 43228

- ❑   Activity: Tours
- ❑   Telephone: (614) 272-9221
    http://www.anthony-thomas.com/tour/index.html
- ❑   Hours: Weekdays, 8:30 am – 3:30 pm
- ❑   Admission: Free
- ❑   Tours: Reservations Required. Minimum 10 people, 60 minutes. Free sample at end of tour.
- ❑   Miscellanous: Factory Candy Shop

H ave you seen "Willy Wonka's Chocolate Factory?" This tour will remind you of that movie, especially when you first see the clean bright white equipment, near spotless flours and dozens of silver insulated pipes running to several production lines. Walk along a glass enclosed mezzanine as you view chocolate and fillings being prepared and molded in rooms remaining at a constant 90 degrees F. with 0% humidity (so workers and chocolate don't sweat!) A couple of wrapping machines are exclusively for fundraisers and airline chocolates, but most of the production line packers can be seen hand packing chocolates for stores. All employees are taste testers – they can pop a morsel anytime to be sure it meets high standards – What a job!

AMERICAN WHISTLE CORPORATION

6540 Huntley Road (I-71 to Route 161 west), **Columbus** 43229

- ☐ Activity: Tours
- ☐ Telephone: (614) 846-2918, **www.americanwhistle.com**
- ☐ Admission: $3.00 per person
- ☐ Tours: Monday-Friday 10:00am-4:00pm (March-September). One hour long, 15-40 people, appointment necessary.
- ☐ Miscellaneous: Gift shop where you'll want to buy a lanyard to go with your new whistle or the World's only 24K gold plated whistle!

Do you know what a lanyard is? Do you know what makes a whistle louder? See and hear the only small metal whistle manufactured in the United States (used by police, referees, coaches, etc.) You'll learn everything you ever wanted to know about whistles and really get to see a small manufacturing operation up close. These people know how to give great tours! Each person gets to take home a whistle they just watched being made!

COLUMBUS POLO CLUB

Columbus (Gahanna) – 43230. *Activity:* Sports. (740) 927-5919 or (614) 855-4288. Oldest team sport in the world. Divot Stomps-half-time stroll by guests on the field to "toe" divots (patches of grass) back into place. Games are played at Headley Park in Gahanna. Headley Park is located off Clark State Road, just south of Morse Road. (Weekends Late May – September)

MOTORCYCLE HERITAGE MUSEUM

Columbus (Pickerington), 13515 Yarmouth Drive (I-70 east exit SR256), 43147. *Activity:* Museums. (614) 856-1900, **www.ama-cycle.org**. *Hours:* Monday - Friday, 9:00 am - 5:00 pm. Weekends 9:00 am - 5:00 pm (March-October). *Admission:* $3.00 Adult, $2.00 Senior (65+). A self-guided tour featuring a wall mural, the history of motorcycles, and the Glory Days.   Kids are most attracted to the 50 motorcycles on display.

COLUMBUS ZOO
9990 Riverside Drive (Route 257, I-270 to Sawmill Road Exit)
Columbus (Powell) 43065

❑   Activity: Animals & Farms

❑   Telephone: (614) 645-3550, **www.colszoo.org**

❑   Hours: Daily, 9:00 am – 6:00 pm (Summer) 9:00 am – 5:00 pm (September – May) 9:00 am – 8:00 pm (Wednesday Family Night)

❑   Admission: $7.00 Adult, $6.00 Seniors, $4.00 Children (2-11). Family Membership available. Parking fee

❑   Miscellaneous: Gift Shops and Concessions. Open 365 days a year

The famous Director Emeritus of the zoo, Jack Hanna, is a regular on "Late Night With David Letterman" and "Good Morning America". Highlights of the zoo include cheetahs, polar bears, lowland gorillas, children's petting zoo (a big hit!), North American Bald Eagles (named George and Barbara) and the Pet-A-Shark exhibit. A 100,000-gallon coral reef exhibit and one of the largest reptile collections in the United States are also featured. New in 1999, is a habitat "Manitee Coast" modeled after famous Island Refuge in Florida. A 190,000 gallon pool with floor to ceiling glass viewing walls!

WYANDOT LAKE ADVENTURE PARK

10101 Riverside Drive (I-270 to Sawmill Road Exit)
Columbus, (Powell) 43065

- ❑ Activity: Amusements
- ❑ Telephone: (614) 889-9283 or (800) 328-9283
  www.sixflags.com/wyandotpark
- ❑ Hours: Daily, 10:00 am - 8:00 pm or 9:00 pm.
  (mid-May – Labor Day)
- ❑ Admission: $16.00 - 20.00. Under Age 3 FREE. Seniors (61+)
  $12.50. After 4:00 pm, $12.50. Season Pass and Combo Packs
  with Columbus Zoo available.
- ❑ Miscellaneous: Concessions, Kiddie rides, and Gift Shops

This is great fun for a summer day. Wyandot offers a huge wave pool, numerous thrilling water slides and a Tadpool water fun area for the little ones. Then, put on your shoes and get on the roller coaster or one of the amusement rides available. All this for one admission charge. Life vests and rafts are available, free, first come.

> <u>CHRISTOPHER ISLAND</u> – Tree house, lagoons, abandoned ships, heated water guns and sprayers, jet steams, and dark speed tunnels.

HANBY HOUSE

Columbus, (Westerville) - 160 West Main Street, (across from Otterbein College), 43081. *Activity:* Ohio History. (614) 882-4291 or (614) 891-6289. **www.ohiohistory.org/places/hanby**. *Tours and Hours:* Saturday 10:00 am - 4:00 pm, Sunday, 1:00 - 5:00 pm. (May – October). Benjamin Hanby was the composer of over 80 folk songs and hymns including "Sweet Nelly Gray" and "Up On the Rooftop". Children will enjoy seeing Ben's original instruments and musical scores. This home was part of the Underground Railroad. Be sure to notice and ask about the roses in a vase by the front window. The tour also includes viewing a short introduction movie. Small admission.

IMAX THEATRE COLUMBUS

Columbus (Worthington) - Crossroads Center (I-270 exit SR-23 north), 43085. *Activity:* Amusements. (614) 840-9800. Enjoy larger-than-life scenes projected on a screen nearly 6 stories tall and 76 feet wide. It also boasts a 12,000 watt sound system and the "feeling" of movement.

OHIO RAILWAY MUSEUM

Columbus, (Worthington) - 990 Proprietors Road (off SR-161), 43085. *Activity:* Museums. **www.trainweb.org/orm**. (614) 885-7345. *Hours:* Sunday, 1:00 – 5:00 pm (mid-May to mid-October). *Admission:* $3.00 Adults, $2.00 Seniors, $1.00 Children (under 12). They have displayed approximately 30 pieces of Ohio Railway History dating from 1897 – 1950. The guide explains that steam engines have their own personality. Get close to one under steam and hear it talk!

ORANGE JOHNSON HOUSE

Columbus, (Worthington) - 956 North High Street, (just north of SR-161), 43085. *Activity:* Ohio History. **www.worthington.org**. 614) 885-1247. *Hours:* (Open House) Sunday, 2:00 - 5:00 pm (mid-February to mid-December). *Admission:* Small donation. The Orange Johnson House is a restored early 1800's home. There are many authentic objects and toys that children can pick up and pretend to use. The guide will describe chores children were given in those days (your own children will think they have it made!). A good time to visit is when they have cooking demonstrations.

ALUM CREEK STATE PARK

Delaware - 3615 South Old State Road (7 miles SE of Delaware off SR-36/37, 1 mile West of I-71), 43015. *Activity:* Outdoors. **www.dnr.state.oh.us/odnr/parks/directory/alum.htm**.(740) 548-4631, 8,600 acres that offers a sandy beach with life-guarded swimming and food service available. Camping, hiking trails, lots of great boating and rentals, fishing and winter sports.

CENTRAL OHIO SYMPHONY ORCHESTRA

Delaware - Ohio Wesleyan University Campus, 43015. *Activity:*
The Arts. (740) 368-3724. Series of concerts with guest artists.
(October - April)

DELAWARE COUNTY HISTORICAL MUSEUM

Delaware - 157 East William Street, 43015. *Activity:* Ohio
History. (740) 369-3831. *Hours:* Wednesday and Sunday, 2:00 –
4:30 pm (mid-March to mid-November). Famous people. "Little
Brown Jug" history.

DELAWARE STATE PARK

Delaware - (6 miles North of Delaware on US-23), 43015.
Activity: Outdoors.(740) 369-2761. 3,145 acres of camping, hiking
trails, boating and rentals, fishing, swimming, and winter sports.
www.dnr.state.oh.us/odnr/parks/directory/delaware.htm.

HAMBURGER INN

Delaware - 16 North Sandusky Street, 43015. *Activity:* Theme
Restaurants. (740) 369-3850. Chrome stools and soda fountains
remain as they were in the 1950's. Great place for a burger and shake.

OLENTANGY INDIAN CAVERNS

1779 Home Road (US-23 North to Home Road (west), follow signs,
6 miles north of I-270), **Delaware** 43015

❑   Activity: Outdoors
❑   Telephone (740) 548-7917, **www.olentangyindiancaverns.com**
❑   Hours: Daily, 9:30 am - 5:00 pm. (April - October)
❑   Admission: $8.00 Adult, $7.20 Senior, $4.00 Children (7-12)
❑   Miscellaneous: Reservations needed for camping. Large picnic
      facilities. FRONTIERLAND with gem mining.

Wyandot Indians used these underground caves until 1810 for
protection from the weather and their enemies. The caves
were formed by an underground river that flows to the Olentangy
River hundreds of feet below the surface. The caves were

originally discovered during a search for oxen that broke loose from a wagon train. Their owner, J. M. Adam's name and date can be seen on the entrance wall. The tour lasts 30 minutes and takes you through winding passages and spacious underground rooms. Then, you visit the museum where Indian artifacts found in the caves are displayed. Gift Shop, playground, sports activities, campsites, picnic grounds and shelter houses are available.

PERKIN'S OBSERVATORY

SR-23 (1 mile south of Delaware), **Delaware** 43015

❑   Activity: Museums
❑   Telephone: (740) 363-1257
    www.perkins-observatory.org/perkins.html
❑   Hours: Friday or Saturday nights, call for schedule.
❑   Admission: $5.00 Adults, $3.00 Seniors, $3.00 Children. To
    order in advance send self-addressed stamped envelope to:
    Perkins Observatory, P.O. Box 449, Delaware OH 43015.

C hildren who have studied astronomy will especially enjoy this. The stars naturally fascinate them at night so this is a real treat to see them this close. The program includes a tour of the observatory, a talk on astronomy, and then telescope observation if it is a clear night.

GRANVILLE HISTORICAL MUSEUM

Granville - 115 East Broadway, 43023. *Activity:* Ohio History. (740) 587-3951. *Hours:* Friday, Saturday, Sunday, 1:00 – 4:00 pm (mid-April to mid-October). Oldest building in the area. Early hand tools and furniture plus a history of the first settlers from Granville, Massachusetts.

GRANVILLE LIFE STYLE MUSEUM

Granville - 121 South Main Street, 43023. *Activity:* Ohio History. (740) 587-0373. *Hours:* Sunday, 1.00 – 4:00 pm (May – September). A grandmother's style home with handed-down and saved possessions for more than 100 years. Adults *(and even children)* are invited to play the 1911 Steinway piano.

MOTTS MILITARY MUSEUM

Groveport - 5075 South Hamilton Road, 43125. *Activity:* Museums. (614) 836-1500. **www.mottsmilitarymuseum.org**. It's purpose is to bring military history into perspective by collecting and preserving memorabilia. Secondly, it educates the public on the importance of past, present and new military events that impact our lives. A wonderful life-long private collection that the public can now enjoy.

BUCKEYE CENTRAL SCENIC RAILROAD

US-40 (3 miles East of Hebron – I-70 to SR-79 North Exit to US-40)
Hebron 43025

- ❑ Activity: Tours
- ❑ Telephone: (740) 928-3827

  www.infinet.com/~pcaravan/railroad/bchome.htm
- ❑ Hours: Weekends and Holidays, 1:00 and 3:00 pm Departures (Memorial Day – October). Seasonal rides also available. Call or visit website for details.
- ❑ Admission: $7.00 Adult, $5.00 Children (2-11)

Take a trip through Ohio farmland for a 90 minute, 10 mile ride on the same route the train traveled in the mid-1800's on the Shawnee line (important line for pioneers heading west). School-aged kids will want to check out the Wild West/Great Train Robbery. Be part of the action as the train is boarded and held up by outlaws. Will the sheriff save the day?

NATIONAL TRAIL RACEWAY

Hebron - 2650 National Road SW (US-40), 43025. *Activity:* Sports. (740) 928-5706. **www.nationaltrailraceway.com**. Drag racing. Super Gas Races & Night Under Fire (jet cars & trucks with fire exhaust, drag racing, fireworks, funny car acts). Weekends & Wednesdays. Day & Evening. (late April - October)

FRANKLIN COUNTY NORTHWEST VILLAGE

Hilliard - Weaver Park, Franklin County Fairgrounds, 43026. *Activity:* Ohio History. Village church, 1850's log cabin, outhouse, caboose, train station, granary, barn and museum. The museum displays vintage household equipment. Open by appointment (April - November) and during the Franklin County Fair.

LANCASTER CHORALE

Lancaster – 43130. *Activity:* The Arts. (740) 687-5855. Choral music and other performances by ensemble of professional singers. (November - July)

THE GEORGIAN / THE SHERMAN HOUSE MUSEUM

Lancaster - 105 East Wheeling and 137 East Main Street, 43130. *Activity:* Ohio History. (740) 654-9923. *Hours:* Tuesday – Sunday. 19th Century homes with period furnishings and war momentos of Civil War General Sherman. Admission.

WAHKEENA NATURE PRESERVE

Lancaster - 2200 Pump Station Road (US-33 to County Road 86 West, follow signs), 43155. *Activity:* Outdoors. (740) 746-8695 or (800) 297-1883. **www.ohiohistory.org/places/wahkeena.** *Hours:* Wednesday - Sunday, 8:00 am - 4:30 pm. (April – October). *Admission:* $2.00 per vehicle. *Miscellaneous:* Museum and Nature Trails. Trees, ferns, mountain laurels, wildflowers and orchids. All that beauty plus 70 species of birds and 15 species of mammals including woodpeckers and white-tailed deer.

MARION COUNTY INTERNATIONAL RACEWAY

LaRue - 2454 Richwood – LaRue Road (Route 37), 43332. *Activity:* **Sports.** (740) 499-3666 or (800) 422 MCIR. **www.mcir.net.** Quarter mile drag racing includes 7up Pro Am and Sunoco IHRA Finals. Admission. Concessions. *Hours:* (Saturdays, April – October)

LITHOPOLIS FINE ARTS ASSOCIATION

Lithopolis - 150 East Columbus Street, 43136. *Activity:* The Arts. (614) 837-7003. **http://cwda.net/LAFAA**. Series of musical concerts and dramatic events in Wagnalls Memorial.

MADISON LAKE STATE PARK

London - (3 miles East of London off SR-665), 43140. *Activity:* Outdoors. **www.dnr.state.oh.us/odnr/parks/directory/madison.htm**. (740) 869-3124. 186 acres of boating, fishing, swimming and winter sports.

HARDING MEMORIAL AND HOME
380 Mount Vernon Avenue (1.5 miles West of SR-23 on SR-95)
Marion 43302

- ❑ Activity: Ohio History
- ❑ Telephone: (740) 387-9630
  www.ohiohistory.org/places/harding
- ❑ Hours: Wednesday - Saturday, 9:30 am - 5:00 pm, Sunday and Holidays Noon - 5:00 pm (Summer). Weekends Only, (September and October). By appointment, (Spring)
- ❑ Admission: $3.00 Adult, $2.00 Senior, $1.25 Youth (6-12)
- ❑ Miscellaneous: Memorial is a circular monument (with columns of white marble) containing the tombs of Mr. and Mrs. Harding. Delaware Avenue.

A great way to learn Presidential history without a fuss from the kids. Do you know what the fancy pot is in the guestroom - the one lying on the floor? They have displayed a podium used at Harding's inauguration in 1920 as our 29th President. See the porch where Harding campaigned what was later called the "Front Porch Campaign", speaking to over 600,000 people overall. The original porch collapsed and a new one had to be built during the campaign. A special small house was built behind the main house for the press associates visiting the area to cover the campaign. Look for the ornate collar worn by their dog "Laddie Boy".

MYSTERIOUS REVOLVING BALL

Marion - Marion Cemetery, 43302. *Activity:* Outdoors. *Hours:* Dawn – Dusk. Can you scientifically solve the "Marion Unsolved Mystery"? Here's the scoop! The ball is a grave monument for the Merchant family (located in the northeast corner of the cemetery) erected in 1896. The 5200-pound granite ball turns mysteriously with continuous movement. There has been no scientific explanation for this revolution and the phenomenon is featured in many newspapers including "Ripley's Believe It or Not"!

PALACE CULTURAL ARTS ASSOCIATION

Marion - 276 West Center Street, 43302. *Activity:* The Arts. (740) 383-2101. Presents theatre, music, dance, and film in restored historic theatre.

WYANDOT POPCORN MUSEUM

169 East Church Street (Heritage Hall – Marion County Museum of History), **Marion** 43302

❑   Activity: Museums

❑   Telephone: (740) 387-HALL, **www.wyandotpopcornmus.com**

❑   Hours: Wednesday – Sunday, 1:00 – 4:00 pm (May – October)
Weekends Only (November – April)

Before you enter the Popcorn Museum, see the hand-made miniature, working carousel and Prince Imperial (a stuffed 25 year old horse from France). You won't believe how they braided his mane! As you enter the large, colorful tent, you'll be enchanted by the antique popcorn poppers and concession wagons. See the first automated popper and the first all electric popper – all in pristine condition. It's the only museum like it in the world and is popular with stars like Paul Newman, who borrowed a Wyandot Concession Wagon to promote his popcorn, "Old Time Style", in Central Park.

BUCKEYE LAKE STATE PARK

Millersport - (9 miles South of Newark off SR-13), 43046. *Activity:* Outdoors. (740) 467-2690. **www.dnr.state.oh.us/odnr/ parks/directory/buckeye.htm**. 3,557 acres of boating, fishing, swimming and winter sports. Many permanent and rental properties are available around the lake.

MOUNT GILEAD STATE PARK

Mt. Gilead - (1 mile East of Mt. Gilead on SR-95), 43338. *Activity:* Outdoors. (419) 946-1961, **www.dnr.state.oh.us/odnr/ parks/directory/mtgilead.htm**. 172 acres of camping, hiking trails, boating, fishing and some winter sports.

DEER CREEK STATE PARK

Mt. Sterling - 20635 Waterloo Road (7 miles South of Mt. Sterling on SR-207), 43143. *Activity:* Outdoors. (740) 869-3124, **www.dnr.state.oh.us/odnr/parks/directory/deercrk.htm**. Nature Programs. Bike Rentals, camping, hiking trails, boating and rentals, fishing, swimming and winter sports available. Lakeview family cabins with A/C. Resort with indoor/outdoor pools, sauna, tennis and fitness areas.

PERRY STATE FOREST

New Lexington - (off of SR-345, 4 miles north of New Lexington) 43764. *Activity:* Outdoors. (740) 674-4035 (Blue Rock office), **www.hcs.ohio-state.edu/ODNR/Forests/stateforests/perry.htm**. Open daily, 6:00 am - 11:00 pm. 4,567 acres in Perry County. Area was formerly strip mined for coal. All purpose vehicle trails (16 miles), bridle trails (8 miles).

LICKING COUNTY ART ASSOCIATION

Newark - 391 Hudson Avenue, 43055. *Activity:* The Arts. (740) 349-8031. Galleries, educational programs and art library.

MOUNDBUILDERS NEWARK EARTHWORKS

99 Cooper Avenue (I-70 to SR-79 north, between Parkview Drive and Cooper), **Newark** 43055

❑   Activity: Ohio History
❑   Telephone: (740) 344-1920
    www.ohiohistory.org/places/moundbld
❑   Hours: Ohio Indian Art Museum, Wednesday – Saturday, 9:30 am - 4:30 pm (April-October). Sunday and Holidays, Noon - 5:00 pm (Summer). Weekends only, (September and October)
❑   Admission: $3.00 Adult, $1.25 Children (6-12)
❑   Miscellaneous: Octagon State Memorial - Small mounds, Wright Earthworks State Memorial. Park open daylight hours.

The Moundbuilders is a circular mound 1200 feet in diameter with walls 8 to 14 feet high. In the museum, we found the primitive stamps most interesting. The engraved tablets were probably used for clothing decorations or tattoos. They feel the tablets were used as stamps because they found colored pigment on them. As you walk outside the museum, you walk right into the mouth opening of a circular mound. Once inside, just imagine the Hopewell Indian ceremonies that occurred many years ago.

DAWES ARBORETUM

Newark - 7770 Jacksontown Road (SR-13), 43056. *Activity:* Outdoors.(800) 443-2937 or (740) 323-2355. **www.dawesarb.org**. *Hours:* Monday – Saturday, 8:00 am – 5:00 pm. Sunday & Holidays, 1:00 – 5:00 pm. Meadows, woods, gardens, cypress swamp, holly and a special Japanese Bonsai garden. If you were flying over the gardens you could see a 2100-foot long series of hedges that spell out "Dawes Arboretum". Free admission.

INSTITUTE OF INDUSTRIAL TECHNOLOGY
55 South First Street (I-70 to SR-13 north)
Newark 43058

❑   Activity: Museums

❑   Telephone: (740) 349-9277, **www.iitnewark.org**

❑   Hours: Tuesday – Friday, 9:00 am - 4:00 pm.
Weekends, Noon – 4:00 pm

❑   Admission: $4.00 Adult, $3.00 Senior (55+), $1.00 Child (4-16).

History of Licking County including the Heisey Glass Studio where artisans create beautiful blown glass. Also displays of molds and tools used to make pressed glass.

❑   TRANSPORTATION AREA – Methods of travel including the shipping canals, railroads, and roads.

❑   PROCESS AND PRODUCTS AREA – Turn a real line shaft. See products made in Licking Country such as Mason jars and engines for farm machines.

❑   MATERIALS AREA – See where local raw materials are used in manufacturing, farming and fuel production. Interactive touch displays educate kids on what, where, and how materials are extracted (raw and finished forms).

❑   STREETS OF YESTERYEAR - (from the old COSI) A varying display of historical Ohio times with interactive volunteers demonstrating crafts like weaving and candle-making.

GREEN'S HERITAGE MUSEUM

Orient - 10530 Thrailkill Road (SR-762), 43146. *Activity:* Ohio History. (740) 877-4254. Historical village with Blacksmith Shop, Antique Farm, 1929 Gas Station, Ice House, Depot, Sawmill, 1871 Church, Country Store with original counters and benches, and original White Castle Gift Shop. Carriage House with 50 antique horse drawn carriages.

VELVET ICE CREAM: YE OLDE MILL ICE CREAM MUSEUM

Velvet Ice Cream (SR-13), **Utica** 43080

❑   Activity: Museums

❑   Telephone: (740) 892-3921or (800) 589-5000
     www.velvet-icecream.com

❑   Hours: Daily, 11:00 am – 9:00 pm (Summer). Daily, 11:00 am –
     8:00 pm (September / October)

❑   Admission: Free

Did you know that the ice cream cone originated by mistake at the St. Louis World's Fair when a waffle vendor rolled waffles into cones for an ice cream vendor who ran out of serving cups? Learn all sorts of ice cream trivia at the Ice Cream Museum located in the restored 1817 mill and water wheel which is surrounded by 20 acres of wooded parklands with ducks and picnic areas. While you are at the mill, stop by the viewing gallery to watch ice cream being made and packaged. Then, catch a light meal and ice cream or yogurt dessert at the 1800's Ice Cream Parlor and gift shop.

Chapter 2
Central East Area

Our Favorites...

- Creegan Company Animation Factory
- Harry London Chocolate Factory
- Longaberger Factory & Homestead
- Glass & Pottery Factory Tours
- Roscoe Village
- Amish Farms
- Warther Carving Museums
- Wendall August Forge

CARNATION BASKET COMPANY

104-112 Prospect Street (US-62 to State Street to Park Street-north), **Alliance** 44601

☐ Activity: Tours

☐ Telephone: (330) 823-7231 or (800) 823-7231

☐ Hours: Weekdays, 9:00 am – 3:00 pm

☐ Admission: Free

☐ Tours: Reservations Suggested. 30 minutes (includes Factory Outlet Store)

☐ Miscellaneous: Factory Outlet Store (Weekdays, 9:00 am – 4:30 pm) Saturday, 10:00 am – 2 pm. Private Label basket for clubs, church or organization available with pre-order. Lasting souvenir that you can use.

See a handmade basket made from start to finish. Includes watching the maple wood clipped and cut to form veneers in different widths and lengths. Watch weavers begin at the bottom of a basket (over a form) and buildup sides. Seamstresses make cloth liners and basket shirts in the sewing department. These accessories finish off the baskets and give them decorating appeal.

GLAMORGAN CASTLE

Alliance - 200 Glamorgan Street, 44601. *Activity:* Tours. (330) 821-2100. **www.aviators.stark.k12.oh.us/History.html**. *Tours:* By Appointment. Generally weekdays at 2:00 pm. Small admission fee. Home of the City School Districts Administration office and once the early 1900's home of the late Col. William Henry Morgan (inventor/businessman). The building measures 185 feet in overall front elevation and truly looks like a giant castle.

BARBARA BARBE DOLL MUSEUM

Barnesville - 211 Chestnut Street (SR-147 and SR-800), 43713. *Activity:* Museums. (740) 425-1760. *Hours:* Wednesday – Sunday, 1:00 – 4:00 pm. (May – September). *Admission:* $2.00 Adult, $1.00 Youth (6-12). Five rooms of a former 1836 women's seminary display 3000 dolls of the late Barbara Barbe's (noted designer and collector) collection. The museum includes dolls made of bisque, wax, tin and plastic. See recent models by Ideal and old European dolls dressed in original costumes.

BELMONT COUNTY VICTORIAN MANSION MUSEUM

Barnesville - 532 North Chestnut Street 43713. *Activity:* Ohio History. (740) 425-2926. Thursday – Sunday, 1:00 – 4:30 pm (May – October). 26 rooms furnished in Gay 90's style home. Admission.

BARKCAMP STATE PARK

Belmont - 65330 Barkcamp Park Road (1 mile East of Belmont off SR-149), 43718. *Activity:* Outdoors. (740) 484-4064. **www.dnr.state.oh.us/odnr/parks/directory/barkcamp.htm**. Nature Programs. 1,232 acres of camping, hiking trails, boating, fishing, swimming and winter sports.

BEHALT

5798 County Road 77 (north of SR-39), **Berlin** 44610

❑   Activity: The Arts
❑   Telephone: (330) 893-3192, **http://pages.sssnet.com/behalt**
❑   Hours: Monday – Saturday, 9:00 am – 5:00 pm
      (until 8:00 pm, June - August)
❑   Tours: 30 minute guided or video (15 minute background to
      Amish area).

Behalt means "the remembering". This 10' x 265' cyclorama mural by artist Heinz Gaugel clearly explains the heritage of Amish and Mennonite people from the beginnings of their faith to the present day. The circular mural took four years to paint using an old technique called "sgraffito" which means scratched. Mr. Gaugel applied five layers of plaster to the wall (green, dark red, dark yellow, white and black). The artist starts scratching through the layers to expose the colors he wants. This makes the mural almost 3D when viewing. The tour is narrated with stories so vivid that you feel as if you are a part of the scene. We were fortunate to meet Heinz Gaugel in the gift shop and it was amazing to meet such a humble man with such apparent and unique artistic talent.

ROLLING RIDGE RANCH

Berlin - 3961 County Road 168 (SR-62 to CR-168), 44610. *Activity:* Animals & Farms. (330) 893-3777. *Hours:* Monday – Saturday, 9:00 am – 1 hour before sunset. Take a 2-mile safari ride in your own vehicle or a horse drawn wagon to see over 200 animals from 6 continents. Feed the animals from the vehicle and stop by the petting zoo before you leave.

SCHROCK'S AMISH FARM AND HOME

4363 State Route 39 (1 mile East of Downtown), **Berlin** 44610

- ❑ Activity: Tours
- ❑ Telephone: (330) 893-3232, **www.amish-r-us.com**
- ❑ Hours: Monday – Friday, 10:00 am - 5:00 pm. Saturday, 10:00 am- 6:00 pm (April - October)
- ❑ Tours and Admission:
  Buggy Ride - $3.00 Adult, $2.00 Children (3-12)
  Home Tour and Slides - $3.00 Adult, $2.00 Children (3-12)
  Farm Only - $1.50 Adult, 1.50 Children (3-12)
  All Three - $6.00 Adult, $4.00 Children (3-12)
- ❑ Miscellaneous: Gifts shops (many)

We started with a buggy ride driven by an Amish man and his horse named "Leroy". After our ride, we were given a sticker to wear that says, "I rode my first Amish buggy ride with Leroy". We then stopped at the farm to pet animals and then watched a slide show about Amish lifestyles. The guide then shows you through the home. Kids, even adults, were surprised to see that all appliances were gas fueled including the lamps (the gas generated light source was hidden in the table under the lamp). We learned why there are no faces on Amish dolls and why only pins and occasional buttons are used in clothing.

WENDALL AUGUST FORGE TOUR

7007 Dutch Country Lane (3 miles West of Berlin – SR-62)
Berlin 44610

❑   Activity: Tours
❑   Telephone: (800) 923-4438 or (330) 893-3713
    www.wendell.com
❑   Tours: Monday – Friday, 9:00 am – 6:00 pm. Saturday,
    (Showroom open and workshop viewing only)

Free tour of the production workshop as metal giftware is taken through a fascinating eleven step process. The gift metal is hammered over a pre-designed template with random hand, or machine operated hammer motions. It was interesting to think someone close to the craft had to design the machine operated hammer for this specific purpose – probably a craftsman who's hands got tired! The impression is now set in one side and the signature hammer marks will stay on the other side. The artist stamps his seal and then the item is forged (put in a log fire) to get smoke marks that bring out the detail of the design. After the item cools, it is cleaned to remove most of the dark smoke color and the metal object is then thinned by hand hammering. For $5.00 you can have a crack at hammering a design into metal. It's well worth the fee to actually try it for yourself and have a personally crafted souvenir. The facility also features a video highlighting the company's history and the showroom has the World's Largest Amish Buggy – over 1200 pounds, and each wheel is over 5 feet tall!

BLUE ROCK STATE FOREST

Blue Rock - 6665 Cutler Lake Road (located 12 miles southeast of Zanesville off SR-60), 43720. *Activity:* Outdoors. (740) 674-4035. **www.hcs.ohio-state.edu/ODNR/Forests/stateforests/bluerock.htm**. Open daily, 6:00 am - 11:00 pm. 4,579 acres in Muskingum County. 26 miles bridle trails. Former fire lookout tower. Blue Rock State Park is adjacent.

FORT LAURENS STATE MEMORIAL AND MUSEUM

(I-77 and SR-212 - Follow Signs), **Bolivar** 44612

☐ Activity: Ohio History

☐ Telephone: (800) 283-8914 or (330) 874-2059
www.ohiohistory.org/places/ftlauren

☐ Hours: Wednesday - Saturday, 9:30 am - 5:00 pm. Sunday & Holidays, Noon - 5:00 pm (Summer). Weekends Only, (September & October). Grounds open, daily (April – October)

☐ Admission: $3.00 Adult, $1.25 Youth (6-12)

Visit the site of the only U.S. Military fort in Ohio during the American Revolution. Also included is a museum (with visual and action packed audiovisual displays), that sits on what was once the fort's west gate. Re-enactment weekends are the best time to visit.

HARRISON STATE FOREST

Cadiz - (3 miles north of Cadiz, east of SR-9), 43907. *Activity:* Outdoors. 330-339-2205 (New Philadelphia office). **www.hcs. ohio-state.edu/ODNR/Forests/stateforests/harrison.htm**. Open daily, 6:00 am - 11:00 pm. 1,345 acres in Harrison County. Area formerly strip mined for coal. Bridle and hiking trails (24 miles), family and horse camping (no fee), fishing ponds.

TAPPAN LAKE RECREATION AREA

Cadiz - (12 miles Northwest of Cadiz off US-250), 43907. *Activity:* Outdoors. (740) 922-3649. Nature programs. 7,597 acres of camping, hiking trails, boating and rentals, fishing, swimming, visitor center, lodge or cabins and food service.

BOYD'S CRYSTAL ART GLASS COMPANY

Cambridge - 1203 Morton Avenue (off SR-209 North), 43725, *Activity:* Tours. (740) 439-2077. **www.boydglass.com**. *Tours:* Monday – Friday, 7:00 am – 11:00 am and Noon – 3:30 pm, 15 minutes, (September – May). The Cambridge area became popular for glass manufacturing because of good sand and abundant wells of natural gas. Boyd's specialty is antique glass reproductions and collectibles. Typical shapes made are trains, airplanes, cars, small animals and Teddy the Tugboat. Watch molten glass being poured into one of 300 molds and put in a furnace. When they cool, they are hand-painted.

GUERNSEY COUNTY HISTORICAL MUSEUM

Cambridge - 218 North 8th Street, 43725. *Activity:* Ohio History. (740) 432-3145. *Hours:* Sunday, 1:00 - 5:00 pm (Memorial Day - Labor Day). Small admission. Famous people and local products.

LIVING WORD PASSION PLAY
6010 College Hill Road (2 miles west of SR-209)
Cambridge 43725

- ❑   Activity: The Arts
- ❑   Telephone: (740) 439-2761
- ❑   Hours: Thursday – Saturday, 8:00 pm (mid-June to Labor Day)
  Saturday Only, 7:00 pm (September)
- ❑   Admission: $12.00 Adult, $9.00 Senior (60+), $6.00 Children
  (under 12)
- ❑   Tours: Free Set Tours, 6:00 pm
- ❑   Miscellaneous: Concessions, Gift Shop, Rain Checks, Free
  Parking.

Experience an evening back in the Holy Land, in 30 AD with an authentic representation of Old Jerusalem. Watch as Jesus and his disciples travel into Jerusalem, he is then crucified, and raises from the dead. The play is full of biblical animals and costumes, even chariots!

MOSSER GLASS
9279 Cadiz Road (I-77 exit 47. US-22 West), Cambridge 43725

- ❑   Activity: Tours
- ❑   Telephone: (740) 439-1827

❑ Tours: Monday – Friday, 8:15, 9:15, 10:15 am, Noon, 1,2,3:00 pm (*Except plant shutdown in July and Christmas Week*). Best not to tour if it's extremely hot outside since the plant is not air conditioned.

M osser makes glass pitchers, goblets, lamps, figurines, auto parts (headlights), and paper weights. Your guide starts the tour explaining the glassmaking process from the beginning when glass powder (sand and cullet-broken glass) are heated to 2000 degrees F. in a furnace. Once melted, the molten glass is pulled on a stick and then iron molded or pressed, fire glazed and finally cooled in a Lehr which uniformly reduces the temperature of the object to prevent shattering. We saw them make old Ford car headlight covers and red heart shaped paperweights. They add selenium to make red glass. A little toothpick holder or doll's glass is typical of the free souvenir of this great tour!

SALT FORK STATE PARK

Cambridge - 14755 Cadiz Road (7 miles Northeast of Cambridge on US-22), 43755. *Activity:* Outdoors. (740) 439-3521. **www.dnr.state.oh.us/odnr/parks/directory/saltfork.htm**. Nature programs. Bicycle rental. 20,181 acres of camping, hiking trails, boating and rentals, fishing, swimming, and winter sports. Family cabins with A/C. Lodge with indoor/outdoor pools, fitness center, tennis, volleyball, and basketball facilities.

ST HELENA III

103 Tuscarawas Village Park (I-77 to Exit 111 Portage Street West, follow signs), **Canal Fulton** 44614

❑ Activity: Tours
❑ Telephone: (800) HELENA-3 or (330) 854-3808
❑ Hours: Daily, 1:00 – 3:00 pm (Summer), Weekends, 1:00 – 3:00 pm (May, September, October)
❑ Admission: $6.50 Adult, $5.50 Senior (60+), $4.50 Children (3-11)

A one-hour horse drawn canal boat freighter ride with a narrative history of the canal system and the local area. Appearing as it did in the 1800's, the view also includes Lock IV, one of the few remaining working locks on old canal routes. Included in the tour is a Canal Museum with pictorial stories of colorful local history and canal memorabilia including tools used to build and repair canal boats.

CANTON BALLET

Canton - 605 North Market Avenue (Palace Theatre), 44702. *Activity:* The Arts. (330) 455-7220. Pre-professional training company performs with professional artists.

CANTON CLASSIC CAR MUSEUM

Canton - Market Avenue at 6th Street entrance, 44702. *Activity:* Museums. (330) 455-3603. *Hours:* Daily, 10:00 am – 5:00 pm. *Admission:* $6.00 Adult, $5.00 Senior (60+), $4.00 Youth (6-18). Housed in Ohio's earliest Ford-Lincoln dealership, this museum offers over 35 antique, classic and special interest cars displayed in the motif of flapper era Roaring 20's. Favorite exhibits are the Rolls Royce and celebrity cars including Queen Elizabeth's tour car, famous movie cars and Amelia Earhart's 1916 Pierce Arrow.

CANTON MUSEUM OF ART

Canton - 1001 North Market Avenue, 44702. *Activity:* The Arts. (330) 453-7666. **www.cantonart.org**. Features traveling exhibitions and permanent collection of American watercolors, works on paper and ceramics.

CANTON SYMPHONY ORCHESTRA

Canton - 2323 17th Street NW, 44702. *Activity:* The Arts. (330) 452-2094. **www.cantonsymphony.org**. Presents classical, holiday, pops and youth concerts/symphony.

CULTURAL CENTER FOR THE ARTS

Canton - 1001 North Market Avenue, 44702. *Activity:* The Arts. (330) 452-4096. Presents FunFest, Family Arts Festival and educational programs.

PLAYERS GUILD CENTER FOR PUBLIC THEATRE

Canton - 1001 North Market Avenue, 44702. *Activity:* The Arts. (330) 453-7619. **www.sssnet.com/playersguild**. Family series presents plays based on award winning children's stories.

MCKINLEY MUSEUM & DISCOVER WORLD

800 McKinley Monument Drive, NW (I-77 south to exit 106, I-77 north to exit 105, follow signs), **Canton** 44708

- Activity: Museums
- Telephone: (330) 455-7043, **www.mckinleymuseum.org**
- Hours: Monday – Saturday, 9:00 am – 5:00 pm (until 6:00 pm Summer). Sunday, Noon – 5:00 pm (until 6:00 pm Summer)
- Admission: $6.00 Adult, $5.00 Senior, $4.00 Children (3-18), $18.00 Family Rate
- Miscellaneous: Planetarium, Research stations with topics like Dinosaurs, Geology, Archaeology, Beavers Life, Baby Shamu, Tornadoes, and a Human Heart.

After you park, take the 108 steps leading up to the bronze doors of the stunning McKinley Memorial where President William McKinley and his wife and children were laid to rest. A few steps away is the McKinley Museum where you can visit McKinley Hall, Historical Hall and the Street of Shops. Walk along the 19th Century Street of homes, general store, print shop, and doctor's office – all indoors on exhibit. Kid's eyes sparkle at the model trains and pioneer toys such as paper dolls or mini cast-iron kitchen appliances. Last, but even more exciting for kids, is Discover World. A large dinosaur robot named "Alice" greets you and a real Stark County mastodon Bondo Betty is around the corner. Find hidden fossil drawers, make a fossil, look for the queen bee in a living beehive, touch a chinchilla, play a tune on tone pipes, or be a weather forecaster – All in one afternoon!

PRO FOOTBALL HALL OF FAME

2121 George Halas Drive NW (I-77 and US-62), **Canton** 44708

❑   Activity: Museums

❑   Telephone: (330) 456-8207, **www.profootballhof.com**

❑   Hours: Daily, 9:00 am – 8:00 pm (Memorial Day – Labor Day)
     Daily, 9:00 am – 5:00 pm, Rest of Year (Closed Christmas Only)

❑   Admission: $10.00 Adult , $6.50 Senior (62+), 5.00 Youth (14 &
     under), $25.00 Family

❑   Miscellaneous: Tailgating Snack Bar – over the counter /
     vending with Top Twenty Tele-trivia and QBI Call-the-Play
     Game.   Special video presentations in the center of each room
     (our favorite – "16 Fantastic Finishes")

If you're an NFL Football Fan, the anticipation builds as you enter the grounds of the sprawling Hall of Fame.   At the top of the curving ramp upstairs you view the first 100 years of football with Pro Football's Birth Certificate and the oldest football (1895) available for display.   Then hit some Astroturf and browse through Pro Football today and Photo Art Gallery (award winning, some amazing, photographs of football heroes in action).   Older children look forward to the Enshrinement Galleries and Super Bowl Room. The newest addition to the Hall is Game Day Stadium.   A 100-Yard film is shown in a two-sided rotating theater.   Start at the Locker Room Show.   Then the entire seating area rotates 180 degrees to the Stadium Show where you become part of a NFL game with a 2 story Cinemascope presentation.   You see, hear and almost make contact with the players!   What a rush!

THE STABLES

Canton - 2317 13th Street NW (I-77 exit 106), 44708. *Activity:* Theme Restaurants. (888) GO-STABLES or (330) 452-1230, **www.thestables.com**. The circular brick building was once the Timken Family Stables.   Festive football and sports atmosphere with many large screen televisions, tableside trivia games, fame room and a huge 10,000 pound carved redwood "football catch" sculpture. "Located a football field away from the Hall of Fame."

GREATER CANTON AMATEUR SPORTS HALL OF FAME

Canton - 1414 North Market Street, 44714. *Activity:* Ohio History. (330) 453-1552. *Hours:* Tuesday – Sunday, Noon – 4:00 pm. Exhibits highlight local area amateur athletes (some are known internationally).

HOOVER HISTORICAL CENTER

1875 Easton Street NW (I-77 Portage Street/North Canton Exit)
Canton 44720

❑   Activity: Museums

❑   Telephone: (330) 499-0287, **www.hoover.com**

❑   Hours: Tuesday – Sunday, 1:00 -5:00 pm

❑   Admission: Free

❑   Miscellaneous: Only known vacuum cleaner museum in the world.

See the Hoover Industry beginnings as a leather tannery. When automobiles came on the scene, W. H. Hoover searched for a new product. He bought the rights to inventor Murray Spangler's upright vacuum cleaner and introduced it in 1908 - The Hoover Suction Sweeper Model O (On display). A short video details the history of the company. Guided tours of the farmhouse include a display of antique vacuums. A favorite is the Kotten Suction Cleaner (1910) that requires a person to rock a bellows with their feet to create suction. An early 1900's electric vacuum weighed 100 pounds (and they advertised it as a portable!).

ELDERBERRY LINE

205 2nd Street (Carrollton – Oneida – Minerva Railroad)
Carrollton 44615

❑   Activity: Tours

❑   Telephone: (330) 627-2282, **www.elderberryline.com**

❑   Hours: Saturday, 11:00 am. Sunday, 1:00 pm. (Memorial Weekend – October)

❑   Admission: $10.00 Adult, $8.00 Children (2-12)

❑   Miscellaneous: No restroom on train. No cooling or heat.
      Elderberry Patch Gift Shop

A scenic round trip of 28 miles lasting 3 hours including the 1 hour layover in Minerva (half-way). The train crosses the historic "Great Trail" of the late 1700's and passengers will pass villages, historic areas, farmland and spacious forests.

MCCOOK HOUSE

Carrollton - Downtown Square, 44615. *Activity:* Ohio History. (330) 627-3345. **www.ohiohistory.org/places/mccookhse**. *Hours:* Friday – Saturday, 10:00 am – 5:00 pm. Sunday, 1 – 5:00 pm (Summer). Weekends only, (Labor Day to mid-October). *Admission:* $3.00 Adults, $1.00 Children (6-12). The family earned the name of "Fighting McCooks" due to their extensive military service in the Civil War.

POMERENE CENTER FOR THE ARTS

Coshocton - 317 Mulberry Street, 43812. *Activity:* The Arts. (740) 622-0326. Art exhibits, music series, community celebration of the arts, art classes, workshops, school and community outreach programs.

ROSCOE VILLAGE

311 Hill Street (SR-16 and 83, near US-36), **Coshocton** 43812

❑   Activity: Ohio History
❑   Telephone: (800) 877-1830, **www.roscoevillage.com**
❑   Hours: Daily, Most village shops open at 10:00 am. Special events
      (May – December). Visitor Center, Daily, 10:00 am – 5:00 pm.
❑   Admission: "Living History Tour" $5-10.00 (ages 5+). Just
      Browsing is Free! Additional charge $3-6.00 for canal boat ride.
❑   Tours: Daily, 10:00 am - 3:00 pm.

L isted as "One of the 20 best sites to discover historic America", - it truly is a place that meets or exceeds your expectations. Experience life in a canal town with canal boat rides (for an additional fee) May through October. Watch craftsmen make brooms, weave or print. In the print shop we pressed our own bookmarks and postcards. Spend gobs of time in the General Store where you can play with and buy old-fashioned toys like harmonicas, paper dolls and wooden toys. Plan to have the kids bring their allowance (and you can too) because you won't be able to resist! During the summer, visit the Hillside where demonstrations of brick-making and woodworking take place. A family style restaurant, the rustic "Warehouse", was once a busy holding house for transport of goods.

THE WILDS

14000 International Road (off SR-284), **Cumberland** 43732

- ❏   Activity: Animals & Farms
- ❏   Telephone: (740) 638-5030, **www.thewilds.org**
- ❏   Hours: Daily, 9:00 am - 5:00 pm (May - October). Hours vary, call first (November - April)
- ❏   Admission: $10.00 Adult, $9.00 Seniors (60+), $7.00 Children (4-12)
- ❏   Tours: 1 hour tours in a shuttle bus

Once a strip mine (donated by American Electric Power) it is now home to the International Center for the preservation of wild animals. Over 9000 acres of forest and grassland with 150 lakes is home to animals in a protected open range habitat (no pens, stables, and cages) designed to create an environment for reproduction. You'll see many animals you don't see in zoos like African gazelles, reticulated giraffes, mountain zebras, tundra swans and red wolves in herds. We saw an Indian rhinoceros that was born in captivity and had foot problems so severe he couldn't be displayed in zoos. With lots of "tender loving care" and adaptation exercises, he now roams free. You might also see real wild horses that look like a rhinoceros and a horse. They are very strong and tough (yet beautiful to watch) animals.

ATWOOD LAKE RESORT

Dellroy - (2 miles Southeast of New Cumberland off SR-212), 44620. *Activity:* Outdoors. **www.atwoodlakeresort.com**. (330) 735-2211 or (800) 362-6406. Nature programs. 4,536 acres of camping, hiking trails, boating and rentals, fishing, swimming, visitor center and winter sports. Beach with paddle boat rentals and food service. Dining at the lodge.

DENNISON RAILROAD DEPOT CANTEEN RESTAURANT

Dennison - 400 Center Street, 44621. *Activity:* Theme Restaurants. (740) 922-6776. **www.dennisondepot.org**. Railroad canteen for WWII servicemen is now used as a museum of local history, a gift shop, an old fashioned candy counter and a theme restaurant. Lunch served Tuesday-Sunday. Small admission to the museum.

BROAD RUN CHEESEHOUSE
6011 County Road 139 NW (4 miles west of I-77, old SR-39)
Dover 44622

❑   Activity: Tours
❑   Telephone: (330) 343-1371, **www.broadruncheese.com**
❑   Admission: $1.50 per person
❑   Tours: Monday – Saturday (Mornings)
❑   Miscellaneous: Gift Shop with novelties, cheese and sausage.

Not just a window view but an actual tour of Swiss, Baby Swiss, Brick, and Muenster productions. They make 640,000 pounds of cheese from 8,000,000 pounds (*yes, pounds!*) of milk each year. After your factory tour you can sample cheese and as a souvenir, get an official cheesemaker paper cap (the one you wore for sanitary reasons during the tour).

WARTHER CARVINGS TOUR

331 Karl Avenue (I-77 to exit 83 to SR-211), **Dover** 44622

- ❑ Activity: Tours
- ❑ Telephone: (330) 343-7513, **www.warthers.com**
- ❑ Hours: Daily, 9:00 am – 5:00 pm (March – November) Daily, 10:00 am – 4:00 pm (December – March)
- ❑ Admission: $6.50 Adults, $3.00 Students (6-17)
- ❑ Miscellaneous: "Tree of Pliers" – 500 interconnecting pairs of working pliers carved out of 1 piece of walnut wood! Mrs. Warther's Button Collection – Over 70,000 in museum! Gift Shop.

A must see tour of the visions of a master craftsman! Mr. Warther started carving at age 5 with a pocketknife while milking cows and during breaks working at a mill. A favorite carving of ours was the steel mill (3 x 5 feet) with moving parts depicting the foreman raising a sandwich to eat, and another worker sleeping on the job. The Abraham Lincoln Funeral Train has thousands of mechanized movements powered by a sewing machine motor. See models of steam locomotives and trains using mostly walnut, ivory, and arguto (oily wood) for moving parts which still run without repairs for over 60 years! He was dissatisfied with the knives that were available, so he developed his own line of cutlery, which is still sold today. The late Mr. Warther loved entertaining children with his carvings (*George actually met him in the 1970's*) and he would carve a pair of working pliers with just a few cuts in a piece of wood in only a few seconds!

POPEYE'S RESTAURANT

Dresden - 416 Main Street, 43821. *Activity:* Theme Restaurants. (740) 754-6330. A 50's décor with hostesses wearing poodle skirts and waitresses in diner dresses and a jukebox at every booth. Soda fountain serving Wimpy Burgers and Homemade Shakes plus many basic favorites. Kids' meals are served in a paper box 50's classic car. Try their 55-cent one bite ice cream sundae – almost too cute to eat!

LONGABERGER MUSEUM AND FACTORY TOUR

5563 Raiders Road (on SR-16), **Dresden/Frazeysburg** 43822l

❑   Activity: Tours
❑   Telephone: (740) 322-5588, **www.longaberger.com**
❑   Hours: Monday – Saturday, 8:00 am – 6:00 pm. Sunday, Noon - 6:00 pm. Closed Easter, Thanksgiving, Christmas, and New Years Day.
❑   Admission: Free
❑   Miscellaneous: Arrive before 1:00 pm Monday – Friday to see actual production. No production on Saturday or Sunday. Weaving demonstrations daily in the Gallery with same setup as one of the factory stations.

JUST FOR FUN SHOP - Tour baskets, souvenirs.
CORPORATE HEADQUARTERS. (State Route 16) Newark.
    A giant 7-story Market Basket design with towering
    heated handles (to melt the winter ice) on top and painted /
    stenciled to look like wood. Incredible!
MAKE A BASKET SHOP. Homestead, Crawford Barn.
    Actually create your own hardwood maple Longaberger
    basket with the help of a Master Artisan. Takes 1 hour.
WORLD'S LARGEST BASKET. Downtown Dresden

F ascinating tours and lots to see in this tiny little town. Longaberger manufactures high quality, handmade hard maple baskets. The one-quarter mile long factory is home to 1000 weavers who make over 100,000 baskets per week (each initialed and dated). It's best to watch a 13 minute video of the company's history and the manufacturing process that takes sugar maple logs (poached and debarked) and cuts them into long thin strips. You'll be mesmerized when you go upstairs to the mezzanine to view 400 crafters, each with their own station, weaving damp wood strips around "forms", Each basket takes about 20-30 minutes to make. Can you guess what a weaving horse is? Before you leave the area you must view the new corporate headquarters and the large basket

– they are difficult to visualize except in person. The Homestead village shops are quaint and the restaurants are cute and fun!

A great new addition for kids at Longaberger...

Children now have a fun place to go while you shop – "LOOK, THINK AND DO CLUB". Ages 8 and up can adventure out into the local nature areas with a guide and provided backpack for each child (usually summertime and special events only). All children like to romp around at the club's headquarters... "The Lookout Treehouse" (located within the Homestead). Listen to the owl and the sights and sounds of nature. Great gift ideas here too.

BEAVER CREEK STATE PARK

East Liverpool - 12021 Echo Dell Road (8 miles North of East Liverpool off SR-7), 43920. *Activity:* Outdoors. (330) 385-3091. **www.dnr.state.oh.us/odnr/parks/directory/beaverck.htm**. 3,038 acres of camping, hiking trails, fishing and winter sports. Pioneer Village - seasonal.

MUSEUM OF CERAMICS

East Liverpool - 400 East 5th Street, 43920. *Activity:* Ohio History. (330) 386-6001. **www.ohiohistory.org/places/ceramics**. *Hours:* Wednesday – Saturday, 9:30 am – 5:00 pm, Sunday and Holidays, Noon – 5:00 pm. *Admission:* $5.00 Adults, $1.25 Children (6-12). Good and bad times of the ceramic industry in town and the effects on its people. Life sized dioramas of kiln, jigger and decorating shops with a collection of old and new ceramics. Slide presentation.

YELLOW CREEK STATE FOREST

West of **East Liverpool**, 43920. *Activity:* Outdoors. (330) 339-2205 (New Philadelphia office). **www.hcs.ohio-state.edu/ODNR/ Forests/stateforests/yellowcreek.htm**. Open daily, 6:00 am – 11:00 pm. 756 acres in Columbiana County. No facilities. Highlandtown Wildlife Area is adjacent.

1880 BUFFALO RANCH

Hartville - 2545 Pontius Street NE, 44632. *Activity:* Animals & Farms. (330) 877-6494 or (800) 870-1880. Take a tour of a working buffalo ranch and learn about the history of the buffalo. Bring a cooler to purchase buffalo meat (if you like that kinda thing - try some samples at their shop - you may love it - some really like the jerky).

QUAIL HOLLOW STATE PARK

Hartville - Congress Lake Road (2 miles North of Hartville), 44632. *Activity:* Outdoors. (330) 877-6652. Nature programs. Bridle trails. 700 acres of hiking trails, winter sports and a visitor center. **www.dnr.state.oh.us/odnr/parks/directory/quailhlw.htm**

GUILFORD LAKE STATE PARK

Lisbon - (6 miles Northwest of Lisbon off SR-172), 44432. *Activity:* Outdoors. (330) 222-1712. **www.dnr.state.oh.us/odnr/parks/directory/guilford.htm**. 488 acres of camping, boating, fishing, swimming and winter sports.

ELSON FLOURING MILL

Magnolia - 261 North Main Street, 44643. *Activity:* Tours. (330) 866-3353. Corn meal has been made at the mill since 1834 and can be purchased still today. *Tours:* Every Thursday at 10:00 am & 2:00 pm, (April – November). *Admission:* $2.00 per person.

MASSILLON MUSEUM

Massillon - 121 Lincoln Way East, 44646. *Activity:* Ohio History. (330) 833-4061. *Hours:* Tuesday – Saturday, 9:30 am – 5:00 pm, Sunday, 2:00 – 5:00 pm. Collection of art with photographs, Ohio quilts, pottery and folk art. History, Sports, Circus (100 Sq. Ft. Miniature), P.T. Barnum's cane, Tom Thumb's clothing.

OHIO SOCIETY OF MILITARY HISTORY

Massillon - 316 Lincoln Way East (US-30 to County Road 172), 44646. *Activity:* Ohio History. (330) 832-5553. *Hours:* Tuesday - Friday, 10:00 am - 5:00 pm. Saturday, 10:00 am - 3:00 pm. *Admission:* Donations. The museum honors people from Ohio who have fought for the United States. A collection of photographs, clothing and medals dating from the recent "Operation Desert Storm" back to the Civil War.

GUGGISBERG CHEESE FACTORY

5060 State Route 557 (Off SR-39, I-77 exit 83), **Millersburg** 44654

- ❑   Activity: Tours
- ❑   Telephone: (330) 893-2500, **www.guggisberg.com**
- ❑   Hours: Daily, 8:00 am – 6:00 pm (Except Sunday, 11:00 am – 4:00 pm) (April – December) Monday – Saturday, 8:00 am – 5:00 pm (December – March)

Home of the original Baby Swiss – you can watch through a window as cheese is being made (best time to view is 8:00 am – 2:00 pm weekdays). We learned milk is brought in the early mornings from neighboring Amish farms. Cultures and enzymes are added to form curd. Curd is pressed into molds and brine salted. Each cheese is aged at least a month for flavor. A short video is always playing that details this process if you can't view it personally.

YODER'S AMISH HOME

6050 State Route 515 (between Trail and Walnut Creek)
Millersburg 44654

- ❑   Activity: Tours
- ❑   Telephone: (330) 893-2541
- ❑   Admission: Tours $3.50 Adult, $1.50 Children (under 12). Buggy Rides $2.00 Adult, $1.00 Children (under 12)

O ne home was built in 1866 and shows authentic furnishings
from that period. Learn what a "hoodle stup" is. Then step
into an 1885 barn with animals to pet. Most popular tends to be
the turkeys – (Yes, you can try to pet turkeys!). Buggy rides are
given by retired real Amish farmers who are personable and tell
stories during the ride.

SHOENBRUNN VILLAGE STATE MEMORIAL

State Route 259 (4 miles East of I-77 exit 81)
New Philadelphia 44663

- ❑ Activity: Ohio History
- ❑ Telephone: (800) 752-2711 or (330) 339-3636
  www.ohiohistory.org/places/shoenbr
- ❑ Hours: Monday – Saturday, 9:30 am – 5:00 pm. Sunday, Noon –
  5:00 pm (Summer). Weekends only, (September and October)
- ❑ Admission: $5.00 Adult, $1.25 Youth (6-12)
- ❑ Miscellaneous: Museum. Video orientation. Gift Shop.

T ake a self-guided tour of the reconstructed log building village
founded by a Moravian missionary in 1772. Church members
tried to convert Delaware Indians to Christianity, but, after 5 years
of Indian hostility, they were forced (300) to abandon the area and
the village was destroyed. Being the first settlement in Ohio,
Shoenbrunn claims the first civil code, the first church, and the
first school.

TRUMPET IN THE LAND

Shoenbrunn Amphitheatre (I-77 to Exit 81)
New Philadelphia 44663

- ❑ Activity: Ohio History
- ❑ Telephone: (330) 339-1132
- ❑ Hours: Daily, (except Sunday). 8:30 pm (mid-June to August)
- ❑ Admission: $13.00 Adult, $6.00 Children (under 12)

I n an Ohio Frontier setting, meet historical characters like David
Zeisgerber (missionary), Simon Girtz (renegade), Captain Pipe
(young warrior who hated white men) and John Heikewelder

(explorer). The Revolutionary War breaks out and Moravian Christians would not take sides. Sadly, in the end, American militia brutally massacre 96 Christian Indians at Gnadenhutten. 70 member cast.

TUSCORA PARK

New Philadelphia - South Broadway Street (I-77 to US-250 east), 44663. *Activity:* Amusements. **http://web.tusco.net/park**. (800) 527-3387. Summertime hours. The central feature is the antique big carousel or the summer showcase concert series. What draws little ones and families is also the Ferris wheel, 6-8 kiddie rides, batting cages and putt-putt - all at low prices. Most rides are 25-50 cents and activities are around $1.00. Great alternative to higher priced amusement "vacations".

356TH FIGHTER GROUP RESTAURANT

North Canton - 4919 Mount Pleasant Road, 44702. *Activity:* Theme Restaurants. **www.starcom2.com/356thFG**. (330) 494-3500. WWII theme with high windows that overlook runways of the Akron/Canton airport.

HARRY LONDON CHOCOLATE FACTORY

5353 Lauby Road (I-77 Exit 113 Airport), **North Canton** 44720

- ❑ Activity: Tours
- ❑ Telephone: (800) 321-0444, **www.londoncandies.com/acb**
- ❑ Hours: Monday – Saturday, 9:00 am – 4:00 pm. Sunday, Noon – 3:30 pm (Actual production only on weekdays)
- ❑ Admission: $2.00 Adult and Senior, $1.00 Youth (6-18)
- ❑ Tour: 45 minutes – 1 hour. Reservations suggested (if group tour) Every half hour.
- ❑ Miscellaneous: Chocolate Hall of Fame, Candy Store

Learn about cocoa beans and the history of chocolate (we didn't know the beans grow in pods on trunks of trees near the equator) Live the fantasy of making, molding, wrapping, and boxing chocolate candy, fudge, and butterscotch. Be sure to try a London Mint (money wrapped candy) or a London Buckeye.

MAPS AIR MUSEUM

5359 Massillon Road, Akron-Canton Airport (I-77 to Exit 113)
North Canton 44720

- ❑ Activity: Museums
- ❑ Telephone: (330) 896-6332
  www.angelfire.com/oh/mapsairmuseum
- ❑ Hours: Monday, 9:00 am – 4:00 pm. Wednesday, 6:00 – 9:00
  pm. Saturday, 8:00 am – 4:00 pm
- ❑ Admission: $4.00 Adults, $3.00 Seniors, $2.00 Children (under 12).
- ❑ Miscellaneous: Gift shop

The staff here are pilots, mechanics, officers, and crew who desire to preserve the legacy of America's aviation heritage. Their slogan "Rebuilding History – One Rivet At a Time" really describes their dedication to acquire and renovate some of the world's greatest military aircraft. MAPS offers not just displays of mint condition aircraft, but also a truly unique "hands on" view of the restoration of some of the world's greatest aircraft by people who may have flown them years ago.

NATIONAL ROAD ZANE GREY MUSEUM

8850 East Pike (US-40 / I-70 Norwich Exit), **Norwich** 43767

- ❑ Activity: Museums
- ❑ Telephone: (740) 872-3143, **www.ohiohistory.org/places/natlroad**
- ❑ Hours: Monday – Saturday, 9:30 am – 5:30 pm. Sunday, Noon –
  5:00 pm (May – September). Daily, Except Monday & Tuesday
  (March, April, October and November)
- ❑ Admission: $5.00 Adult, $1.25 Youth (6 – 12)

"Head West Young Man" in a Conestoga wagon as you explore the history of US-40 National Road. Built based on a concept of George Washington, it stretches between western territories in Illinois to the eastern state of Maryland. It was vital to the development of the frontier heading west and later called "America's Main Street". Play a game where children locate all the different types of bridges on this route (examples. the "Y" and "S" Bridge). The facility also commemorates author Zane Grey and his western novels.

ALPINE POTTERY

Roseville - State Route 93, 43777. *Activity:* Tours. (800) 4-ALPINE. *Tours:* 9:00 am - 3:00 pm (Monday - Friday).

ROBINSON RANSBOTTOM POTTERY

Ransbottom Road (SR-22 south to SR-93 south to County Road 102 east - Follow signs), **Roseville** 43777l

- ❑ Activity: Tours
- ❑ Telephone: (740) 697-7355, **www.ransbottompottery.com**
- ❑ Tours: Weekdays, 9:00 am - 2:00 pm (except for 2 week plant shutdown in the summers and holidays). Guided - By Reservation. Self-guided tours - no appointment necessary. Weekends watch the video tour.
- ❑ Miscellaneous: Pot Shop Gift Shop with below retail prices

Their clay is a special combination of top and bottom clay (what material lies in the middle but isn't used for pottery?). They use 27 tons of clay daily using the processes of casting, ram and spindle pressing, and jiggering. During the tour, you come very near the process, including hot kilns and large press machines. Stay in groups and hold onto small children. Talking with mold castors and watching clay being molded was most interesting. Also very interesting were the beehive kilns (look like brick igloos). Once the items were loaded, the man sealed the doorway with bricks. The pieces are left to heat dry for three days and then four days cooling. This kiln is used for large outdoor pieces (birdbaths, flower pots) that need slow hardening for durability against elements.

SENECAVILLE LAKE RECREATION AREA

Senacaville - (3 miles Southeast of Senecaville on SR-547), 43780. *Activity:* Outdoors. (740) 685-6013. Nature programs. 7,613 acres of camping, hiking trails, boating and rentals, fishing, swimming, visitor center and cabins.

JEFFERSON LAKE STATE PARK

Steubenville - (16 miles Northwest of Steubenville of SR-43), 43944. *Activity:* Outdoors. (740) 765-4459. **www.dnr.state.oh.us/ odnr/parks/directory/jefferson.htm**. 933 acres of camping, hiking trails, boating, fishing, swimming and winter sports.

CREEGAN COMPANY ANIMATION FACTORY

510 Washington Street (I-70 to SR-7 North), **Steubenville** 43952

- ❑ Activity: Tours
- ❑ Telephone Number: (740) 283-3708, **www.weir.net/creegans**
- ❑ Tours: Reservations Preferred. (45 minute tour) Monday – Friday, 10:00 am - 4:00 pm. Saturday, 10:00 am - 2:00 pm.
- ❑ Miscellaneous: Christmas Shop (year round). Retail store sells Creegan's most recent animated figures and scenery. Fancy Food Department (Cake and candy – Free Samples)

Start with the Craft Area where ribbon, yarn, and puppet props abound everywhere. Then, to the Art Department where workers paint faces on molded plastic heads and make costumes. (To make the plastic heads they use a machine press that uses molds to form faces out of sheets of plain white plastic.) In the sculpting area, shelves of hundreds of character head, feet, and hand molds line the walls and a woman sculpts new molds. Finally, peek inside some of the bodies of automated figures to view the electronics that produce body movements. A costumed mascot (Beary Bear) greets and guides your tour. Their theme is "We Make Things Move" and they're the nation's largest manufacturer of animated and costumed characters. (Some customers are Sea World and Walt Disney)

FERNWOOD STATE FOREST

Steubenville - (north of SR-151, southwest of Steubenville), 43952. *Activity:* Outdoors. (330) 339-2205 (New Philadelphia office). Open daily, 6:00 am - 11:00 pm. **www.hcs.ohio-state.edu/ODNR/Forests/stateforests/ fernwood.htm**. 3,023 acres in Jefferson County. 3 mile hiking trail, several picnic areas, 22 family campsites (no fee).

JAGGIN' AROUND

WELSH JAGUAR CLASSIC CAR MUSEUM

Steubenville - 501 Washington Street (off SR-7 - Downtown), 43952. *Activity:* Theme Restaurants. (740) 282-1010. Modern art deco décor with kid's meals served in cardboard classic cars. Attached is the Welsh Jaguar Classic Car Museum. See William Welsh's celebration of the "Glory Days of the Jaguar" that features classic XKs and XKEs. Also, see a Mercedes Gull Wing and 60's Muscle cars. **www.classicar.com/museums/welshjag/welshjag.htm**.

JEFFERSON COUNTY HISTORICAL MUSEUM

Steubenville - 426 Franklin Avenue (Downtown), 43952. *Activity:* Ohio History. (740) 283-1133. Victorian mansion. Steamboat and river history.

STEUBENVILLE - CITY OF MURALS

Steubenville - 501 Washington Street, 43952. *Activity:* The Arts. (740) 282-0938 or (800) 510-4442. **www.steubenvilleoh.com**. *Tours:* Guided tours are available (admission) that includes other tourist spots in the area. During a self-guided tour (free) you can see 25 giant full color (almost 3D) murals with the theme "Preserving a Piece of America" on the sides of downtown buildings. Each has its own name with some of the most interesting being Stanton Park, Ohio River Oil Company and Steam Laundry – these all "jump" right off the wall and appear almost like a photograph. All murals can be seen on their website prior to your visit.

ALPINE HILLS MUSEUM

Sugarcreek - 106 West Main Street, 44681. *Activity:* Ohio History. (330) 852-4113. *Hours:* Daily, 10:00 am – 4:30 pm, except Sundays 1:00-4:00pm (April – November). *Admission:* Donation. 3 floors of Swiss, German and Amish heritage (includes kitchen, cheese house and woodworking displays).

DAVID WARTHER MUSEUM

1387 SR-39 (In the Dutch Valley Complex), **Sugarcreek** 44681

- ☐   Activity: Museums
- ☐   Telephone: (330) 852-3455
- ☐   Hours: Monday – Saturday, 9:00 am - 5:00 pm.

David Warther II is the grandson of Ernest Warther (*see separate listing "Warther Carvings Tour"*). He continues the legacy of carvings with a special emphasis on carving the theme "The History of the Ship" – solid legal ivory model ships. Even the rig lines are carved of ivory (one strand measures $1/10,000^{th}$ of an inch in diameter). David's workshop is on location.

DER DUTCHMAN / DUTCH VALLEY RESTAURANTS

Sugarcreek, 44681, Walnut Creek, Plain City and Bolivar. *Activity:* Theme Restaurants. (330) 893-2926. **www.DutchCorp.com**. Amish kitchen cooking with family style dinners, markets and gift shops. Amish crafts and buggies create an authentic atmosphere. Closed Sundays.

LAZY G RANCH

Toronto - (SR-152 to CR-242), 43964. *Activity:* Animals & Farms. (740) 544-6266. Horseback riding stable. Group rides with campouts.

COBLENTZ CHOCOLATE COMPANY
4917 SR-515 and SR-39, **Walnut Creek** 44687

❑   Activity: Tours
❑   Telephone: (800) 338-9341
❑   Hours: Monday – Saturday,   9:00 am – 6:00 pm (June – October)
     9:00 am – 5:00 pm (November – May)

Watch through the kitchen windows as chocolate is stirred in large vats with automatic paddle stirs. Caramels, fruits, and nuts are hand dipped and layered on large trays to cool and dry. Also, see molds for chocolate forms used to create bars of barks and holiday shapes. Savor the sweet smell of fresh milk and dark chocolate as you decide which treats to buy. Our favorite was the chocolate covered Dutch pretzels with sprinkles or nuts on top.

ALPINE - ALPA

Wilmot - 1504 US-62, 44689. Activity: *Outdoors.* (330) 359-5454 or (800) 546-2572. *Hours:* Daily, 9:00 am - 8:00 pm (Spring - Thanksgiving). Serving lunch and dinner beginning at 11:00 am. This is home of the "World's Largest Cuckoo Clock". The Guinness Book of World Records has it listed as 23 ½ feet high, 24 feet long and 13 ½ feet wide. Trudy, a life-size mannequin with a German accent, opens shutters to greet you. The Swiss Village Market has viewing windows (to watch cheese-making), restaurants and shops. Look for the 40-foot diorama with waterfalls and a moving train.

BUGGY HAUS

Winesburg - County Road 160 (off Route 62), 44690. *Activity:* Tours. *Telephone:* None (Amish). *Hours:* Monday – Saturday, 8:00 am – 5:00 pm. See the world's largest buggy or take a one hour guided tour of a working Amish buggy shop and three floors of warehouse and displays. You'll see over 500 units of buggies, carts, sleighs, and wooden riding horses for sale. Climb aboard them to test them out. Their tour includes the history and cultural differences of buggies around the country.

OHIO AGRICULTURAL RESEARCH AND DEVELOPMENT CENTER

1680 Madison Avenue (off I-71 SR-83 or off US-30)
Wooster 44691

❑ Activity: Tours

❑ Telephone: (330) 263-3700, **www.oardc.ohio-state.edu**

❑ Hours: Monday – Friday, 7:30 am - 4:30 pm (Summer)
Monday – Friday, 8:00 am - 5:00 pm (September – June)

❑ Tours: Guided tours by appointment. Self guided maps at visitor center.

This center is the foremost, nationally known agricultural research Ohio State University facility with inventions to their credit such as crop dusting and adding vitamin D to milk. See the famous cow with the window in it's stomach (actually neuroscopic implant line that allows researchers to study nutrition and digestions) or the electronic sensor detectors that record milk production. Many experiments on insects, greenhouses, honeybees and composting are going on. One project is to turn cornstarch (89 cents/lb.) into xanthum gum ($7.00/lb). This might spark the future scientist within your child.

OHIO LIGHT OPERA

Wooster - Freedlander Theatre, College of Wooster, 44691. *Activity:* The Arts. **www.wooster.edu/OHIOLIGHTOPERA**. (330) 263-2345. Professional company presents 19th & 20th century operettas. (Summer)

SECREST ARBORETUM

Wooster - 1680 Madison Avenue, 44691. *Activity:* Outdoors. (330) 263-3761. Over 2000 species of native and exotic plants and trees, especially Old World roses.

WAYNE CENTER FOR THE ARTS

Wooster - 237 South Walnut Street, 44691. *Activity:* The Arts. (330) 264-2787. Presents chamber music series, dance programs, traditional arts festival, exhibits, classes and workshops.

WAYNE COUNTY HISTORICAL SOCIETY MUSEUM

Wooster – 546 East Bowman Street, 44691. *Activity:* Ohio History. (330) 264-8856. *Hours:* Tuesday – Sunday, 2:00 – 4:30 pm. Log Cabin. Schoolhouse. Indians. Women's Vintage Dress Shop. Carpenter Shop. Admission.

LORENA STERNWHEELER

Moored at Zane's Landing (West End of Market Street – I-70 to Downtown Zanesville Exit – Follow signs), **Zanesville** 43701

❑ Activity: Tours
❑ Telephone: (800) 246-6303 or (740) 455-8883
   www.zanesvilleoh.com/lorena
❑ Hours: Wednesday – Sunday at 1:00, 2:30, and 4:00 pm (June – August). Weekends Only (September / October)
❑ Admission: $5.00 Adult, $2.50 Children (2-12)

There was a mythical sweetheart of the Civil War named Lorena who inspired a song written by the famous Zanesvillian, Rev. Henry Webster. The 104' long, 59-ton boat was christened "Lorena" after that popular song. A one-hour cruise on the Muskingum River at a very reasonable rate.

MAPLETREE BASKETS

Zanesville - 705 Keen Street, 43701. *Activity:* Tours. (888) 2BASKET or (740) 450-8824. **www.mapletreebaskets.com**. *Hours:* Monday – Friday, 8:00 am to 5:00 pm. Saturday by appointment. Manufacturing tours given for groups of 12 or more by advanced reservation only. Watch local artisans hand weave fine quality maple hard wood baskets.

ZANESVILLE ART CENTER

Zanesville - 620 Military Road, 43701. *Activity:* The Arts. (740) 452-0741. **www.zanesvilleoh.com/art/zac.** Visit a 300-year-old English panel room with classic works, glass, ceramics, ancient, Asian, African and contemporary art. Free admission.

MUSKINGUM RIVER STATE PARK

Zanesville - (120 acres along 80 miles of the Muskingum River extending from Devola to Ellis Locks), 43702. *Activity:* Outdoors. **www.dnr.state.oh.us/odnr/parks/directory/muskngmr.htm.** (740) 452-3820. Camping, hiking trails, boating, fishing are available.

BLUE ROCK STATE PARK

Zanesville - (12 miles Southeast of Zanesville off SR-60 and County Road 45), 43720. *Activity:* Outdoors. (740) 674-4794. **www.dnr.state.oh.us/odnr/parks/directory/bluerock.htm.** 350 acres of camping, hiking trails, boating, fishing, swimming and winter sports.

DILLON STATE PARK

Zanesville - (5 miles NW of Zanesville off SR-146), 43830. *Activity:* Outdoors. (740) 453-4377. **www.dnr.state.oh.us/odnr/parks/directory/dillon.htm.** 7690 acres of camping, hiking trails, boating and rentals, fishing, swimming, winter sports. Family cabins with A/C and cable.

ZOAR VILLAGE

198 Main Street (SR-212 – I-77 to Exit 93), **Zoar** 44697

❑ Activity: Ohio History
❑ Telephone (800) 262-6195 or (330) 874-3011
   www.ohiohistory.org/places/zoar
❑ Hours: Wednesday – Saturday, 9:30 am – 5:00 pm. Sunday & Holidays, Noon – 5:00 pm (Summer) Weekends Only, (April, May, September, October)

- ❑ Admission: $5.00 Adult, $4.00 Seniors, $1.25 Youth (6-12)
- ❑ Miscellaneous: Video presentation first explains Zoar history.

Zoar means "a sanctuary from evil". They, as a society of Separatists (separation between church and state), were known for their bountiful gardening designs based on the bible. The 12 block district of 1800's homes and shops include a dairy, bakery, museum, gardens, storehouse, tin shops, wagon shops, and blacksmith. They are actual original buildings in a real town of 75 families. Walk along streets dispersed with restored residences and shops for modern clients.

Chapter 3
Central West Area

Our Favorites...

- Carillion Historical Park
- Caverns
- Clifton Mill
- Freshwater Farms
- Hobart Welded Sculpture
- United States Air Force Museum
- Young's Jersey Dairy Farm

LOGAN COUNTY HISTORICAL MUSEUM

Bellefontaine - 521 East Columbus Avenue, 43311. *Activity:* Ohio History. (937) 593-7557. *Hours:* Wednesday, Friday – Sunday, 1:00 – 4:00 pm (May – October). Weekends only (November-April). Schoolroom, Physician's office, Indians, Battles.

ZANE SHAWNEE CAVERNS

7092 SR-540 (5 miles east of town), **Bellefontaine** 43311

❑ Activity: Outdoors
❑ Telephone: (937) 592-9592
   http://zaneshawneecaverns.homestead.com/introduction.html
❑ Hours: Daily, 10:00 am - 5:00 pm (May - September)
   Weekends only, (April and October)
❑ Admission: $7.00 Adult, $4.00 Children (under age 12)
❑ Miscellaneous: Shawnee and Woodland Nation American Indian Museum - with artifacts from actual tribe members.

The tour and slide show lasts about 45 minutes. See crystals in objects formed like straws, draperies, and popcorn. They boast the only "cave pearls" found in Ohio. Kids will be in awe! There are a lot of extras like hayrides, gift shop, snack bar, and camping. Remember to dress appropriately because the temperature in the caverns is a constant 48-50 degrees F. This property is now owned and operated by the Shawnee People.

MERCER COUNTY HISTORICAL SOCIETY MUSEUM

Celina - 130 East Market Street, 45822. *Activity:* Ohio History. (419) 586-6065. **www.seemore.org/history**. *Hours:* Wednesday – Friday, 8:30 am – 4:00 pm and Sunday, 1:00 – 4:00 (October – April). Chronicles the past 200 years. Riley House. Free admission.

CLIFTON MILL

75 Water Street (I-70 West to SR-72 South), **Clifton** 45316

❑   Activity: Tours

❑   Telephone: (937) 767-5501, **www.cliftonmill.com**

❑   Hours: Monday – Friday, 9:00 am – 5:00 pm. Saturday – Sunday,
    8:00 am – 5:00 pm. (Restaurant), Monday - Friday, 9:00 am –
    3:00 pm. Weekends, 8:00 am – 4:00 pm

❑   Miscellaneous: Restaurant and store.

A surprise treat tucked away in a small town where Woody
Hayes grew up. Built in 1869 on the Little Miami River, it is
the largest operating water powered gristmill in the nation. Before
or after a yummy breakfast or lunch overlooking the river, take a
self-guided tour for a small fee. There are 5 floors to view. Start
in the basement where the turbine takes the flowing water's energy
to move a system of belts to the grindstones. As the stones rotate,
raw grain is poured into the hopper, through a chute and into a
space between the stones which grind it. The most interesting part
of the tour is the belt to bucket elevators that are the "life of the
mill" transporting grain and flour up and down 5 levels. Be sure to
buy some pancake mix to take home!

CLIFTON MILL RESTAURANT

Clifton - (near Springfield) - 75 Water Street (off SR-72), 45316.
Activity: Theme Restaurants. **www.cliftonmill.com**. (937) 767-
5501. An actual working gristmill with restaurant seating with a
view of a waterwheel, river and covered bridge. Pancakes, mush,
grits and bread are made from product produced at the mill. Best
pork barbecue sandwich ever! Breakfast and lunch only.

PAUL LAWRENCE DUNBAR STATE MEMORIAL

219 North Paul Lawrence Dunbar Street (2 blocks north of 3rd
Street, east of US-35), **Dayton** 45401

❑   Activity: Museums

❑   Telephone: (800) 860-0148
    www.ohiohistory.org/places/dunbar
❑   Hours: Wednesday – Saturday, 9:30 am – 4:30 pm. Sunday &
    Holidays, Noon – 4:30 pm (Memorial Day – Labor Day)
    Weekends only, (September, October)
❑   Admission: $3.00 Adult, $1.25 Youth (6-12)

The restored home of the first African American to achieve acclaim in American literature. From a young poet at age 6 to a nationally known figure (until his death at age 33 of tuberculosis), the guide helps you understand his inspiration especially from his mother and her stories of slavery. Personal belongings like his bicycle built by the Wright Brothers and a sword presented to him by President Roosevelt lead you to his bedroom where he wrote 100 novels, poems and short stories.

CITIZEN'S MOTORCAR PACKARD MUSEUM

Dayton - 420 South Ludlow Street – Downtown, 45402. *Activity:* Museums. (937) 226-1917. *Hours:* Tuesday – Friday, Noon – 5:00 pm. Saturday and Sunday, 1:00 – 5:00 pm. See the world's largest collection of Packard automobiles in an authentic showroom. The art deco Packard dealership interior exhibits are spread through 6 settings, Included are the service area and a salesman's office with an old fan blowing and a radio playing early 1900's music.

DAYTON BALLET

Dayton - 140 North Main Street, 45402. *Activity:* The Arts. (937) 449-5060. **www.daytonballet.org**. Professional company performs new works by young American choreographers. (October – April)

DAYTON OPERA

Dayton - 125 East First Street, 45402. *Activity:* The Arts. (937) 228-0662. Presents opera, operetta and musical theatre featuring international and rising young American talent. (October – May)

DAYTON PHILHARMONIC ORCHESTRA

Dayton - 125 East First Street, 45402. *Activity:* The Arts. (937) 224-9000. Plays classical, pops, and chamber series.   Summer outdoor concerts.

DAYTON VISUAL ARTS CENTER

Dayton - 40 West Fourth Street, 45402. *Activity:* The Arts. (937) 224-3822. **www.sinclair.edu/community/duac**. Enjoy programs that showcase regional artists in Terra Cotta District.

OLD COURTHOUSE AND MONTGOMERY COUNTY HISTORICAL MUSEUM

Dayton - 7 North Main Street, Downtown, 45402. *Activity:* Ohio History. (937) 228-6271. *Hours:* Tuesday – Friday, 10:00 am – 4:30 pm, Saturday, Noon – 4:00 pm. Wright Brothers and Pattersons.

DAYTON ART INSTITUTE

Dayton - 456 Belmonte Park North, 45405. *Activity:* The Arts. (937) 223-5277 or (800) 296-4426. **www.daytonartinstitute.org**. *Hours:* Daily, 10:00am - 5:00 pm. Art collection spanning 5000 years. Experiencenter (features 20 hands-on activities) encourages interaction with art and experimentation with artistic elements of line, pattern, color, texture and shape. Free admission.

CARILLON HISTORICAL PARK

1000 Carillon Boulevard (I-75 to Exit 51), **Dayton** 45409

- ❏   Activity: Ohio History
- ❏   Telephone: (937) 293-2841, **www.carillonpark.org**
- ❏   Hours: Tuesday - Saturday, 9:30 am - 5:00 pm, Sunday and Holidays, Noon - 5:00 pm (mid-April to October).
- ❏   Admission: $2.00 Adult, $1.50 Senior, $1.00 Youth (3-17)
- ❏   Miscellaneous: Museum Store. Wooded park with Ohio's largest bell tower, the Carillon Bell Tower (57 bells)

A must see - very comfortable and educational - over 65 acres of historical buildings and outdoor exhibits of history, invention and transportation. Called the "Little Greenfield Village" in Miami Valley and we definitely agree! Our favorites are the Deed's Barn (learn about the Barn Gang and the big companies they started) and the rail cars that you can actually board-the Barney & Smith is ritzy!

SUNWATCH

2301 West River Road (I-75 to Exit 51), **Dayton** 45409

- ❑ Activity: Ohio History
- ❑ Telephone (937) 268-8199
- ❑ Hours: Tuesday – Saturday, 9:00 – 5:00 pm. Sunday and Holidays, Noon – 5:00 pm. (mid-March to November)
- ❑ Admission: $5.00 Adult, $3.00 Youth (6-17) & Seniors
- ❑ Tours: Guided tours daily at 1: 30 pm (Summer)

A n 800 year old reconstructed 12th Century Indian Village with self guided tours of the thatched huts, gardens and artifacts of the lifestyle of a unique culture. Some activities include story telling, archery, multi-media presentation, and best of all, learn to tell time by charting the sun. See how the Indians used flint and bone to create jewelry and tools - then buy some as souvenirs.

WRIGHT CYCLE COMPANY

22 South Williams Street (off West 3rd Street), **Dayton** 45409

- ❑ Activity: Museums
- ❑ Telephone: (937) 443-0793, **www.nps.gov/daav/**
- ❑ Hours: Monday - Saturday, 8:30 am - 4:30 pm. Sunday, 11:00 am - 4:30 pm (Summer). Wednesday - Sunday only, (Rest of year)
- ❑ Admission: Donation

A ctual site where the Wright Brothers had a bicycle business from 1895-1897 and developed their own brand of bicycles. On this site, they also developed ideas that led to the invention of flight almost 7 years later. We walked on the same floorboards that the brothers did and saw actual plans for a flying bicycle!

AULLWOOD AUDUBON CENTER AND FARM

Dayton - 1000 Aullwood Road, 45414. *Activity:* Outdoors. (937) 890-7360. **www.audubon.org**. *Hours:* Monday-Saturday 9:00 am - 5:00 pm, Sunday, 1:00 - 5:00 pm. Closed holidays. *Admission:* $4.00 Adult, $2.00 Child (2-18). Protecting birds and wildlife, they educate on woods, streams, ponds, prairies, meadows and organic farming through guided experiences.

BOONSHOFT MUSEUM OF DISCOVERY

2600 DeWeese Parkway (North of downtown I-75 to exit 57B, follow signs), **Dayton** 45414

❑   Activity: Museums
❑   Telephone: (937) 275-9156
❑   Hours: Monday – Saturday, 9:00 am – 5:00 pm.
     Sunday, Noon – 5:00 pm
❑   Admission: $4.00 Adult, $2.50 Senior, $1.50 Children (3-16),
     $1.00 additional for Space Theater
❑   Miscellaneous: With memberships here, you also can get free or
     discounted admissions to many museums in Ohio & other states.

Includes Museum of Natural History, Children's Museum plus Lasersphere (computer animated planetarium).

> WILD OHIO – An indoor zoo with small animals in natural
> surroundings. Visit the den of bobcat Van Cleve.
> ANCIENT WORLD – Egyptian artifacts with 3000 year old
> mummy.
> SCIENCE CENTER – Inventions stations, preschool area,
> chemistry lab, and discovery tower provides hands on
> adventures.

WRIGHT STATE UNIVERSITY ARTIST SERIES

Dayton - 3640 Colonel Glenn Highway (Student Union), 45435. *Activity:* The Arts. (937) 775-5544. **www.wright.edu/studsvcs/ union/boxoffice/artist.html**. Presents culturally diverse programs and artists.

GENERAL MOTORS CORPORATION ASSEMBLY PLANT

2601 Stroop Road (I-75 south to Springboro Pike South)
Dayton 45439

❑ Activity: Tours

❑ Telephone: (937) 455-2776

❑ Tours: Thursdays, 9:30 am & 1:00 pm. (Reservations Required)
90 minutes long. Lots of walking. Wear closed-toe shoes. Ages
8 and above. Note: No tours are being given until new
construction is complete. Call for updated tour information.

This plant makes GMC Blazers, Chevy Jimmys and Oldsmobile Bravadas. Watch how they take 1500 - 1800 parts and 2 ½ days to make the finished vehicle roll off the assembly line. Lots of larger parts float above you on conveyors. The highlight is the "body drop" where painted frames meet their chassis by robots. Any child into trucks will enjoy this visit!

COX ARBORETUM

Dayton - 6733 Springboro Pike, 45449. *Activity:* Outdoors. (937) 434-9005. **www.dayton.net/metroparks**. *Hours:* Daily, 8:00 am to dusk. Visitor Center, Weekdays, 8:30 am - 4:30 pm and weekends 1:00 - 4:00 pm. 160 acres including the nationally recognized Edible Landscape Garden.

FAIRBORN SUMMER PARK SERIES

Fairborn - 691 East Dayton-Yellow Springs Road, 45324. *Activity:* The Arts. (937) 754-3090. **www.fairborn.k12.oh.us/city/fonf.html**. Free outdoor concerts from big band to jazz to jugglers. (Friday) (June – July)

UNITED STATES AIR FORCE MUSEUM

Wright Patterson Air Force Base (I-75 to SR-4 East to Harshman
Road Exit), **Fairborn** 45433

❑ Activity: Museums

❑ Telephone: (937) 255-3286, **www.wpafb.af.mil/museum**

- ❑   Hours: Daily, 9:00 am - 5:00 pm
- ❑   Admission: Free
- ❑   Miscellaneous: Largest Gift Shop imaginable

    IMAX THEATER - 6 story with hourly 40 minute
        space/aviation films - feel like you're flying with the
        pilots. (Fee $2.00 - $5.00)

    HUFFMAN PRAIRIE FIELD - See where The Wright Brothers
        first attempted flight. Continuous films played at stations
        throughout the complex. National Aviation Hall of Fame
        is next door. Morphis MovieRide Theater - actually
        move, tilt and shout.

For the best in family entertainment / educational value, this museum is definitely a must see! You'll have a real adventure exploring the world's oldest and largest military aviation museum that features over 50 vintage WWII aircraft (*even the huge 6-engine B-36*) and 300 other aircraft and rockets. See everything from presidential planes, to Persian Gulf advanced missiles and bombs, the original Wright Brothers wind tunnel, to the original Apollo 15 command module. Look for the observation balloon (easy to find—just look up ever so slightly), Rosie the Rivetor and "Little Vittles" parachuted goodies. Discovery Hangar Five follows a common museum trend and focuses on the interactive learning of why things fly and different parts of airplanes.

FORT RECOVERY STATE MEMORIAL

Fort Recovery - One Fort Site Street (SR-49 and SR-119), 45846. *Activity:* Ohio History. **www.ohiohistory.org/places/ftrecovr.** (419) 375-4649. *Hours:* Daily, Noon - 5:00 pm (Summer). Weekends Only (May and September). *Admission:* $2.00 Adult, $1.00 Youth (6-12). The remaining blockhouses with connecting stockade wall are where General Arthur St. Clair was defeated by Indians in 1791. A museum with Indian War artifacts and dressed mannequins is also displayed on the property.

BEAR'S MILL

Greenville - Bear's Mill Road (5 miles East on US-36 then South), 45331. *Activity:* Tours. (513) 548-5112. **www.bearsmill.com**. *Tours:* Weekends, 11:00 am – 5:00 pm, (April - November). Thursday - Sunday, 11:00 am – 5:00 pm (December). Store sells flours ground at the mill, gift baskets, handmade pottery. Tour the mill built in 1849 by Gabriel Bear where grinding stones (powered by water flowing beneath the building) grind flour and meal. The process is slow and kept cool to retard deteriorating wholesome nutrients.

GARST MUSEUM, DARKE COUNTY HISTORICAL SOCIETY

Greenville - 205 North Broadway, 45331. *Activity:* Ohio History. (937) 548-5250. *Hours:* Tuesday – Saturday, 11:00 am – 5:00 pm, Sunday, 1:00 – 5:00 pm. Closed January. *Admission:* $1.00. Annie Oakley memorabilia. Lowell Thomas (world famous radio broadcaster), Anthony Wayne, Native American artifacts. Village of shops.

JIM'S DRIVE-IN RESTAURANT

Greenville - 100 Martz Street, 45331. *Activity:* Theme Restaurants. (937) 548-5078. Car hops, root beer, Spanish hot dogs. Lunch and dinner only. (Late March through mid-August)

CARRIAGE HILL FARM AND MUSEUM
7860 East Shull Road (I-70 to Exit 38 – SR-201 north)
Huber Heights 45424

- ❑ Activity: Animals & Farms
- ❑ Telephone: (937) 879-0461, **www.dayton.net/metroparks**
- ❑ Hours: Monday - Friday, 10:00 am - 5:00 pm.
  Saturday - Sunday, 1:00 - 5:00 pm
- ❑ Admission: Donation
- ❑ Miscellaneous: Visitor's Center - Exhibits, videos, picnic area, fishing, horseback riding, cross country skiing, hayrides and bobsled rides.

The self-guided tour of an 1880's working farm is a great benefit to the community. The farm includes a summer kitchen, workshop, black smith and barns. They are best to visit when workers are planting or harvesting gardens. The third Saturday of each month is interactive chore day.

SULLIVAN-JOHNSON MUSEUM OF HARDIN COUNTY

Kenton - 223 North Main Street, 43326. *Activity:* Ohio History. (419) 673-7147. *Hours:* Thursday – Sunday, 1:00 – 4:00 pm (April – December), Saturday and Sunday Only (Rest of Year). Victorian mansion with Indian relics, Alaskan Art, Wilson footballs (manufactured in Ada, OH), iron toys, children's hands-on Discovery Room of history.

INDIAN LAKE STATE PARK

Lakeview   - 2 miles North of Lakeview on SR-235), 43331. *Activity:* Outdoors. (937) 843-2717. **www.dnr.state.oh.us/odnr/ parks/directory/indianlk.htm**. 6448 acres of camping, hiking trails, boating, fishing, swimming and winter sports.

LOCKINGTON LOCKS STATE MEMORIAL

Lockington - 5 miles North of Piqua-Lockington Road (I-75 to exit 83 West on SR-25A), 45356. *Activity:* Ohio History. (800) 686-1535. **www.ohiohistory.org/places/lockingt/index.html**. *Hours:* Daily, Dawn to Dusk. Free admission. View portions of six original locks (elevation adjusters for canal boats) and the aqueduct that lowered boats 67 feet into the Miami-Erie Canal.

MIAMISBURG MOUND

Miamisburg - (I-75 to SR-725 exit 42, follow signs), 45342. *Activity:* Outdoors. **www.ohiohistory.org/places/miamisbur**. (937) 866-5632. *Hours:* Daily, Dawn to Dusk. Park, Picnic. Take the 116 stairs up a 68-foot high and 1.5 acre wide mound built by American Indians. This is the largest conical burial mound in Ohio.

WRIGHT B. FLYER

Miamisburg - 10550 Springboro Pike (SR-741 – Dayton International Airport), 45342. *Activity:* Museums. (937) 885-2327. *Hours:* Tuesday, Thursday, and Saturday, 9:00 am – 2:00 pm. *Admission:* Periodical flights on Wright B available for a charge. Otherwise, only donations. This hangar houses a flyable replica of the 1911 plane built by Wilbur and Orville Wright. They also have a half scale model of the plane and other aviation exhibits and souvenirs.

LAKE LORAMIE STATE PARK

Minster - (3 miles Southeast of Minster off SR-66), 45865. *Activity:* Outdoors. (937) 295-2011. **www.dnr.state.oh.us/odnr/ parks/directory/lkloramie**. 2,055 acres of camping, hiking trails, boating, fishing, swimming and winter sports.

BICYCLE MUSEUM OF AMERICA

New Bremen - West Monroe Street (SR-274), 45869. *Activity:* Museums. (419) 629-9249. **www.bicyclemuseum.com**. *Hours:* Monday – Thursday, 11:00 am – 5:00 pm. Friday, 11:00 am – 8:00 pm. Saturday, 11:00am – 2:00 pm. *Admission:* $3.00 Adult, $2.00 Senior, $1.00 Student. A department store has been converted into a showcase of the world's oldest bike (w/out pedals) to the Schwinn family collection (including the 1,000,000[th] bicycle made). Dayton based Huffy Company also donated many pieces and the owners continue to acquire celebrity bikes.

PIQUA HISTORICAL AREA TOUR

North Hardin Road (I-75 to exit 83 County Road 25A West to SR-66 North), **Piqua** 45356

❑   Activity: Ohio History
❑   Telephone: (937) 773-2522 or (800) 752-2619
    www.ohiohistory.org/places/piqua
❑   Hours: Wednesday – Saturday, 9:30 am – 5:00 pm. Sunday and
    Holidays, Noon – 5:00 pm (Summer) Weekends Only
    (September and October)

❑　　Admission: $5.00 Adult, $1.25 Youth (6-12). Includes canal boat ride.

❑　　Miscellaneous: Rides at 12:30, 2:30, and 4:00 pm

Tour the Johnston Farm which includes a 1808 massive log barn which is probably the oldest such barn in Ohio. In the farmhouse, the kids will probably be most interested in the beds made of rope and hay filled sacks. Eight girls slept in one room (ages 2-20) and three boys in another. Many youth games of that time period are displayed. The Winter Kitchen is also very interesting – especially the size of the walk-in fireplace. The General Harrison canal boat is powered by Cindy and Sammy, two mules, which pull the boat down and back on a section of the Old Miami-Erie Canal (Cincinnati to Toledo). The cargo boat was once used to transport produce and meat at a speed limit of 4 MPH. The boats were fined $10.00 for speeding although many paid the fine and continued going 10 MPH. Once the railroads came, canals became obsolete.

ELDORA SPEEDWAY

Rossburg – 45362. *Activity:* Sports. **www.eldoraspeedway.com.** (937) 338-3815. U.S.A.C. Sprint, UMP Modifieds, and Stock Car racing. (April - October)

THE SPOT

Sidney - 201 South Ohio Avenue, 45365. *Activity:* Theme Restaurants. (937) 492-9181. Freshly ground beef burgers and baked-fresh pies here since 1907. The real appeal for the kids is the curb service at the car hop outside (seasonal). Parents will like the old-fashioned prices - the most expensive item is under $4.00. Lunch/Dinner served. Sit-down Diner too.

CLARK STATE PERFORMING ARTS CENTER

Springfield - 300 South Fountain Avenue, 45501. *Activity:* The Arts. (937) 328-3874. **www.clark.cc.oh.us/pac.htm**. Hosts national and regional performers, recording artists, Broadway shows, and family programs. (September - June)

SPRINGFIELD MUSEUM OF ART

Springfield - 107 Cliff Park Road, 45501. *Activity:* The Arts. (937) 325-4673. **www.spfld-museum-of-art.com**. Permanent collection of 19th & 20th century American/ European art.

SPRINGFIELD SUMMER ARTS FESTIVAL

Springfield - 150 Cliff Park Road, 45501. *Activity:* The Arts. (937) 324-2712. Five weeks of free music and theatre in Veterans Park. (June – July)

SPRINGFIELD SYMPHONY ORCHESTRA

Springfield – 45501. **www.springfieldsym.org**. *Activity:* The Arts. (937) 325-8100. Community orchestra presents series with guest artists.

BUCK CREEK STATE PARK

Springfield - 1901 Buck Creek Lane (4 miles East of Springfield on SR-4), 45502. *Activity:* Outdoors. (937) 322-5284. **www.dnr. state.oh.us/odnr/parks/directory/buckck.htm**. 4030 acres of camping, hiking trails, boating and rentals, fishing, swimming and winter sports. 24 family cabins with A/C.

GRAND LAKE ST. MARY'S STATE PARK

St. Mary's - (2 miles West of St. Mary's on SR-703), 45885. *Activity:* Outdoors. (419) 394-3611. **www.dnr.state.oh.us/odnr/ parks/directory/grndlake.htm**. Nature programs. 14,000 acres of camping, boating and rentals, fishing, swimming and winter sports.

ST. MARY'S FISH FARM

St. Mary's – SR-364 (East Side of Grand Lake), 45885. *Activity:* Animals & Farms. (419) 394-5170. **www.seemore.org/history**. *Hours:* Daily, 9:00 am - 4:00 pm. After boating or swimming on Grand Lake (man-made), wander through 52 acres of ponds where pike, catfish, etc. are raised. The farm is one of the only three in Ohio and is the only farm with a large mouth bass hatchery.

SYCAMORE STATE PARK

Trotwood - (1 mile North of Trotwood on SR-49), 45426. *Activity:* Outdoors. (937) 854-4452. **www.dnr.state.oh.us/odnr/ parks/directory/sycamore.htm**. Snowmobiling. Bridle trails. 2,300 acres of camping, hiking trails, fishing and winter sports.

BRUKNER NATURE CENTER

Troy - 5995 Horseshoe Bend Road, Exit #73 off of I-75 (West on SR-55, 3 miles to Horseshoe Bend Road), 45373. *Activity:* Outdoors. (937) 698-6493. *Hours:* Monday – Saturday, 9:00 am – 5:00 pm. Sunday, 12:30 – 5:00 pm. This 164 acre nature preserve's attractions include 6 miles of hiking trails, a wildlife rehabilitation center and the interpretive center. The 1804 Iddings log house was built by the first settlers in Miami County. The Center's animal rehabilitation has over 65 permanent residents on display. Hiking trails open dawn until dusk.

HOBART WELDED SCULPTURE PARK

400 Trade Square East (SR-41 to Ridge), **Troy** 45373

- ❑ Activity: Outdoors
- ❑ Telephone: (937) 332-5000.
- ❑ Hours: Open dawn to dusk.

An outdoor collection of a dozen welded sculptures from students at the Hobart Institute of Welding Technology (an esteemed welding school). Be sure to check out the "Checkmarks" or "Unity of Man" (one of the nation's largest bronze fountains). The column represents family while the water expresses continuity of life. The "Sound Chamber" actually allows visitors to "play" with the sculpture as its steel and aluminum structure gives an Island Pacific sound when thumped on, strung, or beat with sticks.

KISER LAKE STATE PARK

Urbana - (17 miles Northwest of Urbana on SR-235), 43070. *Activity:* Outdoors. (937) 362-3822. **www.dnr.state.oh.us/odnr/ parks/directory/kisrlake.htm**. 870 acres of camping, hiking trails, boating and rentals, fishing, swimming and winter sports.

CEDAR BOG AND NATURE PRESERVE

Urbana - 980 Woodburn Road (off SR-68 North / I-70 to Springfield / off SR-36), 43078. *Activity:* Outdoors. (937) 484-3744. *Hours:* Wednesday - Sunday, 9:00 am - 4:30 pm (April - September). *Admission:* $3.00 Adult, $1.25 Children (6-12). **www.ohiohistory.org/places/cedarbog**. A bog is a remnant of the Ice Age (glaciers and mastodons) and public tours take you to the boardwalk over this bog. Below you'll see the black, wet, slimy muck and chilly dampness created by a constant water table and cool springs. In contrast, see excellent orchid, prairie and woodland wildflowers.

FRESHWATER FARMS OF OHIO

2624 State Route 68 (north of downtown), **Urbana** 43078

❑ Activity: Animals & Farms
❑ Telephone: (937) 652-3701 or (800) 634-7434
 www.fwfarms.com
❑ Hours: Monday - Friday, 1:00 - 6:00 pm
 Saturday, 10:00 am - 6:00 pm.
❑ Tours: By appointment. Free
❑ Miscellaneous: Supplies for ponds at home - compatible fish, frogs. Produces several hundred thousand trout sold to premium restaurants.

Start your tour by petting a sturgeon fish. Why can you touch them, but not catfish? They raise rainbow trout that are bred in large water tanks. Farmer Smith, a marine biologist with a doctorate in nutrition, and his father (an engineer), developed a system of tracks and tanks using re-circulated pure cleaned water. The fish are really spoiled with a special diet and solar heated hatchery. View the spring water "ponds" with gravel bottoms (outside) and put a quarter in the machine to get fish food to feed the fish. These fish are really spoiled, aren't they?

NEIL ARMSTRONG AIR AND SPACE MUSEUM

500 South Apollo Drive (I-75 to Exit 111), **Wapakoneta** 45895

□   Activity: Museums
□   Telephone: (419) 738-8811 or (800) 860-0142
     www.ohiohisstory.org/places/armstron
□   Hours: Monday – Saturday, 9:30 am – 5:00 pm
□   Sunday, Noon – 5:00 pm. Closed Winter Holidays.
□   Admission: $5.00 Adult, $1.25 Youth (6-12)

The museum honors Neil Armstrong (a Wapakoneta native) and other area aeronauts (like the Wright Brothers) and their flying machines. After greeted by a NASA Skylaneer flown by Armstrong in the early 1960's, trace the history of flights from balloons to space travel. Look at the Apollo crew spacesuits or watch a video of lunar space walks. In the Astro Theater, pretend you're on a trip to the moon. Another favorite is the Infinity Cube – 18 square feet covered with mirrors that make you feel like you've been projected into space. Blast OFF!

MAC-O-CHEE AND MAC-O-CHEEK CASTLES (PIATT CASTLES)

SR-245 (Route 33 West to SR-245 East), **West Liberty** 43357

□   Activity: Tours
□   Telephone: (937) 465-2821
□   Hours - (Each Castle): Daily, Noon – 4 pm (April – October), 11:00 am – 5:00 pm (Summer)
□   Admission: (Each Castle): $6.00 Adult, $5.00 Senior (60+) and Students (13-21), $3.00 Children (5-12), Under 5 Free.

Castles in Ohio? Catch the eerie, yet magnificent old castles furnished with collections ranging from 150-800 years old. Both castles were built in the mid-1800's and give a good sense of what the lifestyle of the upper-class Piatt brothers family was like. This tour is manageable for school-aged (*pre-schoolers not suggested*) children and includes lots of land to explore outside. Telling friends they were in a castle is fun too. Because the furniture is original, the homes have an old smell and the rooms look frozen in time. Ceiling paintings and the kitchen/dining area were most interesting.

MAD RIVER THEATER WORKS

West Liberty - 319 North Detroit, 43357. *Activity:* The Arts. (937) 465-6751. Professional company creates and presents plays that communicate regional ways of life and community concerns.

OHIO CAVERNS

2210 East SR-245 (I-70 to US 68 north to SR-507 east),

West Liberty 43357

❑   Activity: Outdoors
❑   Telephone. (513) 465-CAVE, **www.cavern.com/ohiocaverns**
❑   Hours: Daily, 9:00 am – 5:00 pm (April – October). 9:00 am – 4:00 pm (November – March)
❑   Admission: $7.50 Adult, $4.00 Children (5-12). On the premises is a park and gift shop.

This tour is a one hour guided regular or historic tour of the largest caves in Ohio. The temperature here is 54 degrees F. constantly so dress appropriately. Look for the Palace of the Gods and stalagmites that look like cacti or a pump.

NATIONAL AFRO-AMERICAN MUSEUM AND CULTURAL CENTER

Wilberforce - 1350 Brush Row Road (off US-42 - Next to Central State College), 45384. *Activity:* Ohio History. (800) BLK-HIST. **www.ohiohistory.org/places/afroam**. *Hours:* Tuesday - Saturday, 9:00 am - 5:00 pm. Sunday, 1:00 - 5:00 pm. *Admission:* $4.00 Adult, $1.50 Children. Wilberforce was a famous stop on the Underground Railroad and became the center (Wilberforce

University) for black education and achievements. The University was the first owned and operated by Afro-Americans. Best feature is the "From Victory to Freedom - the Afro-American Experience of 1950 - 1960's".

BLUE JACKET

Caesar's Ford Park Amphitheater (SR-35 to Jasper Road, south to Stringtown Road), **Xenia** 45385

- ❑ Activity: The Arts
- ❑ Telephone: (937) 376-4318, **www.bluejacketdrama.com**
- ❑ Hours: Tuesday – Sunday at 8:00 pm (mid-June to Labor Day). Dinner at the Pavillon, 5:30 – 7:30 pm
- ❑ Tours: Backstage guided tours at 4:00 and 5:00 pm
- ❑ Admission: $8.00 - $14.00 Adult, $ 6.00 Children (1-12), $3.50 Adult, $2.00 Children (Backstage tour). Reservations please.

Over two hour outdoor drama recounts the true story of a pure white man adopted by Indians. Blue Jacket became a Shawnee Indian Chief and fought to keep the land and heritage from frontiersmen like Daniel Boone. To add life to the drama, they use live horses, real muskets, cannons, flaming arrows and torches.

GREENE COUNTY HISTORICAL SOCIETY MUSEUM

Xenia - 74 Church Street, 45385. *Activity:* Ohio History. (937) 372-4606. *Hours:* Tuesday – Friday, 1:00 – 3:30 pm, Saturday and Sunday, 2:00 – 4:00 pm (Summer). Weekends Only, (Rest of Year). Restored Victorian home and 1799 James Galloway cabin where Tecumseh tried to "woo" Rebecca Galloway. Admission.

JOHN BRYAN STATE PARK

Yellow Springs - (2 miles Southeast of Yellow Springs on SR-370), 45387. *Activity:* Outdoors. (937) 767-1274. **www.dnr.state. oh.us/odnr/parks/directory/jhnbryan.htm**. 750 acres of hiking trails, camping, fishing and winter sports.

YOUNG'S JERSEY DAIRY FARM

6880 Springfield-Xenia Rd (SR-68, off I-70), **Yellow Springs** 45387

- ❑ Activity: Animals & Farms
- ❑ Telephone: (937) 325-0629, **www.youngsdairy.com**
- ❑ Hours: Daily, 10:00 am – 10:00 pm
- ❑ Tours: Monday – Friday, (April – October) 1 hour, $2.00 Children – Free for Adults. Short video follows the farming process.
- ❑ Miscellaneous: Retail store began in 1960 and is still operated by members of the Young family. Meet the COW family - Barnabe, Cowtherine, Calfleen, and Cowvin. Udders and Putters Miniature Golf, Driving Range, Batting Cage, Corny Maze (a 3-acre corn field maze in late summer), Wagon Rides, Petting Area – Baby Jersey (pretty-faced calves), cows, pigs and sheep; Water Balloon Toss (summertime).

It is truly amazing at just how much food milk producing cows need! A <u>daily</u> average of 25 gallons of water plus 60 lbs. of silage (fermented hay or corn stalks), 30 lbs. of hay, and 20 lbs. of grain! Silage is stored and fermented in silos. Cows have 4 compartment stomachs. (Find out what "chewing her cud" means!) Cows produce milk after having their first calf and are then milked twice daily to produce 4-5 gallons of milk per day. When milk is fresh out of the cow it is cooled immediately to 35 degrees and then bottled. Raw milk has more nutrients and is more digestible (it still has a lot of enzymes). Learn the biggest secret to making GREAT home made ice cream. Go to the petting area and then the wagon ride with a treat at the end in the restaurant. Our family has fallen in love with this place!

MARMON VALLEY FARM

Zanesfield - 7754 SR-292 (off US-33 northwest), 43360. *Activity:* Animals & Farms. (937) 593-8051. **www.marmonvalley.com**. *Hours:* Call for details. Winter and summer activities are available at Marmon Valley Farm. They have live farm animals and a fun barn with rope bridges, rope swings and barn games. Hiking and horseback riding are available. If it's very cold, try ice-skating. When there's snow, you may want to take your sled along for some great sled riding hills. Horseback riding lessons are also available, along with educational classes on Grooming & Saddling, Arena Riding, Trail Riding and you're promised you'll have fun learning. Their barn dances and hayrides are designed to build relationships and learn about the Lord through bible study.

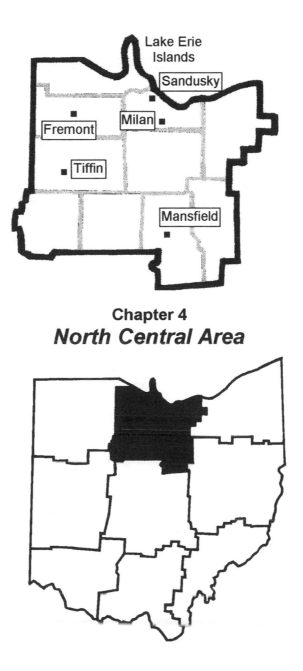

Lake Erie
Islands

Sandusky

Milan

Fremont

Tiffin

Mansfield

Chapter 4
North Central Area

Our Favorites...

- Carousel Magic!
- Kelley's Island
- Mad River & NKP Railroad
- Thomas Edison's Birthplace

ASHLAND COUNTY HISTORICAL MUSEUM

Ashland - 414 Center Street, 44805. *Activity:* Ohio History. (419) 289-3111. *Hours:* Friday and Sunday, 1:00 – 4:00 pm. 1859 house, carriage house, and barn with collections of 19th and 20th Century establishments.

ASHLAND SYMPHONY ORCHESTRA

Ashland - (Ashland University), 44805. *Activity:* The Arts. (419) 289-5115. Community orchestra performs at University (September – May)

ASHLAND WOOSTER DRIVE-IN

Ashland - 1134 East Main Street, 44805. *Activity:* Theme Restaurants. (419) 281-2658. Since 1957 they have been serving root beer, coneys, fries, chicken, onion chips, etc. with carhop service.

LYME VILLAGE

State Route 113 (West of SR-4), **Bellevue** 44811

- ❑ Activity: Ohio History
- ❑ Telephone: (419) 483-4949, **www.lymevillage.com**
- ❑ Hours: Tuesday - Sunday, 1:00 - 5:00 pm (Summer)
    Weekends, 1:00 - 5:00 pm (May and September)
- ❑ Admission: $7.00 Adult, $6.00 Senior (65+), $3.00 Youth (12-18), $20.00 Family
- ❑ Miscellaneous: Gift Shop and concessions.

This 19th Century Ohio Village includes the Wright Mansion, Annie Brown's log home that she owned for 82 years (early Ohio settler exhibits inside), a blacksmith shop, schoolhouse, Grandpa's barn, and the Cooper-Fries general store. All original buildings were moved to this location. Of special interest is the National Museum of Postmark Collector's Club (with the world's largest single collection of postmarks) in a restored post office.

MAD RIVER & NKP RAILROAD SOCIETY MUSEUM

253 South West Street (Just South of US-20), **Bellevue** 44811

❑   Activity: Museums
❑   Telephone: (419) 483-2222, **www.onebellevue.com/madriver**
❑   Hours: Daily, 1:00 – 5:00 pm (Memorial Day - Labor Day)
     Weekends Only, 1:00 – 5:00 pm (May, September, October)
❑   Admission: $2.00 Adult (NKP), $1.00 Children (3-12), $5.00
     Adult (Mad River)

L ook for "Thomas the Tank Engine", "Diesel", or the huge snow plow.   Once you find them, browse through their collections of full-scale locomotives, cabooses, and mail cars – many that you can climb aboard.   Tour guide volunteers are usually retired railway personnel who are knowledgeable and excited to tell you stories about the old railway days.

SENECA CAVERNS

State Route 269, South of (SR-4 off turnpike), **Bellevue** 44828

❑   Activity: Outdoors
❑   Telephone: (419) 483-6711, **www.senecacavernsohio.com**
❑   Hours: Daily, 9:00 am - 7:00 pm (Summer). Weekends, 10:00 am
     - 5:00 pm (May, September, October)
❑   Admission: Yes
❑   Miscellaneous: Light jacket is suggested as the cave is a constant
     54 degrees F.

T ake a one hour tour of the 110 foot deep limestone cave with many small rooms, seven levels and the "Ole Mist'ry River". The cave is actually an earth crack discovered by two boys out hunting in 1872.   To make the tour really fun, stop by Sandy Creek Gem Mining and let your little explorers pan for gems.

COOPER'S MILL AND JELLY FACTORY

Bucyrus - 1414 North Sandusky Avenue (US-30 bypass and SR-4) 44820. *Activity:* Tours. (419) 562-4215. *Hours:* Open Monday - Saturday. *Miscellaneous:* Farm Market - taste test jellies and homemade fudge. Jelly Factory tour lets you watch fruit spreads being made the old fashioned way.

CATAWBA ISLAND STATE PARK

Catawba Island - (off State Route 53), 43452. *Activity:* Outdoors. **www.dnr.state.oh.us/odnr/parks/directory/lakeerie.htm.** (419) 797-4530. Boating, fishing and winter sports.

WILDWOOD WATERPARK

Columbia Station - 11200 East River Road (Route 252), 44028. *Activity:* Amusements. (440) 236-3944. *Hours:* Daily, Daytime. (Mid June – Labor Day). *Admission:* $8.00-$10.00 (ages 5+). A waterpark in the woods with sandy beaches and waterslides, paddle boats, miniature golf, and canoe rides.

HICKORIES MUSEUM

Elyria - Lorain County, 509 Washington Avenue (North of Broad Street), 44035. *Activity:* Ohio History. (440) 322-3341. **www.lcvb.org/101.html.** *Hours:* Tuesday – Friday, 1:00 pm – 4:00 pm. 1894 Tudor home built by inventor Arthur Garford, (padded bicycle seat). Large amount of hickory trees. Admission.

HAYES PRESIDENTIAL CENTER
1337 Hayes Avenue (Rt. 6), **Fremont** 43420

- ❑ Activity: Ohio History
- ❑ Telephone: (800) 998-7737, **www.rbhayes.org**
- ❑ Hours: Monday - Saturday, 9:00 am - 5:00 pm. Sunday and Holidays, Noon - 5:00 pm
- ❑ Admission: $8.50 Adult, $7.50 Senior (60+), $2.50 Youth (6-12) Includes both museum and residence ($5.00 Adult, $1.25 Youth (6-12) separately)

❑   Miscellaneous: Museum Store

The iron gates that greet you at the entrance were the same gates that once stood at the White House during the Hayes administration. The 33-room mansion estate was the home of President and Mrs. Rutherford B. Hayes and is full of family momentos, private papers and books. They give you the sense he dedicated himself to his country. The museum displays the President's daughter's ornate dollhouses and the White House carriage that the family used.

CAR-BET LLAMA RANCH

Galion - 5433 CR-29, 44833. *Activity:* Animals & Farms. (419) 946-4549. Learn about llamas and see demos using llama wool. Llama cart rides.

BUTTERFLY BOX

Kelley's Island - 601 Division Street, 43438. *Activity:* Animals & Farms. (419) 746-2454. Walk through a garden full of hundreds of North American butterflies. Beautiful colored butterflies in an exotic plant environment. Poke you head through the holes of beautiful giant colorful "picture" butterfly paintings for a great photo op. Hours are seasonal, call ahead. Small admission.

KELLEY'S ISLAND STATE PARK

Kelley's Island – 43452. *Activity:* Outdoors. (419) 797-4530, **www.dnr.state.oh.us/odnr/parks/directory/lakeerie.htm**. 661 acres of camping, hiking trails, fishing, swimming, and winter sports. GLACIAL GROOVES are a must see and a great way to study Ohio geology. Located on the north side of the island, the largest easily accessible grooves were formed when ice once covered solid limestone bedrock. Looking safely over fence, you see a giant groove passage that seems unbelievable. Placards along the trail detail the history of glaciers moving through the area.

LAKESIDE ASSOCIATION

Lakeside (Marblehead) - 236 Walnut Avenue, 43440. *Activity:* The Arts. (419) 798-4461. "Chautaqua-like" assembly with programs in historic enclave on Lake Erie. (June – September). The entire area is a Christian family retreat.

MID OHIO SPORTS CAR COURSE

Lexington - Steam Corners Road, 44904. *Activity:* Sports. (800) MID-OHIO. **www.midohio.com**. Indy Car, Sport Car, AMA Motorcycles, Vintage Car Races. General, Weekend, Paddock (walk through garages and see drivers) passes available. Weekends, (June to mid-September)

RICHLAND COUNTY MUSEUM

Lexington - 51 West Church Street (east of SR-42 South), 44904. *Activity:* Ohio History. (419) 884-0277. *Hours:* Weekends only, 1:30 – 4:30 pm (May – October). An 1850 schoolhouse with tools, clothing, children's toys and furniture.

LORAIN PALACE CIVIC CENTER

Lorain - 617 Broadway Avenue, 44052. *Activity:* The Arts. (440) 245-2323. **www.centurytel.net/palace**. Since 1928 it's "the place" for art and theatre events, educational programs. Be sure to ask about their special kids programs.

MOHICAN STATE PARK

Loudonville 3116 State Route 3, 44842. *Activity:* Outdoors. (419) 994-4290.**www.mohicancamp.com** or **www.mohicanresort.com**. Nature programs, scenic, bike rentals, bridle trails. 1,294 acres of camping, hiking trails, boating and rentals, fishing and winter sports. Most people come to stay at riverfront family cabins (with A/C, fireplaces and cable) or the Lodge rooms (with indoor/outdoor pools, sauna, tennis, basketball and shuffleboard facilities). Family playground activity center.

MALABAR FARM STATE PARK

4050 Bromfield Road (I-71 to Exit 169, follow signs)
Mansfield 44843

❑   Activity: Outdoors
❑   Telephone: (419) 892-2784
    www.dnr.state.oh.us/odnr/parks/directory/malabar.htm
❑   Admission: Big House Tour, $3.00 Adult, $1.00 Youth (6-18)
❑   Tour: Tractor Drawn Wagon Tour, $1.00 (12+)
❑   Miscellaneous: Malabar Inn. 1820's stagecoach stop restaurant.
    (*Special note to grandparents... Humphrey Bogart & Lauren*
    Bacall were married on these beautiful grounds).

A writer and lover of nature, Louis Bromfield, dreamed of this scenic land and home. It is still a working farm and the place where Bromfield discovered new farming techniques. The guides at the Big House tell captivating stories. Bridle trails, fishing, hiking trails, camping and winter sports are also available parkwide.

ARTS & SCIENCE DISCOVERY CENTER

Mansfield - 75 North Walnut Street, Richland Academy, (west of carousel, downtown), 44902. *Activity:* Museums. (419) 522-8224. *Hours:* Monday – Thursday, 9:00 am - 9:00 pm, Friday, 9:00 am - 3:00 pm, Saturday, 9:00 am - 1:00 pm. Showcases techno-art - hands-on. Play a gas-powered Fire Organ or follow the perpetual motion Wave Machine.

CAROUSEL MAGIC! FACTORY

44 West Fourth Street (behind the Gift Horse) (I-71 Exit SR-13
North to downtown), **Mansfield** 44902

❑   Activity: Tours
❑   Telephone: (419) 522-2510, **www.carouselmagic.com**
❑   Admission: (Factory Tour) $3.00 Adult, $1.00 Children (5-12)
    (Carousel) $1.00 – (2) ride tokens
❑   Hours: (Factory) Tuesday - Saturday, 10:00 am – 4:00 pm. (30 -
    45 minutes long)

W atch the wood carousel horses being made starting from a "coffin box" with a hollow center, then the carving with special tools, and finally the painting. The artisans are friendly and enjoy showing off their skill and love of the art. Now that you know how they're made, walk over to the wonderful carousel in the center of town (indoor/outdoor style - open daily). For lunch, stop at the Coney Island Diner with its genuine old-time tables, stools and "Blue Plate" specials.

MANSFIELD PLAYHOUSE

Mansfield - 95 East Third Street, 44902. *Activity:* The Arts. (419) 522-8140. Community and guest artists present adult and youth productions.

MANSFIELD SOLDIERS AND SAILORS MEMORIAL BUILDING MUSEUM

Mansfield - 34 Park Ave West, 44902. *Activity:* Ohio History. (419) 525-2491. The building was built in 1888 and is the oldest continuously used memorial building in the state of Ohio. The museum houses artifacts of military history of Richland County as well as civil and natural history artifacts. Donations accepted.

MANSFIELD SYMPHONY

Mansfield - 138 Park Avenue West, Renaissance Theatre, 44902. *Activity:* The Arts. (419) 522-2726. Performs classical works, opera, pops, ballet and special events in restored Renaissance Theatre. Summer musical and outdoor concerts.

RICHLAND ACADEMY OF THE ARTS

Mansfield - 75 North Walnut Street, 44902. *Activity:* The Arts. (419) 522-8224. Performances in black box theatre, recitals, musicals, choral concerts, jazz, and children's plays.

MANSFIELD ART CENTER

Mansfield - 700 Marion Avenue, 44903. *Activity:* The Arts. (419) 756-1700. Displays invitational and juried exhibits. Offers lectures, movies, classes, special programs.

LIVING BIBLE MUSEUM

500 Tingley Avenue (I-71 to US-30 West to SR-545 North)
Mansfield 44905

❏   Activity: Museums
❏   Telephone: (419) 524-0139 or (800) 222-0139
    www.livingbiblemuseum.org
❏   Hours: Monday – Friday, 10:00 am – 5:00 pm (April –
    December). Weekends & Holidays, 10:00 am – 7:00 pm
    (January – December)
❏   Admission: $4.50 Adult, $4.25 Senior, $3.50 Youth (6-18)
❏   Miscellaneous: Gift Shop. Collection of rare bibles and religious
    woodcarvings.

The only life-size wax museum in Ohio – it features figures from the Old and New Testaments. Featured stories include the Life of Christ, Jonah and the whale, and Adam and Eve. The tour guide takes you through dimly lit hallways that add a theatrical, dramatic effect. At the end of the tour you will be left emotional (a small chapel is available to reflect).

KINGWOOD CENTER

Mansfield - 900 Park Avenue West (I-71 exit, SR-30), 44906. *Activity:* Outdoors. (419) 522-0211, *Hours:* Daily, 8:00 am – 5:00 pm. 47 acres of gardens, woods and ponds. Greenhouses with a specialty of tulips and perennials. **www.virtualmansfield.com/ kingwood/index.htm**.

MANSFIELD FIRE MUSEUM

Mansfield - (2 miles west of downtown on W. 4th Street), 44906. *Activity:* Museums. (419) 529-2573 or (800) 211-7231. *Hours:* Saturday – Wednesday, 1:00 - 4:00 pm, (June 1 - September 1). Saturday & Sunday only, 1:00 - 4:00 pm, (September 1 - June 1). No admission charge. A museum of fire fighting history with reproductions of a turn-of-the-century fire station.

OHIO STATE REFORMATORY

100 Reformatory Road (I-71 to SR-30 west & SR-545 North)
Mansfield 44906

❑   Activity: Tours
❑   Telephone: (419) 522-2644, **www.m8.com/mrps**
❑   Hours: Sunday, 1:00 – 4:00 pm (mid - May to October)
❑   Admission: $5.00 per person.
❑   Tours: Phone Reservations Preferred. Ask for East or West Wing Tour. Children under 9 and pregnant women should use caution because of stairs and lead-based paint. 90 minutes. (Groups by reservation only)

A castle prison? Well, maybe from the outside only. This 1886 structure was built as a boy's reformatory. The original cellblocks and offices remain intact and were used to film 3 major motion pictures including "The Shawshank Redemption". What does the architecture have to do with spiritual reform? The East Cell Block houses the world's largest free-standing steel cell block - 6 tiers.

EAST HARBOR STATE PARK

Marblehead - (8 miles East of Port Clinton off SR-269), 43440. *Activity:* Outdoors. **www.dnr.state.oh.us/odnr/parks/directory/ eharbor**. (419) 734-4424. Nature programs. 1,152 acres of camping, hiking trails, boating, fishing, swimming and winter sports.

KELLEYS ISLAND FERRY BOAT LINES

Marblehead - 510 W. Main Street, 43440. *Activity:* Tours. (419) 798-9763 or (888) 225-4325. **www.kelleysislandferry.com**. Daily passenger and automobile transportation to Kelleys Island from Marblehead, departing every half-hour during peak times. Available year-round, weather permitting.

MARBLEHEAD LIGHTHOUSE STATE PARK

Marblehead – 43440. *Activity:* Outdoors. (419) 798-9777. **www.marbleheadpenisula.com**. The oldest working lighthouse on the Great Lakes. Built in 1821 of limestone and uses a large Fresnel lens. Tours available, call for seasonal schedule (usually the 2nd Sunday of the month - Summertime).

NEUMAN'S KELLEYS ISLAND FERRY

Marblehead - (foot of Francis Street), 43440. *Activity:* Tours. (800) 876-1907 or (419) 798-5800. **www.neumanferry.com**. *Hours:* April - November, call ahead or check website. Admission: $5-10.00 round trip.

PREHISTORIC FOREST & MYSTERY HILL

8232 East Harbor Road – SR-163 (8 miles East of Port Clinton off SR-2), **Marblehead** 43440

❑   Activity: Amusements

❑   Telephone: (419) 798-5230, **www.prehistoricforest.com**

❑   Hours: Daily, 10:00 am – Dark (Summer) June – August.
Weekends Only, 10:00 am – Dark (May and September)

❑   Admission: $5 – 7.00 (3 and over)

Learn the eating habits and lifestyles of dinosaurs in a forest full of them. Take a walk through a volcano, dig for dinosaur footprints and bones or get your picture taken with Reggie, the 14' Python snake!   Also included is the Reptile House (pythons, lizards, and alligators) and Mystery Hill (the "Illusion of Nature" House where water runs uphill and chairs stick to the walls).

TRAIN – O – RAMA

Marblehead - 6732 East Harbor Road (Route 161 East), 43440. *Activity:* Museums. (419) 734-5856 **http://hometown.aol.com/ trainorama/index.htm**. *Hours:* Monday – Saturday, 11:00 am – 5:00 pm. Sunday, 1:00 – 5:00 pm (until 6:00 pm in summer). Admission. Gift Shop. Ohio's largest operating model train display open to the public.

OTTO BUFFALO RANCH

Erie County - SR-61, just south of SR-2. *Activity:* Animals & Farms. (419) 588-0028. **www.lakeeriebuffaloranch.com**. *Hours:* Open daily, except Thursdays, (June – October) Weekends, November – May). Call for tour schedule. Learn all about American Bison at one of the oldest buffalo ranches in Ohio. Established in 1964, the Otto family shares information on the history, environment, and habits of the American Buffalo. Trading post, buffalo food concessions, and stocked pond on premises.

EDISON BIRTHPLACE MUSEUM

North Edison Street (off SR-250, Downtown, near exit 7 off
Turnpike), **Milan** 44846

❑   Activity: Museums
❑   Telephone: (419) 499-2135, **www.tomedison.org**
❑   Hours: Tuesday – Saturday, 10:00 am – 5:00 pm. Sunday, 1:00 – 5:00 pm (Summer). Tuesday – Sunday, 1:00 – 5:00 pm (February – May and September – November)
❑   Admission: $5.00 Adult, $4.00 Senior (59+), $2.00 Children (6-12)

Edison was born here in 1847 and raised in this home until age 7. The original family momentos give you a feeling of being taken back in time. The room full of his inventions (he had 1,093 American patents) gives you a sense of his brilliance.   Most famous for his invention of the light bulb and phonograph (1st words recorded were "Mary had a little lamb"), you may not know he was kicked out of school for being a non-attentive/slow learner! So, his mother home-schooled him.   Part of the Edison family belongings include slippers, Derby hat, cane, Mother Edison's disciplinary switch (still hanging in the original spot in the kitchen), butter molds and "Pop Goes the Weasel" yarner. Two practical inventions you'll want to see are the pole ladder (a long pole that pulls out to a full size ladder) and the slipper seat (a cushioned little seat, low to the ground, so it is easier to put your slippers or shoes on).

MILAN HISTORICAL MUSEUM

Milan - 10 Edison Drive (Across the street from Edison's birthplace), 44846. *Activity:* Ohio History. (419) 499-2968, **www.milanhist.org**. *Hours:* Tuesday - Saturday, 10:00 am - 5:00 pm, Sunday, 1:00 - 5:00 pm (Summer). Tuesday - Sunday, 1:00 - 5:00 pm (April, May, September, October). *Admission:* Donations. Small fee for guided group tours. Gift Shop with video and slide presentations. Tour includes several buildings in a complex featuring different themes like the Galpin Home of local history, dolls, toys and a collection of mechanical banks. There are several other homes along with a blacksmith and carriage shop and everything you might want to buy from the 1800's is sold in the general store.

FIRELANDS MUSEUM

Norwalk - 4 Case Avenue (SR-250 and SR-20), 44857. *Activity:* Ohio History. (419) 668-6038. **www.huey.org**. *Hours:* Tuesday – Sunday, Noon – 5:00 pm (Summer). Saturday and Sunday, Noon – 4:00 pm (Spring and Fall). Area that was given as compensation for Revolutionary War fire destruction. 1836 home with firearms, costumes, and toys. Grandpa's newspaper shop upstairs until the 13th grandchild was born. Admission. See over 40 pieces of military history that varies in size from a 60-ton M-60-A1 tank to a 1942 Harley-Davidson military motorcycle. Also see 3 "Huey" UH-1H helicopters and one AH-1A "Cobra" attack helicopter!

FIRELANDS ASSOCIATION FOR VISUAL ARTS

Oberlin - 39 South Main Street (New Union Center), 44074. *Activity:* The Arts. (440) 774-2166. Regional and national artists, art classes, photography and quilt shows.

FRANK LLOYD WRIGHT HOUSE

Oberlin – 44074. Activity: Museums. The only Wright home in Ohio open to the public, an example of Wright's Usonian style. Open 1st Sunday & 3rd Saturday of every month, tours begin on the hour 1:00 –5:00, tickets purchased at Uncommon Objects, 39 South Main Street. (440) 775-2086.

OBERLIN HISTORIC SITES TOUR

Oberlin - 73 South Professor Street (SR-38 and SR-511), 44074. *Activity:* Ohio History. (440) 774-1700. **www.oberlin.edu**. *Hours:* Tuesday – Thursday, 10:30 am and 1:30 pm, 1st Sunday of month, 1:00 and 2:30 pm, 3rd Saturday of month, 1:00 and 2:30 pm. $4.00 Adult. Underground Railroad, former politicians and professor home, little red school house with collection of lunch pails and McGuffey Readers.

MOHICAN-MEMORIAL STATE FOREST

Perrysville - 3060 County Road 939, 44864. *Activity:* Outdoors. (419) 938-6222. Open daily, 6:00 am - 11:00 pm. **www.hcs.ohio-state.edu/ODNR/Forests/stateforests/mohican.htm**. 4,498 acres in Ashland County. Hiking trails (24 miles), bridle trails (22 miles), "Park & Pack" camping sites (10), snowmobile trails (7 miles - weather permitting), state nature preserve. Also War Memorial Shrine and Mohican State Park is adjacent.

AFRICAN WILDLIFE SAFARI PARK

267 Lightner Road (off SR-2 to SR-53), **Port Clinton** 43452

❑ Activity: Animals & Farms
❑ Telephone: (419) 732-3606 or (800) 521-2660
   www.comp-res.com
❑ Hours: Daily, (May – September)
❑ Admission: $7.00 - $11.00
❑ Miscellaneous: Mombassa Café. Jungle Junction Playland. Safari Junction pony and camel rides, petting zoo.

S ee more than 400 animals (including llamas, alpacas, and
zebras) as they wander freely around your vehicle as you drive
through a 100-acre park. This is the only drive through safari park
in the Midwest. The giraffe lean their long necks over to check
you out through your car windows. Another favorite is the
"Porkchop Downs" pig races. Boy, do they snort loud when
they're trying to win!

JET EXPRESS

Port Clinton - 5 North Jefferson Street, 43452. *Activity:* Tours.
(800) 245-1JET. **www.jet-express.com**. Indoor and outdoor
seating on the fastest catamaran to Islands. 22 minute trip with
island history woven in. *Admission:* $1.50 - 10.00 each way. (April
– October)

OTTAWA COUNTY HISTORICAL MUSEUM

Port Clinton - 126 West Third Street, 43452. *Activity:* Ohio
History. (419) 732-2237. Fossils, Indian artifacts, and Military
history.

ALASKAN BIRDHOUSE WILDLIFE AREA

Put-In-Bay - Meechen Road, 43456. *Activity:* Animals & Farms.
(419) 285-9736. *Admission:* $3.00 Adult, $2.00 Senior, $1.50
Youth (6-12). Narrated tours of North American Wildlife including
grizzly bears, moose, geese, walleye fish, whales, cranes, quails,
and ducks. Over 100 stuffed pelts of animals are displayed in their
natural habitats.

LAKE ERIE ISLANDS MUSEUM

Put-in-Bay - 441 Catawba Avenue, 43456. *Activity:* Ohio History.
(419) 285-2804. *Hours:* Daily, 11:00 am – 5:00 pm (May, June
and September). Daily, 10:00 am – 6:00 pm (July and August).
Boating, sailors, and shipping industry artifacts.

MILLER BOAT LINE

Put-in-Bay - Catawba Point (SR-2 to Route 53 north), 43456. *Activity:* Tours. **www.millerferry.com**. (800) 500-2421 or (419) 285-2421. Service to Put-in-Bay and Middle Bass Island. Low rates and most frequent trips.

PERRY'S CAVE

979 Catawba Avenue (South Bass Island, ½ mile from town)
Put-in-Bay 43456

❑   Activity: Outdoors
❑   Telephone: (419) 285-2405, **www.perryscave.com**
❑   Admission: $5.00 Adult, $2.50 Youth (5-11)
❑   Tours: Daily, 10:30 am - 6:00 pm (20 minutes) (Summer)

Inside the cave you'll see walls covered with calcium carbonate (the same ingredient in antacids) that has settled from years of dripping water. Rumor says Perry kept prisoners and stored supplies in the cave during the Battle of Lake Erie. At the Gem Mining Company, buy a bag of sand at the gift shop. Take the bag outside to the mining station and dig through it to find gems. Compare your stones to a display in the survey stations.

PERRY'S VICTORY AND INTERNATIONAL PEACE MEMORIAL

93 Delaware Avenue, **Put-In-Bay** 43456

❑   Activity: Ohio History
❑   Telephone: (419) 285-2184, **www.nps.gov/pevi**
❑   Hours: Daily, 10:00 am - 7:00 pm, (mid-June to Labor Day)
       Daily, 10:00 am - 5:00 pm (Late April to mid-June & September
       and October)
❑   Admission: Observation Deck by elevator, $3.00 per person (age
       17 and up). Must climb two flights of stairs first.

Built of pink granite, 352 feet high and 45 feet in diameter, this memorial commemorates the Battle of Lake Erie and then the years of peace. Commodore Perry commanded the American fleet in the War of 1812. In September of 1813 he defeated the British and Perry then sent his famous message to General William Henry Harrison "We have met the enemy and they are ours". Interpretive actors outside chat with you and there's a small Visitor's Center.

PUT-IN-BAY TOUR TRAIN

Put-In-Bay - (South Bass Island), 43456. *Activity:* Tours. (419) 285-4855. **www.put-in-bay-trans.com/ttmain.htm**. *Hours:* Daily, 10:00 am – 5:00 pm (Memorial Day – Labor Day). Weekends only, (May and September). *Admission:* $8.00 Adult , $1.50 Youth (6-11). A one-hour narrated tour of the island. Departing every 30 minutes, the train trolley allows passengers to depart and re-board (without additional cost) at any time.

CAPTAIN GUNDY'S PIRATE ADVENTURE

Sandusky - 44870. *Activity:* Tours. (419) 625-3193. Set sail for high sea adventure on the El Loro, docked in downtown Sandusky. This one-hour adventure scouts the waters of Sandusky Bay and Lake Erie for pirates' treasure. Hear tales of Bay and Great Lakes history.

CEDAR POINT

SR-4 (I-80 to Exit 7 or Exit 6A. Follow Signs), **Sandusky** 44870

- ❏ Activity: Amusements
- ❏ Telephone: (800) BEST FUN. (419) 627-2350
  www.cedarpoint.com
- ❏ Hours: Vary by season. (May – October)
- ❏ Admission: $10.00-38.00, Small children (under 48") – General (4-59). Separate admission for Soak City and Challenge Park. Starlight rates too!
- ❏ Miscellaneous: Stroller rental. Picnic area. Food Service. Miniature golf.

Amusement extravaganza on the shores of Lake Erie including 12 Roller Coasters and:

> SOAK CITY – wave pool, water slides, Adventure Cove, Eerie Falls (get wet in the dark), swim-up refreshment center.

CHALLENGE PARK – Rip cord Sky coaster (fall 150 feet and
then swing in a 300-foot arc. Grand Prix Raceway.

SPLASH - high dive act in Aquatic Stadium.

LIVE SHOWS – 50's, Motown, Country

CHAOS – turn sideways & upside down at the same time

MILLENIUM - new coaster for the year 2000

CAMP SNOOPY - with piped-in kids music and child sized
play like Red Baron airplanes, Woodstock's express
family coaster, Peanuts 500 Speedway. Also Sing-along
Show with Peanuts characters.

DIXON TICONDEROGA (PRANG) CRAYON FACTORY

1706 Hayes Avenue, **Sandusky** 44870

❑   Activity: Tours
❑   Telephone: (419) 625-9545, **www.dixonticonderoga.com**
❑   Admission: Free
❑   Tours: 10:00 am, Tuesday, Wednesday, Thursday (September –
June). Tours booked a couple of years in advance, so be sure to
plan ahead. Minimum 8 people (maximum 30 people)
Reservations Required. (1 hour tour)

What fun! See how crayons are mixed (colors), poured in
molds, cooled, labeled and then boxed. This is a very
popular factory tour with free samples at the end of your tour.
Dixon is also the manufacturer of the world famous "Yellow #2"
pencil. Why is it yellow? Visit, or stop by their website to find
out!

FIRELANDS SYMPHONY ORCHESTRA

Sandusky – 44870. *Activity:* The Arts. (419) 621-4800.
Professional and semi-professional musicians perform series
concerts, children's concerts at State Theatre. Summer concerts at
Put-in-Bay, Lakeside.

FOLLETT HOUSE MUSEUM

Sandusky – US-6 and 404 Wayne Street, 44870. *Activity:* Ohio History. (419) 627-9608.   **www.sandusky.lib.oh.us**. *Hours:* Tuesday – Sunday, Noon – 4:00 pm (Summer). Weekends only 1:00 – 4:00 pm (Spring and Fall). An 1827 stone mansion built by Oren Follett who fought against slavery and helped to establish the Republican Party. Lake Erie history.

GOODTIME I

Sandusky - 44870 (docked at Jackson Street Pier). *Activity:* Tours. (800) 446-3140. **www.goodtimeboat.com**. *Hours:* Daily, 9:30 am – 6:30 pm (Memorial Day – Labor Day). *Admission:* $10.00 - $20.00 (ages 4 and up). Island hopping 40-meter sight-seeing cruise to Kelley's Island and Put-In-Bay.

ISLAND EXPRESS BOAT LINES

Sandusky - 101 West Shoreline Drive, 44870. *Activity:* Tours. (419) 627-1500 or (800) 854-8121. **www.islandrocket.com**. Ride the Rocket! Sandusky's fastest ferryboat now has direct service to Cedar Point, Kelleys Island, and Put-in-Bay. Frequent departures from downtown Sandusky make the Rocket convenient and fun for the whole family. Enjoy both Kelleys Island and Put-in-Bay with one of the famous island-hopper passes; reservations recommended.

LAGOON DEER PARK

State Route 269 (between SR-2 and US-6), **Sandusky** 44870

- ❑   Activity: Animals & Farms
- ❑   Telephone: (419) 684-5701
     http://sanduskyfunsopts.com/deerpark
- ❑   Hours: Daily, 10:00 am – 6:00 pm (mid-April to mid-October)
- ❑   Admission: $6.00 Adult, $3.00 Children (3-12)
- ❑   Miscellaneous: Pay Fishing available in stocked lake.

H and feed and pet hundreds of deer, llamas, miniature donkeys and other tame species. They have 250 exotic animals from Europe, Japan, Asia, South and North America. Approximately 75 baby animals are born here each year.

MERRY-GO-ROUND MUSEUM

West Washington and Jackson Streets (SR-6), **Sandusky** 44870

- ❏ Activity: Museums
- ❏ Telephone: (419) 626-6111
  www.carousel.net/org/sandusky/index
- ❏ Hours: Monday - Saturday, 11:00 am - 5:00 pm. Sunday, Noon - 5:00 pm (Summer). Weekends Only, (January & February) Wednesday - Sunday (Rest of the Year). Always closed Tuesday.
- ❏ Admission: $4.00 Adult, $3.00 Senior (60+), $2.00 Children (4-14)
- ❏ Miscellaneous: Gift Shop

T his colorful, bright, big museum was the former Post Office. Once inside, you'll see all sorts of carousel memorabilia and history. Next, tour the workshop to watch craftsman make carousel horses with authentic "old world" tools. Finally, ride the Herschel 1930's indoor merry-go-round.

SOUTH BASS ISLAND STATE PARK

South Bass Island - 43452. *Activity:* Outdoors. (419) 797-4530. **www.dnr.state.oh.us/odnr/parks/directory/lakeerie.htm**. A summer ferry takes you to explore over 35 acres on South Bass Island. Camping, boating, fishing, swimming and winter sports.

SENECA COUNTY MUSEUM

Tiffin - 28 Clay Street, 44883. *Activity:* Ohio History. (419) 447-5955. *Hours:* Wednesday and Sunday afternoons. Mid-1800's home. Tiffin Glass.

INDIAN MILL

Upper Sandusky – (SR-23 and SR-67 to Route 47), 43351. *Activity:* Tours. **www.ohiohistory.org/places/indian**. (419) 294-3349. *Hours:* Friday – Saturday, 9:30 am – 5:00 pm. Sunday, 1:00 – 6:00 pm (Memorial Day – October). *Admission:* $1.00 Adult, $.50 Youth (6-12). Original Ohio Historical Society museum of milling housed in a converted gristmill.

WYANDOT COUNTY HISTORICAL SOCIETY

Upper Sandusky - 130 South 7th Street, 43351. *Activity:* Ohio History. (419) 294-3857. *Hours:* Thursday – Sunday, 1:00 – 4:30 pm (May – October). An 1853 mansion with displays including American Indian and pioneer days, antique toys and clothing. Also school house. Admission.

INLAND SEAS MARITIME MUSEUM & LIGHTHOUSE

480 Main St. (3 blocks North of SR-60 / US 6), **Vermillion** 44089

- ❑ Activity: Museums
- ❑ Telephone: (800) 893-1485, **http://www.inlandseas.org**
- ❑ Hours: Daily, 10:00 am – 5:00 pm
- ❑ Admission: $5.00 Adult, $4.00 Senior, $3.00 Youth (6-15), $10.00 Family Rate

The museum celebrates adventures of the Great Lakes including models, photographs, instruments, a steam tug engine, and a 1905 pilothouse. Special artifacts are the timbers from the Niagara (Admiral Perry's 1812 ship) and an 1847 lighthouse built with a 400 foot catwalk to the mainland. The lighthouse began tilting toward the harbor in 1928, so it was dismantled. In 1992, it was rebuilt and the 1891 (leaded glass) lens shines once again!

FINDLEY STATE PARK

Wellington - (3 miles South of Wellington on SR-58), 44090. *Activity:* Outdoors. (440) 647-4490. **www.dnr.state.oh.us/odnr/ parks/directory/findley.htm**. Nature programs. Bike rental. 931 acres of camping, hiking trails, boating and rentals, fishing, swimming and winter sports.

SPIRIT OF '76 MUSEUM

Wellington - 201 North Main Street, 44090. *Activity:* The Arts. (440) 647-4567. *Hours:* Weekends, 2:30-5:00 pm. (April – October) Gallery of paintings and murals done by Archibold Willard (famed painter of "Spirit of '76" painting of three Revolutionary War soldiers playing fife & drum through battle). See objects used as models for works.

CELERYVILLE VEGETABLE FARMS

Willard - 4200 Broadway (Route 224 West to Route 103 South to Celeryville), 44890. *Activity:* Animals & Farms. (419) 935-3633. *Hours:* Weekdays, (June – September) just watching. *Tours:* 20+ people required. Judged one of the best industrial tours in the state, this is a 3000-acre organic "muck" vegetable garden. On tour you'll see greenhouses, celery and radish harvesting machines in action, and vegetable processing (cleaning, pruning) and packaging. Truly unique!

BOOKMASTERS

Mansfield – 2541 Ashland Road, 44905. (800) 537-6727. *Activity* Tours. **www.bookmasters.com**. *Hours:* Monday – Friday, 10:00 am – 2:00 pm. Appointment necessary. Group size (6 – 40). While visiting, kids will learn step-by-step how books (*like the "Kids Love" books*) are produced. Start by seeing what materials are needed, then see the pre-press division, the printing area (*with huge, monster-like printers*), and the final book binding area. See all phases of books being made through production and view finished books at the end of the tour.

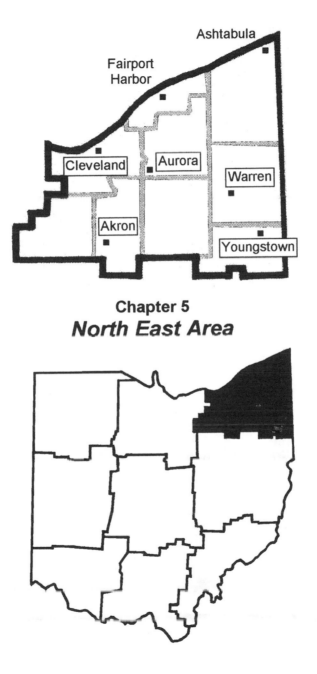

Chapter 5
North East Area

Our Favorites...

- Covered Bridge Pizza
- Fairport Marine Lighthouse
- Hale Farm & Village
- Inventure Place
- Lake Farm Park
- Malley's Chocolates
- Mill Creek Park
- Trolleyville, USA

AKRON RECREATION BUREAU

Akron - 220 South Balch Street, 44302. *Activity:* The Arts. (330) 375-2804. Offers free symphony performances, ballet and summer concerts. **www.ci.akron.oh.us/rec.html**.

STAN HYWET HALL

714 North Portage Path (I-77 or I-71 to SR-18, follow signs into town), **Akron** 44303

❑   Activity: Museums

❑   Telephone: (330) 836-5533, **www.stanhywet.org**

❑   Tours: Daily, 10:00 am – 4:30 pm (April – January)

❑   Admission: $8.00 Adult, $7.00 Senior, $4.00 Children (6-12)

❑   Miscellaneous: Museum Store, Carriage House Café

Want to pretend you're visiting old rich relatives for tea – this is the place.   The long driveway up to the home is beautifully landscaped. You can park right next to the home and carriage house (vs. a block away) and are greeted as an invited guest.   The actual family photographs of the Seiberling Family (Frank was the co-founder of the Goodyear Tire and Rubber Company) scattered throughout the home make you feel as if you know them.   Stan Hywet means "stone quarry" referring to the stone quarry the house was built on and the stone that was supplied for building.   Being an English Tudor, it is rather dark inside with an almost "castle-like" feeling (the detailed wood panels and crown molding are magnificent).   Try to count the fireplaces (23) and discover concealed telephones behind the paneled walls.

SUMMIT CHORAL SOCIETY

Akron - 715 East Buchtel Avenue, 44305. *Activity:* The Arts. (330) 434-7464.   **www.ohio.com/community/choral**.   Children's choir program.

AKRON ZOOLOGICAL PARK

500 Edgewood Avenue (Perkins Woods Park), **Akron** 44307

❑ Activity: Animals & Farms

❑ Telephone: (330) 375-2525, **www.akronzoo.com**

❑ Hours: Monday – Saturday, 10:00 am – 5:00 pm. Sunday – Holidays, 10:00 am – 6:00 pm. (Closed in November)

❑ Admission: $5.00 Adult, $4.00 Senior, $4.00 Children (2-14) $1.00 Parking

A medium-sized zoo featuring Monkey Island, The River Otter Exhibit, and an Ohio Farmyard petting area. New is the Asian Trail with Tiger Valley, the red pandas, and the barking deer.

AKRON AEROS

Akron - Canal Park, downtown. 44308. *Activity:* Sports. (800) 97-AEROS. **www.akronaeros.com**. Minor league baseball with ticket prices ranging $5-8.00.

AKRON ART MUSEUM

Akron - 70 East Market Street, 44308. *Activity:* The Arts. (330) 376-9185. **www.akronartmuseum.org**. An intimate setting for discovering beautiful, new art.

AKRON CIVIC THEATRE

Akron - 182 South Main Street, 44308. *Activity:* The Arts. (330) 535-3179. The ornate interior features a mighty Wurlitzer organ and resembles a Moorish garden complete with blinking stars and moving clouds. The theater features first-rate productions, films and concerts. Group tours of the theater are available and are interesting for all ages. Admission.

AKRON SYMPHONY ORCHESTRA

Akron - 17 North Broadway, 44308. *Activity:* The Arts. (330) 535-8131. **www.akronsymphony.org**. Professional orchestra offers pops, classical and educational concerts. Youth Symphony. (September – July)

TRACKSIDE GRILL (formerly Depot Diner)

Akron - 135 South Broadway Street (Quaker Square), 44308. *Activity:* Theme Restaurants. (330) 253-5970. Sit inside coaches of a former Railway Express Train as the servers (*dressed like conductors*) take your order. Model trains are displayed throughout the restaurant.

INVENTURE PLACE

221 South Broadway Street (off SR-18, Downtown), **Akron** 44308

- ❑ Activity: Museums
- ❑ Telephone: (330) 762-4463, **www.invent.org**
- ❑ Hours: Tuesday – Saturday, 9:00 am – 5:00 pm. Sunday, Noon – 5:00 pm. Closed Christmas Day, New Year's Day, Easter Sunday & Thanksgiving Day.
- ❑ Admission: $7.50 Adult (age 18+), $6.00 Children (3-17) & Seniors (65+). Children FREE ages 2 and under.
- ❑ Miscellaneous: National Inventors Hall of Fame (4 floors of exhibits). Open architecture with 5 tiers of steel and windows.

Start with the Inventor's Workshop. The sign that greets you says it all - "This is a place to mess around. No rights. No wrongs. Only experiments and surprises!" This is honestly the most hands-on, exploring creativity area we've ever visited in Ohio. Kids' (and adults') minds open before your eyes. Therefore, plan to spend at least 2 hours exploring. In the wood shop you can actually work with a hammer, nails, and saws (all real) to build a mini boat, house, or new instrument. The Swap Shop is an area where regular visitors can bring broken appliances, give a description of the problem, then swap for another item to fix or take apart. A favorite exhibit was the "untitled" (metal grasses) which was sculpted of iron powder and danced to music in a magnetic field. Also the animation area where we each made our own "Toy Story" type movies.

WEATHERVANE PLAYHOUSE

Akron -1301 Weathervane Lane, 44313. *Activity:* The Arts. (330) 836-2626. Offers mainstage and children's productions. 3 Youth Theatre shows, Spring Puppet show.

GOODYEAR WORLD OF RUBBER

1144 East Market Street (Downtown, Goodyear Hall, 4th floor of headquarters), **Akron** 44316

❑   Activity: Tours
❑   Telephone: (330) 796-7117
❑   Admission: Free
❑   Tour: Introductory film (by request) of tire production. 1 hour. Individuals may visit anytime between 9:00 am and 5:00 pm. Groups of 10 or more should call ahead for a reservation.
❑   Miscellaneous: Gift Center

Discover how Charles Goodyear vulcanized rubber in his kitchen in a replica of his workshop. Other attractions include a simulated rubber plantation (hands on), Indy race cars, an artificial heart, a moon buggy, history of blimps, history of the trucking industry, and of course an array of Goodyear products. Everyone leaves knowing about at least one unusual new product made from rubber to tell his or her friends about.

PORTAGE LAKES STATE PARK

Akron - (State Route 93 in Akron), 44319. *Activity:* Outdoors. **www.dnr.state.oh.us/odnr/parks/directory/portage.htm**. (330) 644-2220. 4,963 acres of camping, hiking trails, boating, fishing, swimming and winter sports.

OHIO BALLET

Akron - 354 East Market Street, 44325. *Activity:* The Arts. (330) 972-7900. **www.ohioballet.com**. Professional company performs at E.J. Thomas Hall in Akron and Ohio Theatre in Cleveland. Produces free outdoor performances in summer.

UNIVERSITY OF AKRON THEATRE

Akron - University of Akron (Guzzetta Hall), 44325. *Activity:* The Arts. (330) 972-7890. **www.uakron.edu**. Several shows each year in Kolbe/Sandefur Theatres. (October - April)

PYMATUNING STATE PARK

Andover - (6 miles Southeast of Andover off US-85), 44003. *Activity:* Outdoors. (440) 293-6329. **www.dnr.state.oh.us/odnr/ parks/directory/pymatuning.htm**. Nature programs. 17,500 acres of camping, hiking trails, boating and rentals, fishing, swimming and winter sports. Family cabins.

ASHTABULA ARTS CENTER

Ashtabula - 2928 West 13th Street, 44004. *Activity:* The Arts. (440) 964-3396. **www.interlaced.net/aac**. Home of Straw Hat Theatre, (June - August), GB Community Theatre, (September-April). Host of other drama, dance & musical performances.

HUBBARD HOUSE AND UNDERGROUND RAILROAD MUSEUM

Ashtabula Harbor - Walnut Boulevard and Lake Avenue, 44005. *Activity:* Ohio History. (440) 964-8168. *Hours:* Friday - Sunday and Holidays, Noon - 6:00 pm (Summer), Noon - 5:00 pm (September and October). *Admission:* $3.00 Adults, $1.00 Students. A northern terminal that was part of the pathway from slavery to freedom in the pre Civil War era.

SEA WORLD

1100 Sea World Drive (Off SR-43 – Turnpike Exit 13 or 187)
Aurora 44202

- ❑ Activity: Animals & Farms
- ❑ Telephone: (800) 63-SHAMU, **www.seaworld.com**
- ❑ Hours: Daily, 10:00 am – Call for schedule of closing times. (May – September)
- ❑ Admission: $20.00 - $28.00, Under age 3 Free. $4.00 for Parking
- ❑ Miscellaneous: Picnic Areas, Food Service, Restaurants, Diaper Change and Nursing Facilities

A marine life theme park – home of the famous killer whale, Shamu. Also see shows with entertaining trained dolphins, sea lions, penguins, sea otters and walruses. There's lots of other sites to see like the Baywatch water ski show, Dolphin Cove (interactive dolphin habitat), Monster Marsh (life-sized dinosaurs moving in a "Jurrasic Park" setting), "Pirates" (silly 3D movie) and Shamu's Happy Harbor (3-acre pirate boat play ground). Another exhibit you won't want to miss, Shark Encounter is an arched tank that goes overhead making it look like sharks are surrounding you. Non-sea animal shows include "Wild Wings" bird show and Funny Dog tricks.

SIX FLAGS OHIO

1060 Aurora Road, SR-43 (9 miles north of Turnpike Exit 13)
Aurora 44202

- ❑ Activity: Amusements
- ❑ Telephone: (330) 562-8303, **www.sixflags.com**
- ❑ Hours: Open 10:00 am Weekends, 11:00 am Weekdays, (Summer). Weekends Only (May, September, October)
- ❑ Admission: $31.00 (over 48"). Half price for kids (under 48") and Seniors (61+). Kids age 2 and under FREE. $4.00 for Parking
- ❑ Miscellaneous: Lockers and changing rooms. Paddleboat and Aquacycle rentals. Stroller and wagon rental. Picnic area. Food service. Towel rental. Proper swimwear required. Swimwear available in gift shops.

Take a ride on a backward loop or 13-story plunge roller coaster. Water play at Hurricane Harbor: 2-½ acre pool with surfs, water chutes, wet slides, toboggan run, or white water rapids. Little ones can splash in mini-waterfalls and slides (even a feeding area for babies). Hooks Lagoon is a 5-story tree house with 150+ water gadgets to shoot. Newer rides are the Superman mega coaster or the Villain. Also Batman Stunt Show, Bugs Bunny appearances, Looney Tunes Boom Town (family soft play area), and Shipwreck Falls boat ride.

MAGICAL THEATRE COMPANY

Barberton - 565 West Tuscarawas Avenue, 44203. *Activity:* The Arts. (330) 848-3708. Northeast Ohio's only professional resident and touring theater for children and families, is comprised of professional adult actors, directors and designers. This dynamic company also takes its spirited productions to schools, churches, country clubs, recreation centers, civic centers and beyond.

HALE FARM AND VILLAGE

2686 Oak Hill Road (I-77 exit 143 or I-271 exit 12 (SR-303), follow signs), **Bath** 44210

- ❑ Activity: Ohio History
- ❑ Telephone: (800) 589-9703 or (330) 666-3711
  www.wrhs.org/sites/hale.htm
- ❑ Hours: Tuesday - Saturday, 10:00 am - 5:00 pm. Sunday and Holidays, Noon - 5:00 pm. (late-May – October)
- ❑ Admission: $9.50 Adult, $8.50 Senior (59+), $5.50 Youth (3-12)
- ❑ Miscellaneous: Museum Shop and Snack Bar. Map and sample questions to ask towns people provided.

Tour a living museum with original buildings moved to the area to form a village. Jonathan Hale moved to the Western Reserve from Connecticut and prospered during the canal era building a brick home and farm typical of New England. The gate house prepares guests with an orientation movie, then begin your adventure around the homestead area with an old-fashioned sawmill and wood shop (where lumber is produced). Period tools and machines provide wood-working demonstrations. Other barns serve as shops for a blacksmith and basket maker (post-1850 transitional cut baskets). The Hall House (made of bricks made on site by Hale family and are still made today) has candle, broom making and pioneer cooking (and sampling!) demonstrations. You will feel like you're part of mid-1800's life as crops are planted and harvested, glass items blown, textiles spun, barters made, and church and school attended. Kids are asked to help with chores and schoolwork.

HUNTINGTON BEACH RECREATION AREA

Bay Village - Cleveland MetroParks, 44140. *Activity:* Outdoors. (440) 871-2900. LAKE ERIE NATURE AND SCIENCE CENTER. Hiking trails, boating, fishing, swimming, food service.

BALDWIN-WALLACE COLLEGE ACES

Berea - 275 Eastland Road, 44017. *Activity:* The Arts. (440) 826-2157. **www.baldwinw.edu**. Performing arts series with multi-cultural appeal and cross-cultural interaction features known artists performing with local talent.

BEREA SUMMER THEATRE

Berea - 95 East Bagley Road, 44017. *Activity:* The Arts. (440) 826-2240. Community theatre with musicals and dramas during the summer.

WHITEHOUSE OSTRICH FARM AND NOAH'S LOST ARK ANIMAL PARK

Berlin Center - 8424 Bedell Road (off SR-224), 44401. *Activity:* Animals & Farms. (330) 584-7835. One of Ohio's largest breeders of ostrich invite you to tour the Exotic Animal Park. Hands-on interaction with unusual, uncommon international animals.

MAPLESIDE FARMS - APPLE FARM RESTAURANT

Brunswick - 294 Pearl Road, 44212. *Activity:* Theme Restaurants. (330) 225-5576. 5000 apple tree orchard view at the restaurant. Apple house, gift house and ice cream parlor.

CENTURY VILLAGE MUSEUM AND COUNTRY STORE

14653 East Park Street (SR-87 and SR-700), **Burton** 44021

❑ Activity: Ohio History

❑ Telephone: (440) 834-1492

www.geaugalink.com/geaugahistory

❑ Hours: Tuesday – Sunday, 1:00 – 5:00 pm (June – October)
Weekends only, (November – March)

❑ Admission: $5.00 Adult, $4.00 Senior, $3.00 Children (6-12)

❑ Tours: Tuesday - Friday 10:30 am, 1:00 and 3:00 pm (May –
October only). No 10:30 am tour on weekends.

A restored community with 12 buildings containing 19th Century historical antiques and a working farm. Best to attend during Apple Syrup Festivals, Civil War Festival, or Pioneer School Camp.

YELLOW DUCK PARK

Canfield - 10590 Columbiana-Canfield Road (3 miles north of SR-1, on SR-46) 44406. *Activity:* Amusements. (330) 533-3773. *Hours:* Daily, 11:00 am – 7:00 pm (Summer). *Admission:* Ages 3+. Season passes or daily admission. Enjoy a family swim club, Little Tikes Beach, Yellow Duck and Jackrabbit Waterslides.

PIONEER WATERLAND AND DRY PARK

10661 Kile Road (off US-6 or SR-608 / US-322), **Chardon** 44024

❑ Activity: Amusements

❑ Telephone: (440) 951-7507

❑ Hours: Daily, 10:00 am – 8:00 pm (Memorial Day – Labor Day)

❑ Admission: $11.95 and up. Dry activities are a few additional
dollars each. Less than 40" tall - FREE.

❑ Miscellaneous: Picnic Area, Food Service, and Video Arcade

L ittle ones frequent the toddler play area and waterland. Others can explore the water slides, paddleboats, inner tube rides, volleyball nets, Indy raceway, batting cages, miniature golf or driving range. All adjoining a chlorinated crystal clear lake with beaches.

CLEVELAND BROWNS

Cleveland - Browns Stadium Downtown, Lakefront. *Activity:* Sports. (440) 891-5000. **www.clevelandbrowns.com**. NFL Football, New Dawg Pound.

CLEVELAND BOTANICAL GARDEN

Cleveland - 11030 East Blvd. (University Circle), 44106. *Activity:* Outdoors. (216) 721-1600. **www.cbgarden.org**. Display gardens as well as a great resource for advise on horticulture, landscape design and floral design. Free admission. Grounds open daily, dawn to dusk.

CLEVELAND CENTER FOR CONTEMPORARY ART

Cleveland - 8501 Carnegie Avenue, 44106. *Activity:* The Arts. (216) 421-8671. **www.contemporaryart.org**. Displays of avant-garde paintings, sculpture, drawings, prints, and photographs by regional and national artists. Free. Open daily except Monday.

CLEVELAND INSTITUTE OF MUSIC

Cleveland - 11021 East Blvd, 44106. *Activity:* The Arts. (216) 791-5000. **www.cim.edu**. Concert series offers broad range of performances including family concerts. Most events are free.

CLEVELAND MUSEUM OF ART

Cleveland - 11150 East Boulevard, 44106. *Activity:* The Arts. (216) 421-7340. **www.clemusart.com**. See collection of objects from all cultures and periods including European and American paintings, medieval, Asian, Islamic, pre-Columbian, African masks, Egyptian mummies and Oceanic art. Free general admission; charge for parking.

CLEVELAND ORCHESTRA

Cleveland - 11001 Euclid Avenue, 44106. *Activity:* The Arts. (800) 686-1141. **www.clevelandorch.com**. Concerts in Severance Hall (September - May), at Blossom Music Center (Summer).

CLEVELAND SIGNSTAGE THEATRE

Cleveland - 8500 Euclid Avenue, 44106. *Activity:* The Arts. (216) 229-2838. **www.signstage.org**. Performances combine the beauty of sign language, mime and the theatre to create cultural experiences shared by deaf and hearing people.

KARAMU THEATRE

Cleveland - 2355 East 89th Street, 44106. *Activity:* The Arts. (216) 795-7070. **www.karamu.com**. Community based arts and education organization rooted in African American cultural heritage.

CHILDREN'S MUSEUM OF CLEVELAND

10730 Euclid Avenue University Circle (I-90 to Chester Avenue Exit), **Cleveland** 44106

- ❑ Activity: Museums
- ❑ Telephone: (216) 791-KIDS, **www.museum4kids.com**
- ❑ Hours: Daily, 10:00 am – 5:00 pm
- ❑ Admission: $5.00 Adult (age 16+), $4.50 for Seniors (65+) & Children (18 months to 15 years). Kids under 18 months FREE.

The Children's Museum of Cleveland offers innovative and educational exhibits and programs for children ages 0-10 years and their families with unique ways of discovering the world through play.

CLEVELAND MUSEUM OF NATURAL HISTORY

1 Wade Oval Drive (University Circle), **Cleveland** 44106

❑   Activity: Museums
❑   Telephone: (216) 231-4600 or (800) 317-9155, **www.cmnh.org**
❑   Hours: Monday - Saturday, 10:00 am – 5:00 pm. Sundays, Noon
     – 5:00 pm, Wednesday until 10:00 pm (September – May)
❑   Admission: $6.50 Adult, $4.50 Youth (7-18), $3.50 Children
     (3-6), Senior/College Students
❑   Miscellaneous: Gift shop. Planetarium $1.50 extra

Meet "Happy" the 70 foot long dinosaur or "Lucy" the oldest human fossil. Birds and Botany outdoors and a Gem Room and Hall of Man (human skeletons) highlight your visit. The newest gallery, "Planet e", and Discovery Center are the hottest spots now.

HEALTH MUSEUM

8911 Euclid Avenue, University Circle (I-90 Exit on Chester), **Cleveland** 44106

❑   Activity: Museums
❑   Telephone: (216) 231-5010, **www.healthmuseum.org**
❑   Hours: Monday – Friday, 9:00 am – 5:00 pm. Saturday, 10:00 am
     – 5:00 pm. Sunday, Noon – 5:00 pm
❑   Admission: $4.50 Adult, $3.00 Senior and Youth (6-17)
❑   Miscellaneous: Heath related books and games. Group tours
     suggested as they present specially designed age specific topics
     for your group.

Learn from Stuffie, the stuffed doll, with a zippered window to his organs that can be removed and played with. Have you met "Juno" the transparent talking woman or seen the world's largest tooth (an 18 foot walk-through). Touch Island is interactive and the Children's Health Fair features "Stop That Germ", Food Guide Pyramid and Cardiovascular Fitness.

WESTERN RESERVE HISTORICAL SOCIETY

10825 East Boulevard, University Circle, **Cleveland** 44106

❑ Activity: Ohio History
❑ Telephone: (216) 721-5722, **www.wrhs.org**
❑ Hours: Monday– Saturday, 10:00 am – 5:00 pm
  Sunday, Noon – 5:00 pm
❑ Admission: $7.50 Adult, $6.50 Senior, $5.00 Youth (6-12)
  Free on Tuesday, 3:00 – 5:00 pm
❑ Miscellaneous: Crawford Auto-Aviation Museum. Library to
  discover your family tree.

Cleveland's oldest cultural institution boasts a tour of a grand mansion recreating the Western Reserve from pre-Revolution War to the 20th Century. The look (but mostly don't touch) displays include: baseballs, roller coasters, farming tools, clothing and costumes and over 150 classic automobiles (Cleveland built cars, oldest car, and heaviest car) and airplanes.

CLEVELAND LAKEFRONT STATE PARK

Cleveland - (off I-90, downtown), 44108. *Activity:* Outdoors. **www.dnr.state.oh.us/odnr/parks/directory/clevelkf.htm**. (216) 881-8141. 450 acres of boating and rentals, fishing, swimming, and winter sports.

CLEVELAND METROPARKS ZOO

3900 Wildlife Way (I-71 exit Fulton Road or East 25th Street) **Cleveland** 44109

❑ Activity: Animals & Farms
❑ Telephone: (216) 661-6500, **www.clemetzoo.com**
❑ Hours: Daily, 10:00 am – 5:00 pm. Until 7:00 pm Weekends
  (Summer). Closed only Christmas and New Year's Day.
❑ Admission: $7.00 Adult (12+), $4.00 Children (2-11). Free Parking
❑ Miscellaneous: Outback railroad train ride. Concessions.
  Crocodile or Roaring Lion Café. Free zoo only admission for
  county residents on Mondays.

A rainforest with animal and plant settings like the jungles of Africa, Asia, and South America is the most popular exhibit to explore. The rainforest boasts a storm every 12 minutes, a 25-foot waterfall, and a walk-through aviary. Altogether, the whole zoo holds more 3300 animals from all continents including Africa and Australia. Wolf Wilderness is a popular educational study exhibit.

EAST CLEVELAND THEATER

Cleveland - 14108 Euclid Avenue. 44112. *Activity:* The Arts. (216) 851-8721. Produces theatre programs for adults and children that further racial understanding and create a sense of community. (September – May)

CLEVELAND TROLLEY TOURS

Cleveland - North Marginal Road (Burke Lakefront Airport) Downtown, 44113. *Activity:* Tours. (800) 848-0173 or (216) 771-4484. *Hours:* Late morning or Early afternoon departures. **www.lollytrolley.com** *Admission:* $5.00 and up. *Tours:* 1 or 2 hours, Reservations Required. *(1 hour tour is suggested for preschoolers).* "Lolly the Trolley", an old fashioned bright red trolley, clangs its bell as you take in over 100 sights around the downtown area. A great way to show off the city to visitors!

TOWER CITY CENTER OBSERVATION DECK

Cleveland - 50 Public Square, 42nd Floor, Terminal Tower. 44113. *Activity:* Outdoors. (216) 621-7981. *Hours:* Weekends, 11:00 am - 4:30 pm (Summer). 11:00 am - 3:30 pm (Rest of Year). *Admission:* $2.00 Adult, $1.00 Youth (6-16). The Tower deck offers a full view of the city (best if you choose a clear day) with a few displays of the history of the Terminal Tower and downtown.

GOOD TIME III

825 East 9th Street Pier (Behind Rock & Roll Hall of Fame)
Cleveland 44114

- ❏ Activity: Tours
- ❏ Telephone: (216) 861-5110, **www.goodtimeiii.com**
- ❏ Hours: Daily, Noon, 3:00 pm, Sundays at 6:00 pm (mid-June to Labor Day). Weekends only in May and September.
- ❏ Admission: $12.50 Adult, $11.50 Senior, $7.50 Children (2+)
- ❏ Miscellaneous: Food Service Available. Lower deck is airconditioned and heated.

The quadruple-deck, 1000 passenger boat takes a two hour excursion of city sights along the Cuyahoga River and Lake Erie. The word Cuyahoga is Indian for "crooked". You'll see tugboats and the largest yellow crane boats in the country. See all the industry in the Flats including concrete, pipe, transportation, limestone, and coke businesses. Collision Bend used to be so narrow that many boats got tangled up. Since then, they have dredged the curve and it's now very wide.

GREAT LAKES SCIENCE CENTER

601 Erieside Avenue (E 9th Street and I-90, North Coast
Harbor, Downtown), **Cleveland** 44114

- ❏ Activity: Museums
- ❏ Telephone: (216) 694-2000, **www.glsc.org**
- ❏ Hours: Monday – Sunday, 9:30 am – 5:30 pm, open one hour later on Saturdays.
- ❏ Admission: $7.75 Adult, $5.25 Children (3-17), $6.75 Seniors. Memberships Available
- ❏ Miscellaneous: Gift Shop – We picked up Astro Food (freeze dried ice cream and french fries). OmniMax Theater – 6 story domed screen image and sound. McDonald's and Bytes sandwich restaurants on location.

O ver 300 interactive exhibits – especially fun on the second floor. Pilot a blimp, test your batting skills, or bounce off the walls in the Polymer Funhouse. The science playground museum focuses on the Great Lakes region and its environment. Young lab scientists (guests) can create a tornado or create light.

HORNBLOWER'S

Cleveland - 1151 North Marginal Road (Cleveland Lakefront), 44114. *Activity:* Theme Restaurants. (216) 363-1151. Dine in an actual barge used on Lake Erie. Indoor/Outdoor dining with a view of the harbor from every seat.

NAUTICA QUEEN

1153 Main Avenue (West Bank Flats), **Cleveland** 44114

- ❑ Activity: Tours
- ❑ Telephone: (800) 837-0604 or (216) 696-8888
  www.nauticaqueen.com
- ❑ Hours: Monday – Thursday, Noon, 7:00 pm. Friday Noon, 7:30 pm. Saturday 11:00 am, 7:30pm. Sunday, 11:00 am, 4:00 pm. Reservation Required. (April – New Years Eve)
- ❑ Admission: $12-17 Children (Adult prices are approx. double)

3 Hour Dinner Cruise or 2 hour Lunch/Brunch Cruise. Many cruises include entertainment with special themes.

ROCK AND ROLL HALL OF FAME MUSEUM

One Key Plaza (9th Street exit north, downtown waterfront), **Cleveland** 44114

- ❑ Activity: Museums
- ❑ Telephone: (216) 781-ROCK or (888) 764-ROCK
  www.rockhall.com
- ❑ Hours: Daily, 10:00 am - 5:30 pm. (open until 9:00 pm on Wednesdays). Closed Thanksgiving and Christmas.
- ❑ Admission: Adults: $14.95, Seniors/Children: $11.50. Free Museum admission for children 8 and under with the purchase of an adult admission.

❑   Miscellaneous: Museum Store. Café & Outdoor Terrace
    restaurants for ticketed guests.

A s parents reminisce, kids will probably giggle, at most of the
     many exhibits including: Rock & Roll and the Media, It's
Only Rock & Roll, Cinema (documentary films), Induction
Videos, Radio Station and the Hall of Fame. Please check in with
Visitor's Services before you explore here - they'll let you know
which areas have PG and above ratings - you'll know which areas
to overlook.

U.S.S. COD

1809 East 9th Street (North Marginal Road next to Burke Lakefront)
Cleveland 44114

❑   Activity: Museums
❑   Telephone: (216) 566-8770, **www.usscod.org**
❑   Hours: Daily, 10:00 am - 5:00 pm (May - September)
❑   Admission: $5.00 Adult, $4.00 Seniors (62+), $3.00 Student
    (under 5 Free)

W e started our visit at the Aristotle periscope on shore that
     gives you a view of Lake Erie and puts you in the mood to
explore the WW II submarine that sank enemy shipping boats.
The ninety-man crew lived in cramped quarters - an amazing
reminder of the price of freedom.   The eight separate
compartments, tight quarters, ladders to climb and plenty of knobs
to play with give an authentic feeling of submarine life.

WILLIAM G. MATHER MUSEUM

Docked at 1001 East 9th Street Pier (Northcoast Harbor)
Cleveland 44114

❑   Activity: Museums
❑   Telephone: (216) 574-6262
    http://little.nhlink.net/wgm/wgmhome.html
❑   Hours: Daily, 10:00 am - 5:00 pm, except Sunday, Noon - 5:00
    pm (Summer). Weekends only, (Friday - Sunday) in (May,
    September, October)

❑   Admission: $5.00 Adult, $4.00 Senior (60+), $3.00 Youth (5-18)
❑   Miscellaneous: Best for preschoolers and older because of
     dangerous spots while walking. Films play continuously.

The floating Mather is an iron boat once used to carry ore, coal and grain along the Great Lakes. Little eyes will open wide in the 4 story engine room and they will have fun pretending to be the crew (or maybe guests) in the cozy sleeping quarters or the elegant dining room. Group tours are treated to programmed learning fun in the Interactive Cargo Hold area. Make a sailor hat or a boat made from silly putty (why does a boat float?). Learn to tie sailors' knots with real rope or pretend you're at sea as you move the ship's wheel. In the pilothouse area, kids use navigation charts, working radar, and a marine radio to plan a trip.

CLEVELAND BALLET

Cleveland - One Playhouse Square, Suite 330, 44115. *Activity:* The Arts. (216) 426-2500. **www.csjballet.org**. Resident ballet company presents classical and contemporary dance. (September – March)

CLEVELAND CAVALIERS

Cleveland - Gund Arena, 44115. *Activity:* Sports. (216) 420-2200. **www.nba.com/cavs**. Professional Basketball. (September – April). Cav's Hot Shots kid's fan club.

CLEVELAND INDIANS

Cleveland - 2401 Ontario (Jacobs Field), 44115. *Activity:* Sports. (216) 420-4200. **www.indians.com**. Professional Baseball. Kids Club. (April – October). Tours include Kidsland, a press box, a suite, a dugout, a fun video and you're escorted by Slider.

CLEVELAND LUMBERJACKS

Cleveland - One Center Ice (Gund Area), 44115. *Activity:* Sports. (216) 420-0000. **www.jackshockey.com**. International League Hockey. Jack Park Youth Club. (October – May)

CLEVELAND OPERA

Cleveland - State Theatre, 1519 Euclid Avenue, 44115. *Activity:* The Arts. (216) 241-6000. Internationally famous professional resident company. **www.clevelandopera.org**. (October-March)

CLEVELAND PLAYHOUSE

Cleveland - 8500 Euclid Avenue, 44115. *Activity:* The Arts. (216) 795-7000. **www.playhousesquare.com**. America's longest running regional theatre presents contemporary and classical plays; children's series and student festival.

CLEVELAND ROCKETS

Cleveland - Gund Arena, 44115. *Activity:* Sports. (216) 263-ROCK. **www.wnba.com/rockers**. WNBA women's basketball. Tickets range from $8-19.00.

DANCE CLEVELAND

Cleveland - 1148 Euclid Avenue, Suite 311, 44115. *Activity:* The Arts. (216) 861-2213. **www.dancecleveland.org**. The nation's oldest modern dance association presenting the best in contemporary dance.

GREAT LAKES THEATER FESTIVAL

Cleveland - 1501 Euclid Avenue, Suite 423, 44115. *Activity:* The Arts. **www.greatlakestheater.org** (216) 241-5490 or Tickets: (216) 241-6000. Professional resident company produces Shakespeare, Shaw, Ibsen, Chekov, Moliere, Greek dramatists and modern classics. (October – May)

100TH BOMB GROUP

Cleveland - 20000 Brookpark Road, 44135. *Activity:* Theme Restaurants. (216) 267-1010. A WWII English farmhouse décor with a view of Hopkins Airport runways.

MALLEY'S CHOCOLATES

13400 Brookpark Rd. (I-480 & West 130th Street), **Cleveland** 44135

☐   Activity: Tours
☐   Telephone: (800) 835-5684 or (216) 362-8700
    www.malleys.com/tours3.html
☐   Admission: $2.00
☐   Tours: Monday-Friday, 10:00 am –3:00 pm (By appointment).
    Also some Saturdays. Strollers allowed, No cameras. 45-60
    minute tour. 15-50 person limits.

See and hear about the story of chocolate from a professional at Malley's family business (since 1935).   We learned it takes 400 cocoa beans to make one pound of chocolate.   You'll watch them roast nuts, dip chocolates, and wrap goodies along with samples at the beginning and end of the tour (plus a candy bar to take home).   They sell one half million pounds per year with the most sales at Easter, then Christmas, then Valentine's Day.   Allow time to shop in their factory store.

NASA GLENN RESEARCH VISITOR CENTER

21000 Brookpark Road (I-480 to Exit 9, next to
Cleveland Hopkins Airport), **Cleveland** 44135

☐   Activity: Museums
☐   Telephone: (216) 433-2001, **www.grc.nasa.gov**
☐   Hours: Weekdays, 9:00 am – 4:00 pm. Saturday, 10:00 am –
    3:00 pm. Sunday and Holidays, 1:00 – 5:00 pm
☐   Admission: Free
☐   Tours: Available, call for details

The main exhibit space called the Microgravity Materials Science Laboratory houses a space shuttle, satellites, zero gravity chamber, wind tunnels, and space environmental tanks.   Look for the moon rock and space suit used by astronauts (audio explanation). A fun treat is to watch the "Astrosmiles" video – you'll learn clever space jokes told by astronauts. ACTS satellite control room and the space shuttle live broadcasts are what keep people coming back.

MEMPHIS KIDDIE PARK

Cleveland - 10340 Memphis Avenue (I-71 to West 117th/Memphis Avenue Exit), 44144. *Activity:* Amusements. (216) 941-5995. *Hours and Admission:* 10:00 am - 8 or 9:00 pm, seasonal. Pay per ride. Little tots rides like a Ferris wheel, roller coaster (our little girl's first!), carousel and miniature golf.

CONNEAUT HISTORICAL RAILROAD MUSEUM

Conneaut - 363 Depot Street and Mill Street (East of Route 7), 44030. *Activity:* Museums. **www.accvb.org/museums.html**. (440) 599-7878. *Hours:* Daily, Noon – 5:00 pm (Memorial – Labor Day). *Admission:* Donation. Old New York Central depot with an old steam engine and railroad cars.

CUYAHOGA VALLEY YOUTH BALLET

Cuyahoga Falls - (Akron Civic Theatre), 44223. *Activity:* The Arts. (330) 996-1100. **www.cvyb.org**. Pre-professional youth ballet presents ballet/modern dance. (September – May)

BOULEVARD OF FLAGS

Eastlake - 35150 Lake Shore Boulevard, City Hall, 44095. *Activity:* Ohio History. (440) 951-1416. Believe it or not, 500 American flags lining the entrances to City Hall. It's the largest display in The United States!

FAIRPORT MARINE MUSEUM
129 Second Street (I-90 to SR-44 north to SR-2),
Fairport Harbor 44077

❑   Activity: Museums
❑   Telephone: (440) 354-4825, **www.ncweb.com/org/fhlh**
❑   Hours: Wednesday, Saturday, Sunday and Holidays. 1:00 – 6:00 pm (Memorial Weekend – Weekend after Labor Day)
❑   Admission: $2.00 Adult, $1.00 Senior and Student. Under 6 – Free.

Pretend you're on a sea voyage as you explore an old pilothouse with navigation instruments, maps and charts and a large ship's wheel. Find out what number of whistles you use to indicate the ship's direction. This room was large enough to really romp around. The highlight of this museum has to be the real lighthouse (although it's a steep, tough climb up and out to the deck). After you proudly climb the 69 steps, catch your breath with a beautiful view of Lake Erie.

GARRETTS MILL

Garrettsville - 8148 Main Street (Route 82 and Route 88), 44231. *Activity:* Tours. (330) 527-5849. *Hours:* Monday – Friday, 11:00 am – 10:00 pm. Saturday, 11:00 am - 2:00 pm / 4:00 - 11:00 pm. Sunday, 11:00 am - 4:00 pm. Free admission. Food Service Store. Take a self-guided tour of a working gristmill built in 1804 on the banks of the rushing Silver Creek. The first floor grinds grain to flour with milling stones that are 3000 pounds each. The second floor is where they sift, bag and store flour. A system of flights (cup conveyor mechanism) transport the grain and flour to different floors.

ERIEVIEW PARK

Geneva-on-the-Lake - 5483 Lake Road (I-90 to Geneva Exit 218 to SR-531), 44041. *Activity:* Amusements. (440) 466-8650. **www.ncweb.com/biz/erieview**. *Hours:* Daily, Noon to 10:00 pm (Memorial Day – Labor Day). Weekends only, Mother's Day to late May). *Admission:* "Day Pass" $5-7.00, Group Rates, Individual rides are $1.20. Food Service, Picnic Area. Located on the "strip" with old-fashioned classic rides, kiddie rides, bumper cars and water slides.

GENEVA STATE PARK

Geneva-on-the-Lake - Padanarum Road (Shore of Lake Erie), 44041. *Activity:* Outdoors. (440) 466-8400 **www.dnr.state.oh.us/ odnr/parks/directory/geneva.htm**. 698 acres of camping, hiking trails, boating, fishing, swimming, winter sports. Large cabins.

AC & J SCENIC RAILROAD

State Route 46 to East Jefferson Street, **Jefferson** 44047

❑   Activity: Tours
❑   Telephone: (440) 576-6346, **www.accvb.org/museums.html**
❑   Hours: Weekends, 12:30, 2:00, and 3:30 pm.
    (mid-June to October)
❑   Admission: $7.00 Adult, $6.00 Senior (60+),
    $5.00 Children (3-12)
❑   Miscellaneous: Gift Shop/ Concessions

R ide on a 1951 Nickel Plate train with a bright red caboose on a one hour ride through woodlands and farmland. Stop halfway at a staging yard for coal and iron ore in Ashtabula Harbor.

VICTORIAN PERAMBULATOR MUSEUM

Jefferson - 26 East Cedar Street (off SR-46), 44047. *Activity:* Museums. (440) 576-9588. **www.accub.org/museums.html**. *Hours:* Saturday, 11:00 am – 5:00 pm. Wednesday, 11:00 am – 5:00 pm (Summer Only). Admission is around $3.00. First of all, do you know what a perambulator is? If you were like us, we just had to know! Answer...a baby carriage. Two sisters have collected and displayed almost 140 carriages dating from the mid-1800's to the early 1900's. Some are shaped like swans, gondolas, seahorses, and antique cars (made from wicker, which was the Victorian style). This is supposedly the nation's only baby carriage museum.

KENT STATE UNIVERSITY MUSEUM

Kent - East Main & South Lincoln Streets (Rockwell Hall), 44242. *Activity:* The Arts. **www.kent.edu/museum/anne/ksum**. (330) 672-3450. Features work of the world's greatest artists and designers. Fashion, ethnic costumes, and textiles are highlighted. Open Wednesday – Sunday. *Admission:* $3-5.00.

PUFFERBELLY RESTAURANT

Kent & Berea 44240, *Activity:* Theme Restaurants. (330) 673-1771 & (440) 234-1144. Sit down and dine in a restored historic train depot and firehouse.

HOLDEN ARBORETUM

Kirtland - 9500 Sperry Road, 44094. *Activity:* Outdoors. (440) 946-4400. **www.holdenarb.org**. *Hours:* Tuesday – Sunday, 10:00 am – 5:00 pm. 3000 acres of gardens and walking trails. Focus on woody plants. Admission over age six.

LAKE FARM PARK

8800 Chardon Road (I-90 to SR-306 south to Route 6 east)
Kirtland 44094

- ❑ Activity: Animals & Farms
- ❑ Telephone: (800) 366-FARM, **www.lakemetroparks.com**
- ❑ Hours: Daily, 9:00 am - 5:00 pm Closed Mondays (January - March) and all major holidays.
- ❑ Admission: $6.00 Adult, $5.00 Senior (65+), $4.00 Children (2-11)
- ❑ Miscellaneous: Gift Shop. Restaurant. Comfortable walking or tennis shoes are best to wear on the farm. Wagon rides throughout the park are included. Wagon rentals are available. Barnyard - ostriches, poultry, sheep petting. Pony rides are $2.00.

Not really a farm - it's a park about farming (and the cleanest farm/park you'll ever visit!).   Most of their focus is to discover where food and natural products come from. In the Dairy Parlor, you can milk a real cow and make ice cream from the cow's milk. Wander over to the Arena and watch the sheep show. What products can be made with the help of sheep? - How about feta cheese from their milk and yarn from their wool coats. Use special brushes to clean their wool and then spin some by hand. Exhibits are ready to be played with all day in the Great Tomato Works. A giant tomato plant (6 feet wide with 12-ft. leaves) greets you and once inside the greenhouse, you can go down below the earth in the dirt to see where plants get their start. Sneak up on a real honeybee comb, but mind the words on the sign, "DO NOT DISTURB - HONEYBEES AT WORK". This visit generates lots of questions about the food you eat. Great learning!

MAILBOX FACTORY

Kirtland - 7857 Chardon Road (US-6), 44094. *Activity:* Outdoors. (440) 256-MAIL. **www.mailboxfactory.com**. *Hours:* Monday - Friday, 10:00 am - 6:00 pm. Saturday, 9:00 am - 5:00 pm. You can't miss this place! As you approach the workshop, finished decorative mailboxes are adorning the lawn and many boxes and totem poles (yes!) are works in progress. Owner Wayne Burrwell used to drive a snow plow and occasionally knocked down mailboxes during his work. When he replaced them, he did it with such a unique mailbox that others on the street became envious. Now his livelihood is making mailboxes shaped like cows (with a cowbell), pelicans, trucks, flamingoes, and our favorite (and the special of the week), a "pig box". A must see!

LAKE MILTON STATE PARK

Lake Milton - (1 mile South of I-76 off SR-534), 44429. *Activity:* Outdoors. **www.dnr.state.oh.us/odnr/parks/directory/lkmilton.htm**. (330) 654-4989. 2,856 acres of boating, fishing, swimming and winter sports. At the beach are scenic cruises with live narration of history of the lake and Craig Beach Village. (330) 547-5555, 1 hour long, about $5.00 per person.

BECK CENTER FOR THE CULTURAL ARTS

Lakewood - 17801 Detroit Avenue, 44107. *Activity:* The Arts. (216) 521-2540 **www.lkwpl.org/beck**. Visual and performing arts center offers community theatre, gallery, artists' collective, education, outreach programs, and children's theatre.

MAGICAL FARMS

Litchfield - 5280 Avon Lake Road (SR-83), 44253. *Activity:* Animals & Farms. (330) 667-3233. **www.alpacafarm.com**. *Tours:* Daylight hours, Daily. 2nd largest alpaca breeding farm in North America.

TENDER SHEPHERD FARMS

Lodi - 7434 Lafayette Road, 44254. *Activity:* Animals & Farms. (330) 948-4218. **www.ohio.net/~tsfpacas.** Alpaca farm with over 40 acres to tour. Learn about their care and fiber products made from their fur.

WESTERN RESERVE FINE ARTS ASSOCIATION

Madison - 49 Park Street, 44057. *Activity:* The Arts. (440) 428-5913. Presents performances, art shows and student recitals plus education in music, art, and dance.

ZOO-4-U

Madison - 5414 River Road, 44057. *Activity:* Animals & Farms. (440) 428-6556. Exotic and rare domestic petting zoo. 150 different kinds of handleable, petable, rideable animals. Playground, picnic area & pony rides. (May 1 - October 31)

MEDINA COUNTY HISTORICAL SOCIETY
JOHN SMART HOUSE MUSEUM

Medina - 206 North Elmwood Street and Friendship Street, 44256. *Activity:* Ohio History. (330) 722-1341. *Hours:* Tuesday and Thursday, 9:00 am – 5:00 pm, 1st Sunday of Month, 1:00 – 4:00 p.m. East Lake style home. Victorian, Civil War, pioneer and Indian artifacts. Life-size photographs of real "giants", Anna Julian and Martin Bates (also boots and helmet).

GARFIELD'S LAWNFIELD NATIONAL HISTORIC SITE

8095 Mentor Avenue (2 miles East on US-20), **Mentor** 44060

❑ Activity: Ohio History

❑ Telephone: (440) 255-8722, **www.wrhs.org/sites/garfield.htm**

❑ Hours: Monday - Saturday, 10:00 am - 5:00 pm.
Sunday, Noon - 5:00 pm

❑ Admission: $6.00 Adult, Seniors $5.00, $4.00 Youth (6-12)

❑ Miscellaneous: Gift Shop

The Victorian mansion was the home of President James A. Garfield. Shortly after his election, an opponent at a railroad station in Washington D.C. assassinated him. Catch the funeral wreath sent by Queen Victoria when Garfield was killed. See the video showing Garfield's campaign on the front porch of his home in 1880. Journalists standing on the lawn covering the campaign nicknamed the property "Lawnfield".

LAKE COUNTY HISTORY CENTER

Mentor - 8610 King Memorial Road, 44060. *Activity:* Ohio History. (440) 255-8979. Housed in Shadybrook, a one-time summer home for a wealthy family in the early part of the century, the history center chronicles Lake County's past in a museum and research library.

MIDDLEFIELD CHEESE HOUSE

Middlefield – SR-608, 44062. *Activity:* Tours. (216) 632-5228. *Hours:* Monday – Saturday 7:00 am – 5:30 pm. Free admission. Over 20 million pounds of Swiss cheese are produced here each year. Your tours begins with the film "Faith and Teamwork" describing the cheese-making process. Then wander through the Cheese House Museum with Swiss cheese carvings, antique cheese-making equipment, and Amish memorabilia. Lastly, sample some cheese before you buy homemade cheese, sausage and bread.

PUNDERSON STATE PARK

Newbury - (2 miles East of Newbury off SR-87), 44065. *Activity:* Outdoors.**www.dnr.state.oh.us/odnr/parks/directory/punderson.htm**. (440) 564-2279. Nature programs. Tennis. 996 acres of camping, hiking trails, boating and rentals, fishing, swimming and winter sports. Family cabins with A/C and fireplaces. Punderson Manor House Resort has indoor/outdoor pools, tennis, basketball, toboggan and winter chalet.

NATIONAL MCKINLEY BIRTHPLACE MEMORIAL AND MUSEUM

Niles - 40 North Main Street (SR-46 to downtown), 44446. *Activity:* Ohio History. (330) 652-1704. **www.mckinley.lib.oh.us.** *Hours:* Monday - Thursday, 9:00 am - 8:00 pm. Friday & Saturday, 9:00 am - 5:30 pm. (Also, Sunday, 1:00 - 5:00 pm – September – May). Free admission. Auditorium and Library. The classic Greek structure with Georgian marble which houses a museum of McKinley memorabilia. Also see artifacts from the Civil War and Spanish-American War.

COVERED BRIDGE PIZZA

North Kingsville and **Andover** – SR-193 & US-20, North Kingsville or 380 East Main Street, Andover, 44114. *Activity:* Theme Restaurants. (440) 224-0497 or (440) 293-6776. Actual covered bridges with built-in pizza shops!. Located in the heart of Ashtabula County (*area features 14 covered bridges that can be toured*). Daily, except Monday for Lunch/Dinner. Moderate prices. Casual.

TROLLEYVILLE, USA

7100 Columbia Road (SR-252 off I-480 West)
Olmstead Township 44138

❑   Activity: Tours

❑   Telephone: (440) 235-4725, **www.trolleyvilleusa.org**

❑   Hours: Wednesday, Friday, 10:00 am – 3:00 pm (Late May – September) Saturday, Sunday, and Holidays, Noon – 5:00 pm (May – November)

❑   Admission: $5.00 Adult , $4.00 Senior, $3.00 Children (3-11). Includes unlimited rides in all cars.

The 1914 Cleveland Station Railway Depot is home to more than 34 pieces of electric railway equipment. Note the switchboard from the Penn Railroad Station downtown. Take rides on the 2 ½ mile train ride on a #304, #409 or #460 Interurban (electric rail car) at 72 MPH speeds. You'll have a chance to stop at a depot built in 1896 with a replica of a Pittsburgh streetcar.

HEADLANDS BEACH STATE PARK

Painesville – SR-44 (2 miles Northwest of Painesville), 44060. *Activity:* Outdoors. **www.dnr.state.oh.us/odnr/parks/directory/ headlnds.htm**. (440) 881-8141. 125 acres of hiking trails, fishing, swimming and winter sports.

INDIAN MUSEUM OF LAKE COUNTY

Painesville - 391 West Washington Street (Lake Erie College), 44077. *Activity:* Ohio History. (440) 352-1911. *Hours:* Monday – Friday, 10:00 am – 4:00 pm, Saturday and Sunday, 1:00 – 4:00 pm. Interactive matching game of Indian tribes. Dig for arrow heads in sand. Grinding corn to flour. Small admission.

LAKE ERIE COLLEGE FINE AND PERFORMING ARTS DEPARTMENT

Painesville - 391 West Washington Street, 44077. *Activity:* The Arts. (440) 352-3361. **www.lec.edu**. Offers theatre, dance, music and art programs. (September – April)

PAINESVILLE SPEEDWAY

Painesville - 500 Fairport Nursery Road, 44077. *Activity:* Sports. (440) 354-3505. 1/5 mile asphalt track.

GREENBRIER THEATRE

Parma Heights - 6200 Pearl Road, 44130. *Activity:* The Arts. (440) 842-4600. Semi-professional community theatre offers mainstage and café-style productions, usually Broadway hits. (September – June)

CUYAHOGA VALLEY SCENIC RAILROAD

Cuyahoga Valley National Recreation Area (Peninsula and Independence – off I-77 or I-271, follow signs) **Peninsula** 44264

❑   Activity: Tours
❑   Telephone. (800) 468-4070, **www.cvsr.com**

- ❏ Hours: Departs Wednesday – Sunday, Morning and early Afternoon (Summer – October). Weekends, Morning and early Afternoon (Rest of the Year)
- ❏ Admission: $11.00 - $20.00 Adult, $10.00 - $18.00 Senior, $7.00 - $12.00 Children (3+)
- ❏ Miscellaneous: Gift Shop at Depot, Gift Shop Car, Concession Car, Park Ranger/Volunteer available for transportation or nature information.

Ride in climate controlled coaches built between 1939 and 1940 on the very scenic 2 - 6 ½ hour ride to many exciting round trip destinations. Meadowlands, pinery, marsh, rivers, ravines, and woods pass by as you travel to Hale Farm and Village, Quaker Square, Inventure Place, Canal Visitor Center, Stan Hywet Hall or just a basic scenic tour (best if small kids take shorter or trips with layovers). This is a fun way to spend the day family style (grandparents too!) and see one other attraction along the way. Be sure your little engineers get a blue or pink cap to wear along the trip as a memory of their first train ride!

TINKER'S CREEK STATE PARK

Portage - Aurora-Hudson Road (2 miles West of SR-43), 44266. *Activity:* Outdoors. (330) 296-3239. **www.dnr.state.oh.us/odnr/ parks/directory/tinkers.htm**. 760 acres of hiking trails, fishing trails, swimming and winter sports.

PORTAGE COUNTY HISTORICAL SOCIETY

Ravenna - 6549 North Chestnut Street, 44266. *Activity:* Ohio History. **www2.clearlight.com/~pchs/index.phtml**. (330) 296-3523. *Hours:* Tuesday, Thursday & Sunday, 2:00 - 4:00 pm. Besides the Lowrie-Beatty museum, the society's 12-acre site includes the Carter House, an early pioneer homestead, John Campbell Land Grant Office, 1810-1811 the Mahan Barn, an 1810 New England-type barn, Ford Seed Company Museum, housed in an old photographer's studio, an Advance-Rumely Steam Traction Engine, the unique Proehl-Kline Clock Tower housing the 1882 Portage County Courthouse Seth-Thomas clock & courthouse bell; & various farm buildings.

WEST BRANCH STATE PARK

Ravenna - (5 miles East of Ravenna off SR-5), 44266. *Activity:* Outdoors. **www.dnr.state.oh.us/odnr/parks/directory/westbrnc.htm**. (330) 296-3239. Nature programs. Bridle trails. 8,002 acres of camping, hiking trails, boating and rentals, fishing, swimming and winter sports.

DOVER LAKE WATERPARK

Sagamore - 7150 West Highland Road (access I-77, I-271, SR-303 or SR-82) 44067. *Activity:* Amusements. (330) 655-SWIM. **www.DoverLake.com**. *Hours:* Daily, 10:00 am - 8:00 pm (mid-June to August). *Admission:* $9 - 11.00 per person (42" and under are free). Parking $2.00. 7 mountain slides, tube rides, speed slides, kiddie play, wave pool, paddleboats and a nice small lake and beach.

SHAKER HISTORICAL MUSEUM

Shaker Heights - 16740 South Park Boulevard (off I-271), 44120. *Activity:* Ohio History. **www.ohiohistory.org/places/shaker**. (216) 921-1201. *Hours:* Tuesday – Friday and Sunday, 2:00 – 5:00 pm. Free admission. Shaker Community remnants. Furniture and inventions (apple peeler, flat broom, tilter chair, clothes pins).

HUDSON BANDSTAND CONCERT SOCIETY

Stow - 4936-C Friar Road, 44224. *Activity:* The Arts. (330) 673-5985. Sunday series includes band concerts, dance, bluegrass, jazz, choral and youth groups on Hudson Green or Barlow Community Center. (Summer)

MOSQUITO LAKE STATE PARK

Warren - (10 miles North of Warren off SR-305), 44410. *Activity:* Outdoors. **www.dnr.state.oh.us/odnr/parks/directory/mosquito.htm**. (330) 637-2856. Bridle trails. 11,811 acres of camping, hiking trails, boating and rentals, fishing, swimming and winter sports.

WARREN CIVIC MUSIC ASSOCIATION

Warren – 44481. *Activity:* The Arts. (800) BUCKEYE. Presents yearly concert series of instrumental and vocal music, opera and dance. (September – May)

NATIONAL PACKARD MUSEUM

Warren - 1899 Mahoning Avenue NW, 44482. *Activity:* Museums. (330) 394-1899. **www.packardmuseum.org**. *Hours:* Tuesday - Sunday, Noon - 5:00 pm. *Admission:* $5.00 Adult, $3.00 Senior (65+), $3.00 Children (7-12). Watch a video about Packard's family of vehicles and personal family stories. See memorabilia about the manufacturer's history from 1899 – 1958. Also Packard Electric history display.

MCDONALD'S

Warren - 2891 Elm Road NE, 44483. *Activity:* Theme Restaurants. (330) 372-6282. Ohio's largest McDonald's Play Place with five slides over two stories high, talking equipment (mirrors, trash cans), two ball pits and interactive computers. Open daily.

TRUMBULL COUNTY HISTORICAL SOCIETY

Warren - 303 Monroe Street NW, 44483. *Activity:* Ohio History. (330) 394-4653. *Hours:* Saturday & Sunday, 1:00 – 4:00 pm. (April –October) John Stark Edwards/Thomas Denny Webb House.

MOST MAGNIFICENT MCDONALD'S IN AMERICA

Warren - 162 North Road SE, 44484. (330) 856-3611. *Activity:* Theme Restaurants. A 3-story building (mostly glass) complete with brass and marble fixtures, a glass elevator, an indoor waterfall, and even a baby grand piano! A must see…open daily.

WILLOUGHBY FINE ARTS ASSOCIATION

Willoughby - 38660 Mentor Avenue, 44094. *Activity:* The Arts. (440) 951-7500. Cultural center gives opportunity to see, hear and participate in the arts.

MILL CREEK PARK

(South of Mahoning Ave. off Glenwood Ave.) **Youngstown** 44406

- ❑ Activity: Outdoors
- ❑ Telephone: (330) 740-7115 (Lanterman's Mill). (330) 740-7107 (Ford Nature Center) or (330) 740-7109 (Winter) **www.cboss.com/millcreek**
- ❑ Hours: Tuesday - Friday, 10:00 am - 5:00 pm. Saturday and Sunday, 11:00 am - 6:00 pm
- ❑ Miscellaneous: Gift Shop. Lanterman's Mill (May - October). Admission.

This park has your basic scenic trails, lakes, falls, gardens and covered bridges but it also has more. The Ford Nature Center is a stone house with live reptiles and hands-on exhibits about nature. Lanterman's Mill is a restored 1845 water-powered gristmill with a 14-foot oak wheel. As you travel through the park, be on the look out for the Silver Bridge (reminiscent of Old England and Mary Poppins). The best community park system (and very well kept) you'll find anywhere!

BUTLER INSTITUTE OF AMERICAN ART

Youngstown - 524 Wick Avenue, 44502. *Activity:* The Arts. (330) 743-1711. **www.butlerart.com**. *Hours:* Tuesday – Saturday, 11:00 am - 4:00 pm, Sunday, Noon - 4:00 pm. Showcases American art from colonial times to the present. Children's Gallery (hands-on) and American Sports Art Gallery.

MAHONING VALLEY HISTORICAL SOCIETY MUSEUM

Youngstown - 648 Wick Avenue (Arms Family Museum), 44502. *Activity:* Ohio History. (330) 743-2589. *Hours:* Tuesday – Friday, 1:00 – 4:00 pm, Saturday – Sunday, 1:30 – 5:00 pm. Small Admission. "The Valley Experience".

MCDONOUGH MUSEUM OF ART

Youngstown - Youngstown State University, 44503. *Activity:* The Arts. (330) 742-1400. Presents visual art works of old and new artists. (September – July)

YOUNGSTOWN HISTORICAL CENTER OF INDUSTRY & LABOR

151 West Wood Street, **Youngstown** 44503

- ❑   Activity: Museums
- ❑   Telephone: (800) 262-6137 or (330) 743-5934
     www.ohiohistory.org/places/youngst/
- ❑   Hours: Wednesday – Saturday, 9:00 am – 5:00 pm
     Sunday, Noon – 5:00 pm
- ❑   Admission: $5.00 Adult, $4.00 Senior, $1.25 Youth (6-12)

If your family has a heritage of steelworkers in the family, then this is the place to explain their hard work. The history of the iron and steel industry in the Mahoning Valley area can be viewed easily looking at the life-sized dioramas titled, "By the Sweat of Their Brow". Rooms are set up like typical steel mill locker rooms, company houses, and a blooming room. They certainly give you the "feel" of the treacherous work at the mill.

YOUNGSTOWN SYMPHONY

Youngstown - 260 Federal Plaza West, 44503. *Activity:* The Arts. (330) 744-4264. Performs Pops Concerts with guest artists in Powers Auditorium (tours).

YOUNGSTOWN PLAYHOUSE

Youngstown – 44511. *Activity:* The Arts. (330) 788-8739. Community theatre offers mainstage, summer musical and youth shows.

GORANT CANDIES

8301 Market Street (SR-7, Boardman), **Youngstown** 44512

- ❑ Activity: Tours
- ❑ Telephone: (800) 572-4139 Ext. 236
- ❑ Tours: Weekdays until 1:30 pm. Maximum 50 people.
  1st grade and above
- ❑ Miscellaneous: Candy store. Displays of chocolate history.

Put on your paper hat and watch up to 375,000 pieces of chocolate candy being made each day. See the 2000-pound chocolate melting vats and color-coded rooms. The brown walls are the molding room where chocolate is poured and shook on vibrating tables (takes out the air bubbles). The yellow room is the coating room. A personalized hand dipper (only one) dips 3600 candies a day. Receive a free candy bar at the end of the tour.

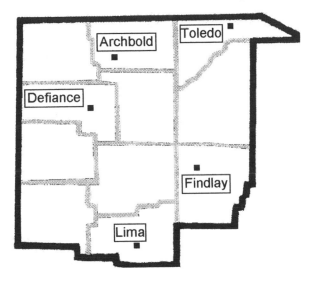

Chapter 6
North West Area

Our Favorites...

- COSI Toledo
- Sauder Farm & Village
- S.S. Willis Boyer
- Tony Packos Café

MOM'S DINER

Archbold - 213 North Defiance Street, 43502. *Activity:* Theme Restaurants. (419) 445-5060. Open daily at 11:00 am. Milkshakes, burgers, 50's style décor, jukebox music and servers that wear poodle skirts.

SAUDER FARM AND CRAFT VILLAGE

22611 SR-2 (off SR-66, 2 miles Northeast on SR-2 or off turnpike exit 25), **Archbold** 43502

❑   Activity: Ohio History

❑   Telephone: (800) 590-9755, **www.saudervillage.com**

❑   Hours: Monday – Saturday, 10:00 am – 5:00 pm. Sunday, 1:00 – 5:00 pm (mid-April to October)

❑   Admission: $9.50 Adult, $9.00 Senior, $4.75 Youth (6-16)
$1.00 Carriage, Train or Wagon rides. Group Rates available (25+)

❑   Miscellaneous: Barn Restaurant. Gift Shop. Bakery. Country Inn.

The farm consists of a barnyard house with a summer kitchen full of antique tools and hardware. Walk along the craft village where you can meet a weaver, glassblower, broom maker, tinsmith, blacksmith and potter all dressed in early 20th Century clothing.

BOWLING GREEN STATE UNIVERSITY
FINE ARTS CENTER GALLERIES

Bowling Green - Fine Arts Building, 43403. *Activity:* The Arts. (419) 372-8525. Galleries and a Japanese ceremonial room exhibit national/student art.

AUGLAISE VILLAGE FARM MUSEUM

Off US-24 (3 miles SW of Defiance - follow signs), **Defiance** 43512

❑   Activity: Ohio History

❑   Telephone: (419) 784-0107, **www.defiance-onlint.com/auglaise**

❑   Hours: Weekends, 11:00 am - 4:00 pm (June - Labor Day)

❑   Admission: $2.00 Adult, $1.00 Youth (6-16)

A recreated late 19th Century village - 17 new, restored or reconstructed buildings that serve as museums. The Red Barn with the Street of Shops and Hall of Appliances is probably the most interesting - especially the old-fashioned appliances and authentic period food they serve. Best to visit during festivals or special events when there is an abundance of costumed guides.

INDEPENDENCE DAM STATE PARK

Defiance – SR-424 (4 miles East of Defiance), 43512. *Activity:* Outdoors.**www.dnr.state.oh.us/odnr/parks/directory/indpndam. htm**. (419) 784-3263. 604 acres of camping, hiking trails, boating, fishing, and winter sports.

JIGGS DRIVE IN

Defiance - 111 Holgate Avenue, 43512. *Activity:* Theme Restaurants. (419) 782-4393. A 50's carhop drive in with servers dressed in Jiggs shirts and jackets that come out to your car and hook trays to your car window. They serve food like chili dogs and rootbeer. Daily for lunch and dinner. (mid-April through August)

DELPHOS CANAL COMMISSION MUSEUM CENTER

Delphos - 111 West Third Street, 45833. *Activity:* Ohio History. (419) 695-7737. *Hours:* Monday, Wednesday, Friday, 9:00 am – Noon. Tuesday & Thursday, 6:00 - 8:00 pm. Canals and canal boats. Stained glass artist. Quilt club work in progress.

MUSEUM OF POSTAL HISTORY

Delphos - 131 North Main Street (Lower Level of Post Office), 45833. *Activity:* Museums. (419) 695-2811. *Hours:* Monday, Wednesday, Friday, 1:30 – 3:30 pm. 7000 square feet of displays plus media presentations that show development of American history and the influences of the U.S. Mail. See the progress of mail processing, development of the letter, stamps, postmarks and the idea of a post office. You can actually sit in a 1906 rural mail coach.

HARRISON LAKE STATE PARK

Fayette - (4 miles South of Fayette off SR-66), 43521. *Activity:* Outdoors. **www.dnr.state.oh.us/odnr/parks/directory/harrison. htm**. (419) 237-2593, 249 acres of camping, hiking trails, boating, fishing, swimming, and winter sports.

DIETSCH BROTHERS

Findlay - 400 West Main Cross Street (SR-12), 45839. *Activity:* Tours. (419) 422-4474. *Tours:* Tuesday – Sunday (Daytime). ½ hour long, 20 people maximum. Reservations required. Three brothers (2nd generation) run an original 1937's candy and ice cream shop. In the summer, see ice cream made with real cream. They make 1500 gallons per week. Fall, heading into the holidays, is the best time to see 500 pounds of chocolate treats made daily.

GHOST TOWN MUSEUM PARK

Findlay - (US-68 to County Road 40 West), 45840. *Activity:* Ohio History. (419) 326-5874. *Hours:* Tuesday - Sunday, 9:30 am - 6:00 pm (Memorial Day Weekend - mid-September). *Admission:* $4.00 Adult, $2.00 Children (under 12). A ghost town recreation with 28 buildings from the 1880's including a general store and barbershop.

ISAAC LUDWIG MILL

Providence Park (US-24 and SR-578), **Grand Rapids** 43522

- ❑ Activity: Tours
- ❑ Telephone: (419) 535-3050
- ❑ Hours: Wednesday – Friday, 10:00 am – 4:00 pm. Saturday – Sunday, 11:00 am – 5:00 pm (May – October)
- ❑ Admission: Free demonstrations of mill. 45 minute mule drawn canal boat rides leave every hour until 4:00 pm. Narrated. $4.00 Adult , $3.00 Senior (59+), $2.00 Children (3-12)

A nother one of the few mills left in Ohio. This 19th century mill sits on the Maumee River and demonstrates how a flour mill, sawmill and electric generator can be powered by water from the old canal below.

MARY JANE THURSTON STATE PARK

Grand Rapids – SR-65 (2 miles West of Grand Rapids), 43534. *Activity:* Outdoors. **www.dnr.state.oh.us/odnr/parks/directory/ mjthrstn.htm**. (419) 832-7662. 555 acres of hiking trails, boating, fishing and winter sports.

CULBERTSON'S MINI ZOO SURVIVAL CENTER

Holland - 6340 Angola Road (SR-2 to Holland-Sylvania Road, North to Angola West), 43537. *Activity:* Animals & Farms. (419) 865-3470. *Hours:* Monday – Saturday, 9:00 am – 6:00 pm. *Admission:* $2.00 Adult, $0.75 Children (3-14). Specializes in the rescue and refuse of exotic animals like cougars, lions, tigers, baboons, buffaloes, deer, birds, and fish.

ALLEN COUNTY MUSEUM

Lima - 620 West Market Street, 45801. *Activity:* Ohio History. (419) 222-9426. **www.worcnet.gen.oh.us/~acmuseum**. *Hours:* Tuesday – Sunday, 1:30 – 5:00 pm. Indian and pioneer artifacts. Antique automobiles and bicycles. Barber Shop, Doctor's office, country store, log house on grounds. Next door is MacDonell House (wall of purses). Lincoln Park Railroad exhibit locomotive and Shay Locomotive (huge train) is something the kids will love.

ARTSPACE/LIMA

Lima - 65/67 Town Square, 45801. *Activity:* The Arts. (419) 222-1721. Features exhibits of local/regional artists and classes. Art fair in September. Holiday festival in December.

KEWPEE

Lima - (three locations), 45801. *Activity:* Theme Restaurants. (419) 228-1778. Burgers since 1928 with wrappers that say "Hamburger with pickle on top, makes your heart go flippity flop".

LIMA SYMPHONY ORCHESTRA

Lima - 67 Town Square, 45801. *Activity:* The Arts. (419) 222-5701. Plays series of concerts plus holiday, family, children's and summer concerts. (October – May)

LIMALAND MOTOR SPEEDWAY

Lima - 1500 Dutch Hollow Road (off SR-81), 45805. *Activity:* Sports. Race Headquarters, (419) 998-3199 or Raceday, (419) 339-6249. **www.limaland.com**. ¼ mile, high-banked, clay oval track. (April - September)

OLD BARN OUT BACK

Lima - 3175 West Elm Street, 45805. *Activity:* Theme Restaurants. (419) 991-3075. A local favorite with large timbers, cedar-aged barn siding, and lanterns hanging from wagon wheels create a true feeling of being "down on the farm". Groups can eat together in the "Chicken Coop", "Milking Parlor", or "Pig Pen". Grandma's famous recipe fried chicken or cinnamon rolls along with great homemade favorites and a large variety of fresh food served on their salad bar. Local family owned. Come with ready appetites, as the portions are farm-style generous. Don't miss this family-friendly Lima tradition!

POPCORN GALLERY

Lima - 927 North Cable Road, Suite H-1, 45805. *Activity:* Tours. (419) 227-2676. Free admission. *Tours:* Monday – Friday, Mornings. Reservations required. (45 minute tour and store browsing). See how 40 flavors of popcorn are made. Begin with an explanation of why corn pops. Then see industrial poppers spill out oodles of popped corn that is then flavored using a slurry that is cooked onto corn. The American Indians had over 700 varieties of popcorn and brought some to the first Thanksgiving.

FORT MEIGS

29100 West River Road (1 mile Southwest of SR-25,
I-475 to exit 2), **Perrysburg** 43552

❑   Activity: Ohio History
❑   Telephone: (419) 874-4121
    www.ohiohistory.org/places/ftmeigs
❑   Hours: Wednesday - Saturday, 9:30 am - 5:00 pm. Sunday,
    Noon - 5:00 pm (Memorial Day Weekend - Labor Day)
    Weekends only, (September and October)
❑   Admission: $5.00 Adult, $1.25 Youth (6-12)
❑   Miscellaneous: Visitor's Center with Gift Shop at the stone
    shutterhouse.

A War of 1812 era authentic castle-like log and earth fort with seven blockhouses that played an important role in guarding the Western frontier against the British. The walls of the blockhouses are 2 feet thick with 4-inch deep windows and cannon hole ports on the second floor. See actual cannons fired as the air fills with smoke.

MAUMEE STATE FOREST

Swanton - 3390 County Road D, 43558. *Activity:* Outdoors. (419) 822-3052.   **www.hcs.ohio-state.edu/ODNR/Forests/stateforests/ maumee.htm**. Open daily, 6:00 am - 11:00 pm. 3,068 acres in Fulton, Henry and Lucas counties. Bridle trails (15 miles), All-purpose vehicle area with 5 miles of trails (also snowmobile-weather permitting), Windbreak arboretum area.

FRANCISCAN CENTER

Sylvania - 6832 Convent Boulevard, 43560. *Activity:* The Arts. (419) 885-1547. **www.franciscancenter.org**. Summer arts camp. Presents season of music and theatre. (September – May)

JEWISH COMMUNITY CENTER
JUNIOR THEATRE GUILD

Sylvania - 6465 Sylvania Avenue, 43560. *Activity:* The Arts. (419) 885-4485. See professional touring artists from the US and Canada in productions ranging from classics to new works in theatre, puppetry, opera and dance.

MAUMEE / TOLEDO TROLLEY TOUR

Toledo – Downtown. *Activity:* Tours. (419) 245-5225. *Tours:* Wednesday & Sunday (Weekly, June – September). 2 ½ hours long. Tour downtown Toledo & Maumee on an 1880 streetcar replica.

TOLEDO MUD HENS BASEBALL

Toledo - Ned Skeldon Stadium, *Activity:* Sports. (419) 893-9483. **www.mudhens.com**. Maumee. Semi-professional baseball (farm team for the Detroit Tigers). See "Muddy" the mascot.

TOLEDO STORM

Toledo - Toledo Sports Arena. *Activity:* Sports. (419) 691-0200. **www.thestorm.com**. Semi-Professional hockey part of East Coast Hockey League (affiliate for Tampa Bay Lightning or Detroit Vipers). Season starts in October.

COSI TOLEDO

One Discovery Way (Downtown riverfront, corner of Summit and Adams Streets), **Toledo** 43604

- ❑ Activity: Museums
- ❑ Telephone: (419) 244-COSI, **www.cositoledo.org**
- ❑ Hours: Monday - Saturday, 10:00 am - 5:00 pm. Sunday, Noon - 5:30 pm. Closed Thanksgiving, Christmas, New Years & Easter
- ❑ Admission: $7.00 Adult (19-64), $5.50 Senior (65+) and Children (2-18)
- ❑ Miscellaneous: Science 2 Go Gift Shop. Atomic Cafe - restaurant of food, "Science where you're encouraged to play with your food".

Seven learning worlds including Mind Zone (distorted Gravity Room, Animation, T-Rex), Sports (improve your game using science), Life Force (secrets of parts of the body like your skin, brain, and stomach), Water Works (water arcade, water travel, rainstorms), KidSpace, and BabySpace (18 months and under). The older kids will love Whiz-Bang Engineering and Science Park (greeted by Ed the animatronic security guard, feel hydraulics with motion simulator, take the Science on the Go Challenge!).

TOLEDO OPERA

Toledo - 406 Adams Street (Historic Valentine Theatre), 43604. *Activity:* The Arts. (419) 255-7464. Professional regional company presents three shows with guest artists.

TOLEDO SYMPHONY ORCHESTRA

Toledo - 2 Maritime Plaza, 43604. *Activity:* The Arts. (800) 348-1253 or (419) 246-8000. **www.toledosymphony.com**. Regional symphony performs orchestral masterpieces with guest artists, chamber, contemporary, pops, youth and summer concerts.

SS WILLIS B BOYER MARITIME MUSEUM

26 Main Street, International Park (East side of Maumee River – Downtown), **Toledo** 43605

❑   Activity: Museums
❑   Telephone: (419) 936-3070
❑   Hours: Daily, 10:00 am – 5:00 pm (May – October)
      Wednesday – Saturday, 10:00 am – 5:00 pm, Sunday, Noon - 5:00 pm (November – April)
❑   Admission: $6.00 Adult, $4.00 Student

The 617-foot freighter depicts how ships of the Great Lakes worked in the early to mid-1900's. It was the biggest, most modern ship on the Great Lakes (in its day) and as you drive up, it takes up your whole panoramic view. A nautical museum of Lake Erie resides inside with photographs, artifacts and best of all for kids, hands-on exhibits.

TONY PACKO'S CAFÉ

Toledo - 1902 Front Street, 43605. *Activity:* Theme Restaurants. (419) 691-6054. **www.tonypackos.com**. Corporal Klinger (Jamie Farr) in the TV series M*A*S*H raved about it. See it for yourself and try some ethnic Hungarian style food such as cabbage rolls, chicken paprikash, chili dogs and Packo's famous chili. Be sure to look for the hundreds of hot dog buns signed by TV stars that have visited the café.

U.S. GLASS SPECIALTY OUTLET

Toledo - 1367 Miami Street (I-75 exit 199), 43605. *Activity:* Tours. (419) 698-8046. *Hours:* Retail: Monday – Friday, 9:00 am – 5:30 pm. Saturday – Sunday, 11:00 am – 4:00 pm. *Viewing:* Tuesday – Sunday, 11:00 am – 4:00 pm. Watch glass blowers at work. Gift Shop sells decorated glass and ceramics.

SANDPIPER CANAL BOAT

Toledo - 2144 Fordway, Riverfront, 43606. *Activity:* Tours. (419) 537-1212. *Hours:* Hourly, Wednesday – Sunday, 10:00 am – 4:00 pm (May – October). *Admission:* $4.00 Adult, $3.00 Senior, $2.00 Children (12 and under). Replica of a Miami and Erie Canal boat. Cruise up river past riverside estates or down river to Lake Erie.

ARAWANNA II

Toledo - Rossford City Marina (Cherry Street & Front Street on the Maumee River), 43607. *Activity:* Theme Restaurants. (419) 691-7447. **www.arawannabelle.com**. *Hours:* Weekends, Departs at 1:00 pm (April – November). Board a true sternwheeler used in Disney's "Huck Finn". Narrated tour of Maumee Valley river estates or skyline of downtown Toledo. 2 deck boat (lower deck is sheltered) with meal included (lunch/dinner). Higher prices ($16-$28.00) because food is served on the tour.

OHIO THEATRE

Toledo - 3114 LaGrange Street, 43608. *Activity:* The Arts. (419) 241-6785. Former vaudeville/movie house presents classical music, live stage, film and children's series.

TOLEDO ZOO

2700 Broadway (I-75 to US-25 - 3 miles South of downtown)
Toledo 43609

❑   Activity: Animals & Farms

❑   Telephone: (419) 385-5721, **www.toledozoo.org**

❑   Hours: Daily, 10:00 am - 5:00 pm (April - Labor Day)
      Daily, 10:00 am - 4:00 pm (Rest of the Year)

❑   Admission: $6.00 Adult, $3.00 Senior (60+) and Children (2-11)

❑   Miscellaneous: Carnivore Cafe (dine in actual cages once used to house big cats!). Children's Zoo - petting zoo & hands on exhibits.

They have areas typical of a zoo but they are known for their Hippoquarium (the world's first underwater viewing of the hippopotamus) along with a well-defined interpretive center and hands-on exhibits. The Kingdom of Apes and African Savanna are other popular exhibits. The renovated Aviary, new Primate Forest and Arctic Encounter are hot spots too.

TOLEDO FIREFIGHTERS MUSEUM

Toledo - 918 Sylvania Avenue, 43612. *Activity:* Museums. (419) 478-FIRE. *Hours:* Saturday, Noon – 4:00 pm (Summer), Saturday and Sunday, Noon – 4:00 pm (Winter). Feel what 150 years of history of fire-fighting must have meant to the fireman. Learn fire safety tips. See actual vintage pumpers, uniforms, and equipment used that trace the growth of the Toledo Fire Department. Located in the former No. 18 Fire Station.

TOLEDO SPEEDWAY

Toledo - 5639 Benore Road, 43612. *Activity:* Sports. (419) 729-1634. Stock car racing. ½ mile, asphalt, high-banked oval. (May – October)

TOLEDO BOTANICAL GARDENS

Toledo - 5403 Elmer Drive (off North Reynolds Road), 43615. *Activity:* Outdoors. (419) 936-2986. Open dawn to dusk. 57 acres of meadows and gardens. Gallery and gift store.

MAUMEE BAY STATE PARK

Toledo - 1400 Park Road #1 (8 miles East of Toledo, then 3 miles North off SR-2), 43618. *Activity:* Outdoors. (419) 836-7758. **www.dnr.state.oh.us/odnr/parks/directory/maumebay.htm**. 1,845 acres of camping, hiking trails, boating, fishing, swimming and winter sports. Resort cottages and rooms, golf, racquetball, sauna, whirlpool, fitness, tennis, volleyball and basketball are available.

TOLEDO MUSEUM OF ART

Toledo - 2445 Monroe at Scottwood (off I-75), 43620. *Activity:* The Arts. (419) 255-8000. **www.toledomuseum.org**. Discover treasures from the riches of the medieval, the splendors of a French chateau and the tombs of Egypt. Also glass, sculpture, paintings. Free admission.

WOLCOTT HOUSE MUSEUM

Toledo (area) - 1031 River Road, 43537. *Activity:* Ohio History. (419) 893-9602. *Hours:* Wednesday – Sunday, 1:00 – 4:00 pm, (April – December). Life in the mid-1800's in the Maumee Valley. Log home, depot, church and gift shop. Admission

VAN BUREN LAKE STATE PARK

Van Buren – SR-613 (1 mile East of Van Buren), 45889. *Activity:* Outdoors. **www.dnr.state.oh.us/odnr/parks/directory/vanburen. htm**. (419) 299-3461. 296 acres of camping, hiking trails, boating, fishing, and winter sports.

BLUEBIRD PASSENGER TRAIN
49 North 6th St. (& *3rd* & *Mill Street* - ***Grand Rapids***)
Waterville 43566

❑   Activity: Tours

❑   Telephone: (419) 878-2177

❑   Hours: Tuesday - Thursday, Saturday, Sunday & Holidays,
      Afternoon Departures. (Summer). Weekends & Holidays Only,
      (May, September, October)

❑   Admission: $8.00 Adult, $7.00 Senior (65+), $4.50 Children (3-12)

Can you guess why they call it "Bluebird"? Answer: The bluebirds come back to Ohio in the spring and leave in the early fall. That's when the train runs. The 45-minute trip (each way) on a 1930's era passenger train includes a spectacular view from a 900-foot long bridge over the Maumee River.

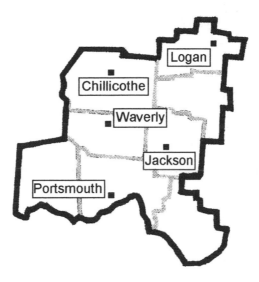

Chapter 7
South Central Area

Our Favorites...

- Hocking Hills Area
- Mitchellace Shoestring Factory
- Portsmouth Murals
- State Parks

TAR HOLLOW STATE FOREST

(northeast of **Chillicothe**, south of **Adelphi**), 43101. *Activity:* Outdoors. (740) 663-2523 (Waverly office). **www.hcs.ohio-state.edu/ODNR/ Forests/stateforests/tarhollow.htm**. Open daily, 6:00 am - 11:00 pm. 16,120 acres in Ross, Vinton and Hocking counties. Bride trails (33 miles), horse campground, hiking trails (22 miles), grouse management area. Tar Hollow State Park is adjacent.

SCIOTO TRAIL STATE FOREST

124 North Ridge Road (south of **Chillicothe**, off US-23), 44690. *Activity:* Outdoors. (740) 663-2523. **www.hcs.ohio-state.edu/ ODNR/Forests/ stateforests/sciototrail.htm**. Open daily, 6:00 am - 11:00 pm. 9,390 acres in Ross and Pike counties. Mountain bike and bridle trails (26 miles), hiking trails (1 mile). Former fire lookout tower. Scioto Trail State Park is adjacent.

TAR HOLLOW STATE PARK

Adelphi - (10 miles South of Adelphi off SR-540), 43135. *Activity:* Outdoors. (740) 887-4818. **www.dnr.state.oh.us/odnr/ parks/directory/tarhollw.htm**. 634 acres of camping, hiking trails, boating, fishing, swimming.

MAGIC WATERS AMPHITHEATRE

Bainbridge - 7757 Cave Road, 45612. *Activity:* The Arts. (937) 365-1388. **www.highlandcounty.com/magic.htm**. Summertime enjoy magic shows and kid's theatre (i.e. The Wizard of Oz). On December weekends they run Journey to Bethlehem - A Christmas Walk of Joy.

PIKE LAKE STATE PARK

Bainbridge - 1847 Pike Lake Road (6 miles Southeast of Bainbridge), 45612. *Activity:* Outdoors. **www.dnr.state.oh.us/ odnr/parks/directory/pikelake.htm**. (740) 493-2212. Nature programs. 613 acres of camping, hiking trails, boating and rentals, fishing, swimming and winter sports. Family cabins.

SEVEN CAVES

7660 Cave Rd. (US-50, 4 miles NW, follow signs), **Bainbridge** 45612

- ❑   Activity: Outdoors
- ❑   Telephone: (937) 365-1283
- ❑   Hours: Daily, 9:00 am - Dusk
- ❑   Admission: $8.00 Adult, $4.00 Youth (5-11)
- ❑   Miscellaneous: Many stairs. Self-guided tours make this an adventure. Snack bar and shelter house.

Three trails lead to caves with cemented walkways, handrails, and lighting showing specific formations. See cliffs, canyons, and waterfalls.

ADENA STATE MEMORIAL

(West of SR-104 off Adena Road), **Chillicothe** 45601

- ❑   Activity: Ohio History
- ❑   Telephone: (740) 772-1500
     www.ohiohistory.org/places/adena
- ❑   Hours: Wednesday - Saturday, 9:30 am - 5:00 pm (Summer)
     Sundays and Holidays, Noon - 5:00 pm (Summer)
     Weekends only, (September and October)
- ❑   Admission: $5.00 Adult, $1.25 Youth (6-12)

View the overlook of the hillside that was used to paint the picture for the Ohio State Seal. See the 1807 stone mansion built by the 6th Ohio governor Thomas Worthington. Also visit a tenant house, smoke house, wash house, barn and spring house.

GREAT SEAL STATE PARK

Chillicothe - Marietta Pike (3 miles Northeast of Chillicothe), 45601. *Activity:* Outdoors. (740) 773-2726. **www.dnr.state.oh.us/ odnr/parks/directory/grtseal.htm**. 1,864 acres of camping, bridle trails, hiking trails, and winter sports.

HOPEWELL CULTURE NATIONAL HISTORICAL PARK

Chillicothe - 16062 SR-104, 3 miles north of Chillicothe), 45601. *Activity:* Outdoors. (740) 774-1125. **www.nps.gov/hocu**. *Hours:* Daily, 8:00 am - 6:00 pm (Summer). Daily, 8:30 am - 5:00 pm (Rest of year). *Admission:* $2.00 per person. Maximum charge per vehicle is $4.00. Visitor Center with a 15 minute "Legacy of the Moundbuilders" orientation film. The 120-acre park with 13-acre earthwall enclosure is home to 23 prehistoric burial and ceremonial mounds of the Hopewell Indians.

JAMES M. THOMAS TELEPHONE MUSEUM

Chillicothe - 68 East Main Street, 45601. *Activity:* Museums. (740) 772-8200. **www.horizontel.com/museum.htm**. *Hours:* Monday – Friday, 8:30 am – 4:30 pm. Free admission. Run by the Chillicothe Telephone Company, it shows the telephone from its invention stages to modern times. Especially note the display of early telephone sets.

PUMP HOUSE ART GALLERY

Chillicothe - Enderlin Circle, Yoctangee Park, 45601. *Activity:* The Arts. (740) 772-5783. **www.bright.net/~pumpart**. Visit art gallery and cultural center in restored water pumping station.

ROSS COUNTY HISTORICAL MUSEUM

Chillicothe - 45 West 5th Street, 45601. *Activity:* Ohio History. (740) 772-1936. **www.rosscountyhistorical.org**. *Hours:* Daily, (except Monday), 1:00 – 5:00 pm (April – September), Weekends, (December – March). See the table upon which Ohio's Constitution was signed. Civil War. Franklin House women's museum. Admission.

SCIOTO TRAIL STATE PARK

Chillicothe - (10 miles South of Chillicothe off US-23), 45601. *Activity:* Outdoors. (740) 663-2125. **www.dnr.state.oh.us/odnr/ parks/directory/sciototr.htm**. 248 acres of camping, hiking, boating, fishing and winter sports.

SUMBURGER RESTAURANT

Chillicothe - 1487 North Bridge Street, 45601. *Activity:* Theme Restaurants. (740) 772-1055. Casual lunch or dinner menu items ordered from table telephones.

TECUMSEH

Sugarloaf Mountain Amphitheater (Delano Road off SR-159)
Chillicothe 45601

❑   Activity: The Arts

❑   Telephone: (740) 775-0700, **www.tecumsehdrama.com**

❑   Hours: Monday – Saturday, Show time, 8:00 pm. Reservations please. (mid-June to Labor Day)

❑   Admission: $15.00 General (slightly reduced during Monday - Thursday), $6.00 Children (under 10)

❑   Tours: Backstage Tours 2 –5:00 pm. $3.50 Adult. $2.00 Children. One hour long, demonstrations on weaponry, stunts & makeup.

❑   Miscellaneous: Mountain Valley Gift Shop. Restaurant with buffet served a few hours before the show.

This production has received national attention. More than 1.6 million people have already seen the outdoor re-enactment of Shawnee Leader, Tecumseh's life and death. Fast action horses, loud firearms and speeding arrows make the audience part of the action especially when costumed actors enter the scene from right, left and behind.

LAWRENCE COUNTY MUSEUM

Ironton - 506 South 6th Street (6th and Adams Street), 45638. *Activity:* Ohio History. (740) 532-1222. *Hours:* Friday – Sunday, 1:00 – 5:00 pm (mid-April to mid-December). 1870 Victorian home of Rev. Runkin and served as a station for the Underground Railroad. Iron industry. Free admission.

NOAH'S ARK ANIMAL FARM

1527 McGiffins Road (5 miles East on SR-32), **Jackson** 45640

❑   Activity: Animals & Farms

❑   Telephone: (800) 282-2167, **www.zoomnet.net/~noah**

❑   Hours: Monday – Saturday, 10:00 am – 6:00 pm.

   Sunday, Noon – 6:00 pm (April – October)

❑   Admission: $5.00 Adult, $4.00 Children (3-12)

❑   Miscellaneous: A-1 Diner.

Exotic animals and birds (more than 150), miniature golf, Pay Fishing lake and ¼ mile train ride (additional $1.00). Most love the black bears and their cubs best.

PIKE STATE FOREST

Latham - 334 Lapperrel Road (on SR-124, just west of Latham), 45646. *Activity:* Outdoors. (740) 493-2441. **www.hcs.ohio-state. edu/ODNR/Forests/stateforests/pike.htm**. Open daily, 6:00 am - 11:00 pm. 11,961 acres in Pike and Highland counties. Bridle trails (33 miles), APV trails (15 miles), Pike Lake State Park is adjacent.

HOCKING HILLS STATE PARK

Logan - 20160 SR-664 (Route 33 south to Route 664, follow signs), 43138. *Activity:* Outdoors. (800) HOCKING. *Hours:* 6:00 am - Sunset (Summer), 8:00 am (Winter). Overnight accommodations, bed and breakfasts, camping, cabins with A/C and fireplaces, recreation, picnic grounds, and hiking, Nature trails are found throughout the park, many of them lead to obscure, out- of- the-way natural creations. The park includes: Ash Cave (an 80 acre cave and stream), Cantwell Cliffs, Cedar Falls, Conkle's Hollow, Rock House, and the most popular, Old Man's Cave (a wooded, winding ravine of waterfalls and caves). Your children's sense of adventure will soar! Concessions available at Old Man's Cave or dining in the Lodge (with outdoor pool). We recommend close supervision on the hiking trails for your child's safety.

LAKE LOGAN STATE PARK

Logan - (4 miles West of Logan off SR-664), 43138. *Activity:* Outdoors. **www.dnr.state.oh.us/odnr/parks/directory/lklogan. htm.** (740) 385-3444, 717 acres of hiking, boating and rentals, fishing, swimming and winter sports.

LAKE HOPE STATE PARK

McArthur - 27331 SR-278 (12 miles Northeast of McArthur on SR-278), 45651. *Activity:* Outdoors. (740) 596-5253. **www.dnr. state.oh.us/odnr/parks/directory/lakehope.htm**. Nature programs. 3,223 acres of camping, family cabins, hiking, boating and rentals, fishing, swimming.

SMOKE RISE RANCH RESORT

Murray City - (US-33 to SR-78 to CR-92), 43144. *Activity:* Animals & Farms. (800) 292-1732. **www.smokeriseranch.com**. Full service campground or cabins. Working Cattle Ranch (Ridin' & Ropin'), Riding Arenas, Trail riding, heated pool and hot tub.

JACKSON LAKE STATE PARK

Oak Hill - (2 miles West of Oak Hill on SR-279), 45656. *Activity:* Outdoors. **www.dnr.state.oh.us/odnr/parks/directory/jacksonl. htm**. (740) 682-6197. 335 acres of camping, boating, fishing, swimming and winter sports.

DEAN STATE FOREST

Pedro - 149 Dean Forest Road, 45659. *Activity:* Outdoors. (740) 532-7228. **www.hcs.ohio-state.edu/ODNR/Forests/stateforests/dean.htm**. Open daily, 6:00 am - 11:00 pm. 2,745 acres in Lawrence County. 20 miles bridle trails, Wayne National Forest is adjacent.

BRUSH CREEK STATE FOREST

Peebles 45660. *Activity:* Outdoors. (740) 372-3194. **www.hcs.ohio-state.edu/ODNR/Forests/stateforests/brushcreek.htm**. Open daily, 6:00 am - 11:00 pm. 12,749 acres in Scioto, Adams and Pike counties. 12 miles bridle trails, 3 miles hiking trails.

SERPENT MOUND STATE MEMORIAL

3850 State Route 73, **Peebles** 45660

- Activity: Outdoors
- Telephone: (937) 587-2796, **www.ohiohistory.org/places/serpent**
- Hours: Daily, 10:00 am - 5:00 pm (April - October)
- Admission: $5.00 per vehicle
- Miscellaneous: Profile of the "cyptoexplosion" doughnut shape can be seen off State Route 770 - East of Serpent Mound.

The largest earthwork in the United States, it measures 1335 feet from head to tail and is about 15 feet high. The mound appears as a giant serpent uncoiling in seven deep curves. The oval doughnut at one end probably represents the open mouth of the snake as it strikes.

MITCHELLACE SHOESTRING FACTORY

830 Murray Street (Corner of Gallia Street off US-52)
Portsmouth 45662

- Activity: Tours
- Telephone: (740) 354-2813 or (800) 848-8696 **www.mitchellace.com**

❑   Tours: Groups of 10 (no more than 50). One hour tour. Age 8+
❑   Miscellaneous: Company store (laces for 25 cents) - end of tour.

The former shoe factory works 2-3 shifts per day to make more than 4,000,000 pairs of shoelaces per week. They are the world's biggest shoelace manufacturers for shoes and skates (especially RollerBlades). Family descendants still run the company started in 1902. Start the tour by watching weaving and braiding machines (over 1300) producing strands of fabric. This process takes up an entire floor and when you step onto the floor, all you see are flashes of color. The tipping department takes long strands and cuts them into different lengths and then they are tipped with aglets of nylon or metal. Automatic machines band, fold, label and seal. Other laces are blister packed (plastic pouch over laces is melted onto backing card). The shortest lace is 10 inches. The longest made is 120 inches (for ice skates).

PORTSMOUTH MURALS

Portsmouth – SR-23 South (Washington Street to Ohio River - follow green mural signs), 45662. *Activity:* The Arts. **www.portsmouth.org**. Artist Robert Dafford (internationally known muralist) can be seen working on new murals in the months of May – September. Look for the scaffold and the artist dressed in paint-dotted white painter's pants and shirt. Our two favorites were Chillicothe Street 1940's (a very colorful, tremendously detailed, cartoon-like mural) and Twilight (a modern day view of the bridge over the river, looks like a photograph).

SOUTHERN OHIO MUSEUM & CULTURAL CENTER

Portsmouth - 825 Gallia Street, 45662. *Activity:* The Arts. (740) 354-5629. **www.portsmouth.org**. Changing exhibits in fine arts and history, performing arts events.

HOCKING STATE FOREST

Rockbridge - 19275 SR-374 (off SR-374 and 664, northeast of Laurelville), 43149. *Activity:* Outdoors. (740) 385-4402. www.hcs.ohio-state.edu/ODNR/Forests/stateforests/hocking.htm. Open daily, 30 minutes before sunrise - 30 minutes after sunset. 9,267 acres in Hocking County. Hiking trails (9 miles), Bridle trails (40 miles), horse campground, see a former fire lookout tower, rock climbing a rappelling area, and state nature preserves. Hocking Hills State Park is adjacent.

LAKE WHITE STATE PARK

Waverly - (4 miles Southwest of Waverly on SR-104), 45690. *Activity:* Outdoors. (740) 947-4059. www.dnr.state.oh.us/odnr/ parks/directory/lkwhitew.htm. 358 acres of camping, boating, fishing, swimming and winter sports.

BUCKEYE FURNACE MUSEUM

123 Buckeye Park Road (Off SR-124), **Wellston** 45692

- ❏ Activity: Museums
- ❏ Telephone: (740) 384-3537
  www.ohiohistory.org/places/buckeye
- ❏ Hours: Wednesday – Saturday, 9:30 am – 5:00 pm. Sundays and Holidays, Noon – 5:00 pm. (Summer). Weekends Only, (Labor Day – October)
- ❏ Admission: $3.00 Adult, $1.25 Youth (6 12)

Visit Ohio's only restored charcoal furnace which remains from the original 80 furnaces in Ohio. In the mid – 1800's, this industry took root as trees were converted into charcoal to make iron for railroads and ammunition. The self-guided tour of the furnace shows you where raw materials (charcoal, iron ore, etc.) were brought to the top of the hill and poured into the furnace to be heated to 600 degrees F. Impurities (slag) stayed on the top while liquid iron (which is heavier) flowed to the base.

LAKE ALMA STATE PARK

Wellston - (3 miles Northeast of Wellston on SR-349), 45692. *Activity:* Outdoors. (740) 384-4474. **www.dnr.state.oh.us/parks/ directory/lakealma.htm**. 279 acres of camping, hiking, boating, fishing and swimming.

RICHLAND FURNACE STATE FOREST

Wellston - (off SR-327, near Byer, NW of Wellston), 45692. *Activity:* Outdoors. (740) 596-5781 (Zaleski office). **www.hcs.ohio-state.edu/ODNR/Forests/stateforests/richlandfurnace.htm**. Open daily, 6:00 am - 11:00 pm. 2,448 acres in Jackson and Vinton counties. APV trails (7 miles).

SHAWNEE STATE FOREST

West Portsmouth -13291 US-52, 45663. *Activity:* Outdoors. (740) 858-6685. **www.hcs.ohio-state.edu/ODNR/Forests/stateforests/ shawnee.htm**. Open daily, 6:00 am - 11:00 pm. 62,583 acres in Scioto and Adams counties. Ohio's largest state forest. Backpack trails (60 miles) with 8 walk-in camp areas (self-registration permit - no fee), Bridle trails (75 miles), horse campground (no fee), 5 small forest lakes, 8000 acre wilderness area. Shawnee State Park is adjacent.

SHAWNEE STATE PARK

West Portsmouth - 4404 SR-125 (8 miles West of Portsmouth), 45663. *Activity:* Outdoors. (740) 858-6652. **www.dnr.state. oh.us/odnr/parks/directory/shawnee.htm**. Nature programs. 1,168 acres of camping, hiking, boating and rentals, fishing, swimming, winter sports and food service. Family cabins, lodge with indoor/outdoor pools, sauna, whirlpool, fitness center, tennis and basketball.

ZALESKI STATE FOREST

Zaleski - SR-278 (south of Logan), 45698. *Activity:* Outdoors. **www.hcs.ohio-state.edu/ODNR/Forests/stateforests/zaleski.htm.** (740) 596-5781. Open daily, 6:00 am - 11:00 pm. 26,827 acres in Vinton and Athens counties. Bridle trails (50 miles), Backpack trails (23 miles), 3 walk-in camp areas (self-registration permit - no fee), Forest of Honor, Hunter's campground (in season - no fee), grouse management area, and sawmill. Lake Hope State Park is adjacent.

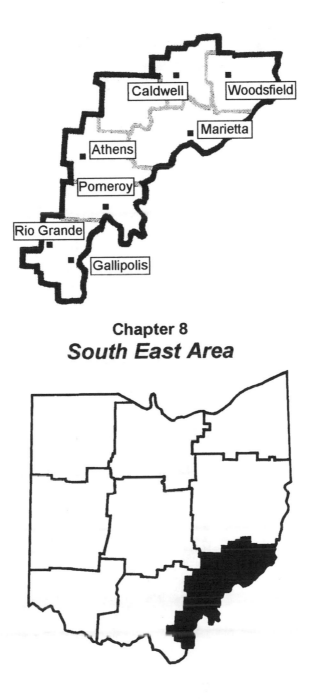

Chapter 8
South East Area

Our Favorites...

- Butch's Coca-Cola Museum
- Campus Martius Museum
- Lee Middleton Doll Factory
- Rossi Pasta Factory

SUNFISH CREEK STATE FOREST

(off SR-7, south of **Powhattan Point**), 43942. *Activity:* Outdoors. (740) 593-3341 (Athens office). **www.hcs.ohio-state.edu/ODNR/ Forests/stateforests/sunfishcreek.htm**. Open daily, 6:00 am - 11:00 pm. 637 acres in Monroe County. No facilities. Steep terrain along the Ohio River.

DAIRY BARN CULTURAL ARTS CENTER

Athens - 8000 Dairy Lane (US-33 & 501), 45701. *Activity:* The Arts. (740) 592-4981. **www.dairybarn.org**. Festivals. Hayrides and storytellers for kids. Arts and crafts exhibits.

OHIO UNIVERSITY

Athens – 45701. *Activity:* Tours. (740) 593-2097. **www.ohiou. edu/athens/index.html**. College Green tour starts at Visitor Center. Self-guided tour includes walk to oldest part of Campus buildings. Also tree tour shows 50 of the 115 different species of trees on campus (some are from Japan, China, and Siberia).

OHIO UNIVERSITY OFFICE OF PUBLIC OCCASIONS

Athens - Templeton-Blackburn Memorial Auditorium, 45701. *Activity:* The Arts. (740) 593-1760. **www.ohiou.edu**. Presents theatre, music, dance, ethnic & folk art programs. (October – May)

STROUD'S RUN STATE PARK

Athens - County Road 20 (8 miles Northeast of Athens off US-50A), 45701. *Activity:* Outdoors. (740) 592-2302. **www.dnr.state. oh.us/odnr/parks/directory/strouds.htm**. 2,767 acres of camping, hiking trails, boating and rentals, fishing, swimming and winter sports.

WOLF RUN RECREATION AREA

Belle Valley - (1 mile East of Belle Valley off I-77), 43717. *Activity:* Outdoors. (740) 732-5035. 1,363 acres of camping, hiking trails, boating, fishing, swimming and winter sports.

<u>LEE MIDDLETON ORIGINAL DOLL FACTORY</u>

1301 Washington Boulevard (I-77 to SR-50/618), **Belpre** 45714

❑   Activity: Tours

❑   Telephone: (740) 423-1481 or (800) 233-7479

www.leemiddleton.com

❑   Tours: Monday – Friday, 9:00 am – 2:00 pm (Hourly). March – December. Approximately 20 minutes. Reservations Suggested. Free admission.

❑   Miscellaneous: Factory Store with bargain buys and Nursery where you can adopt a life-sized Middleton infant baby doll complete with papers, promises and pictures.

Hopefully during your visit you'll get to experience a little girl adopting her first Middleton baby. It's so real, you'll swell with emotion as you see the new "Mom" promise the nursery worker to care for her baby properly. Lee Middleton started making dolls at her kitchen table in 1978 and modeled them after her children and children she knew. On tour a guide (dressed like a Middleton doll) shows you techniques critical to the distinctiveness of these expensive collectable dolls that look and feel almost real. One machine makes feet, hands and heads out of liquid vinyl cured in molds. Watch them put eyes in by blowing up the mold head like a balloon (with an air compressor) and popping in the eyes. Then they release the air and the eye is set in place. See the artists hand paint each doll's face using stencils and paint makeup. What a fun "girl's place" to visit. Prepare to fall in love with a doll and want one for your own!

GIFFORD STATE FOREST

Chesterhill -17221 SR-377 (17 miles northeast of Athens), 43728. *Activity:* Outdoors. (740) 554-3177. **www.hcs.ohio-state.edu/ ODNR/Forests/stateforests/gifford.htm**. Open daily, 6:00 am - 11:00 pm. 320 acres in Athens County. Experimental tree seed production area. 4 mile hiking trail.

ARIEL THEATRE

Gallipolis - 426 Second Avenue, 45631. *Activity:* The Arts. (740) 446-2787. Restored opera house is home to Ohio Valley Symphony, Ariel Players.

OUR HOUSE MUSEUM

Gallipolis - 434 1ˢᵗ Avenue (off SR-7), 45631. *Activity:* Ohio History. (740) 446-0586. **www.ohiohistory.org/places/ourhouse**. *Hours:* Tuesday – Saturday, 10:00 am – 5:00 pm, Sunday, 1:00 – 5:00 pm (Summer). Weekends, (May, September, October). *Admission:* $0.50-$3.00. A restored river inn with furnishings of early Americana. Admission.

BURR OAK STATE PARK

Glouster - 10220 Burr Oak Lodge Road (6 miles Northeast of Glouster off SR-13), 45732. *Activity:* Outdoors. (740) 767-3570. **www.dnr.state.oh.us/odnr/parks/directory/burroak.htm**. Nature programs, Bridle trails, Family cabins with A/C, and Guest rooms with an indoor pool, tennis and basketball courts are highlights of this park. Also camping, hiking trails, boating and rentals, fishing, swimming, and winter sports.

BUTCH'S COCA-COLA MUSEUM

118 Maple Street, Harmar Village, **Marietta** 45750

- ❑ Activity: Museums
- ❑ Telephone: (740) 376-COKE
   www.harmarvillage.com/harmarcoke
- ❑ Hours: Tuesday – Saturday, 10:00 am – 4:30 pm.
   Sunday, Noon - 4:30 pm (Spring – Fall)
   Friday and Saturday, 10:00 am – 4:30 pm (Winter)
- ❑ Admission: Donation

Memorabilia from 1900 to the present traces the history of this beverage and its marketing. Buy a bottle of COKE or Sarsaparilla (vanilla Root Beer) and sip it while you browse. The Icy-O-Cooler (1900) looks like a top-loading washing machine and was the 1st style of COKE coolers (one of only 6 left in the country). Although it's rusted, you can still see the COCA-COLA logo on the front. Of special interest to us was the 2 Liter glass bottle and all of the single serving bottles from foreign countries. We asked about a plastic can of COKE and Butch told us it was test marketed in Atlanta, GA for 3 weeks. The idea was "trashed" when the recyclers became upset because the can would not recycle effectively (the top was aluminum and the can, plastic).

<u>CAMPUS MARTIUS: MUSEUM OF NORTHWEST TERRITORY</u>

601 2nd Street (2nd and Washington Street), **Marietta** 45750

- ❑   Activity: Ohio History
- ❑   Telephone: (740) 373-3750
     www.ohiohistory.org/places/campus
- ❑   Hours: Monday - Saturday, 9:30 am - 5:00 pm. & Sundays and Holidays, Noon - 5:00 pm (May – September) Wednesday - Saturday, 9:30 am - 5:00 pm and Sunday, Noon - 5:00 pm (Spring and Fall)
- ❑   Admission: $4.00 Adult, $3.20 Senior (65+) $1.00 Children (6-12)

Campus recreates early development of Marietta as the first settlement in the Northwest Territory. The Putnam House is the oldest residence in Ohio. The home and land office display replicas of the hardships of early pioneer life including old surgical and musical instruments. A new exhibit titled "Paradise Found and Lost: Migration in the Ohio Valley", highlights migration from farms to cities and from Appalachia to industry. See the stage jacket worn by Appalachian born Country Singer, Dwight Yoakum. Videos and interactive computer games on migration. You can actually create a feeling of being taken back in time by walking through the train passenger car and listening to actual stories of passengers taking a trip to the "big city" for business or jobs (stories are told on telephone handsets). See actual huge photographs of downtown Columbus and Marietta in the early 1900's that take up an entire wall - you'll feel as if you're walking into them!

HISTORICAL HARMAR MODEL RAILROAD STATION MUSEUM

Marietta - 220 Gilman Street, Harmar Village, 45750. *Activity:* Museums. (800) 288-2577. **www.eekman.com/harmarstation**. *Hours:* Daily, 11:00 am – 5:00 pm. *Admission:* $5.00 General (4th grade and older). $15.00 Family. More than 1500 linear feet of authentic toy electric trains on several levels of track. Up to 15 trains operate simultaneously and over 200 vintage locomotives are on display. The museum is housed in the original town station depot. Operating electric train exhibit with different sized trains. Some operations are hands-on.

MARIETTA TROLLEY TOURS

Marietta - 127 Ohio Street (Levee House Café), 45750. *Activity:* Tours. (740) 374-2233. **www.mariettaonline.com/attractions/ tours.htm**. *Hours:* Afternoon, 12:30 and 2:30 pm (April – October). Schedule can vary. Call or visit website for details. *Admission:* $7.50 Adult, $7.00 Senior (55+), $5.00 Youth (5-12). Narrated one-hour tours describing and viewing historic architecture, shops along Front Street, Marietta College and more.

OHIO RIVER MUSEUM

601 Second Street (St. Clair & Front Street), **Marietta** 45750

❑   Activity: Museums
❑   Telephone: (740) 373-3717
    www.ohiohistory.org/places/ohriver
❑   Hours: Wednesday – Saturday, 9:30 am – 5:00 pm
    (October – November / March - April).
    Daily, 9:30 am – 5:00 pm, Sunday, Noon – 5:00 pm.
    (May – September)
❑   Admission: $5.00 Adult, $4.00 Senior (65+),
    $1.25 Children (6-12)

The WP Snyder, Jr. moored along the museum is the last surviving stern-wheeled towboat in America. Also, see a model of a flat boat and other scale models of many riverboats. A video titled, "Fire on the Water" describes dangerous early times when boilers might explode, killing many.   Diorama (full scale) of wildlife along the Ohio River.

ROSSI PASTA

114 Greene Street (Downtown), **Marietta** 45750

- ❑   Activity: Tours
- ❑   Telephone: (740) 376-2065, **www.rossipasta.com**
- ❑   Hours: Monday - Saturday, 9:00 am - 7:00 pm.
  Sunday, Noon - 5:00 pm. (June - December)
  Daily, 10:00 am - 6:00 pm (January - May)
- ❑   Tours: Pasta making times vary, best weekdays before 3:00 pm.
  Call ahead for best times to tour.
- ❑   Miscellaneous: Upscale gourmet pasta with unusual twists of
  flavors like Artichoke, Wild Mushroom, Calamari, Linguini. Free
  sample bag of pasta to first time visitors.

They hand roll dough adding fresh flavor ingredients as they "turn" the dough.   Their secret is using spring wheat flour instead of highly manufactured semoline flour. A machine cuts the pasta into very long and wide strips (linguini) or thin soup noodles. Teardrop shapes are stamped out. Next, the cut pasta goes into one of two large drying chambers which are precisely regulated to insure even temperatures.   Finally, the pasta is packaged in clear Rossi-labeled bags. Be sure you invite your favorite gourmet cook along for this tour - it's a new level of pasta to experience!

SHOWBOAT BECKY THATCHER

Marietta - 237 Front Street on the River, 45750. *Activity:* The Arts. (877) 540-BOAT. **www.marietta-ohio.com/beckythatcher**. Vintage early 1900's sternwheeler that has a theater that was once a boiler room. Talented performers create a "Mark Twain" mood with melodramas like "Little Mary Sunshine" and favorites of composer Stephen Foster ("Oh Susanna" and "Camptown Races"). Funny signs appear during the performance instructing you when to "boo" or "cheer". The restaurant on board serves basic American food and Riverboat Pie (secret recipe) for dessert! Hours: Daytime/Evening (Summer and Fall)

THE CASTLE

Marietta - 418 Fourth Street, 45750. *Activity:* Ohio History. (740) 373-4180. **http://mcnet.marietta.edu/~castle**. *Hours:* Monday - Sunday, (Summer), Thursday – Monday, (April, May, September - December), Weekdays, 10:00 am – 4:00 pm, Weekends, 1:00 – 4:00 pm. *Admission:* $3.50 Adult, $3.00 Senior(60+), $2.00 Student (6+). Historic area furnishings. Impressive parlor and chandelier. Video.

VALLEY GEM STERNWHEELER

601 Front Street (SR-60 and SR-7) (Docks next to the Ohio River Museum under the Washington Street Bridge), **Marietta** 45750

❏ Activity: Tours
❏ Telephone: (740) 373-7862, **www.marietta.edu/~Vgem**
❏ Hours: Tuesday – Sunday. Departs every hour from 1:00 – 5:00 pm. No 5:00 pm departure on Saturday. (Summer) Rest of Year and Holidays, call for schedule.
❏ Admission: $5.50 Adult , $3.00 Children (2-12)
❏ Miscellaneous: Gift and snack area on board. Fall foliage cruises very popular in October. Heated main cabin.

Take the 300 passenger, 50 minute cruise on the Valley Gem where the captain points out historic interests. See who can find the large stone blocks spelling "Marietta" on the landing welcoming steamboats. Why was the boat named after a piano company?

HOCKING VALLEY SCENIC RAILWAY

(Off US-33), **Nelsonville** 45764

❏ Activity: Tours
❏ Telephone: (800) 967-7834 or (740) 753-9531 (Saturday and Sunday), **www.hvsr.com**
❏ Hours: Weekends, Noon and 2:30 pm, (June – October). Special Holiday Schedule

❑   Admission: $7.50 - $10.50, Adult, $4.75 - $7.50 Children (2-11)

R ide through the hills of scenic Hocking Valley on an authentic
1916 steam locomotive or a 1950 diesel locomotive (both
trips are 25 miles roundtrip). Both rides include a 30-minute stop
over at Robbins Crossing Visitor's Center (small settler village).

FORKED RUN STATE PARK

Reedsville - (3 miles Southwest of Reedsville off SR-124), 45772.
Activity: Outdoors. (740) 378-6206. **www.dnr.state.oh.us/odnr/
parks/directory/forkedrn.htm**. 817 acres of camping, hiking,
boating and rentals, fishing, swimming, winter sports and food
service.

SHADE RIVER STATE FOREST

17221 - SR-377 (southeast of Athens, near **Reedsville**), 45772.
Activity: Outdoors. (740) 554-3177. **www.hcs.ohio-state.edu/
DNR/Forests/stateforests/shaderiver.htm**. Open daily, 6:00 am -
11:00 pm. 2,602 acres in Meigs County. Hiking trail (2 miles).
Forked Run State Park is adjacent.

BOB EVAN'S FARM
State Route 588 (off US-35 to SR-325 South), **Rio Grande** 45674

❑   Activity: Animals & Farms
❑   Telephone: (800) 944-FARM, **www.bobevans.com**
❑   Hours: Daily, 8:30 am - 5:00 pm (Summer).
     Weekends in September
❑   Admission: Free for tour - Activities additional.
❑   Tours: By wagon - 10:00 am, Noon, 2:00 and 4:00 pm

B egin or end your visit at the restaurant, once named "The
Sausage Shop"-Bob's first restaurant. Then, wander round to
visit the Farm Museum (implements of yesteryear farms and a
pictorial history of the company). See a log cabin village with a
one-room school house, small animal barn yard, hay rides,
horseback riding, canoe trips, craft barn and demonstrations, plus

the Homestead (an old stagecoach stop and former home of Bob and Jewel Evans). Nearby in Bedwell (State Route 50/35) is Jewel Evan's Mill where you can view millstones grinding flour.

CAPTAIN HOOK'S TOMB

Stockport - State Route 376 (Old Brick Cemetery - along river), 43787. *Activity:* Outdoors. Legend says that Captain Isaiah Hook designed his grave monument to be sharp on top so that it would be impossible for his wife to dance on his grave!

THE BARN

Stockport - State Route 78, 43787. *Activity:* The Arts. (740) 962-4284. **www.chuckglass.com**. 1904 stained glass studio used by nationally known artist, Chuck Borsari. *Hours:* Sunday - Thursday, 1:00 - 5:00 pm.

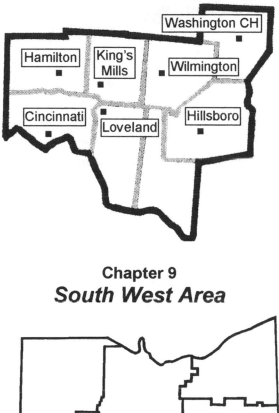

Chapter 9
South West Area

Our Favorites...

- Cincinnati Fire Museum
- Cincinnati History Museum
- Cincinnati Museum of Natural History & Science
- Harriet Beecher Stowe & Rankin House
- Loveland Castle
- Ohio River Cruises
- Turtle Creek Railway
- United Dairy Farmer's Factory

DELTA QUEEN STEAMSHIP COMPANY

Activity: Tours. (800) 215-0805. **www.deltaqueen.com**. "Delta Queen", "Mississippi Queen", or "American Queen". Overnight paddlewheel steamboat trips with regional food service and old time river music played on the calliope and banjo. Also can explore tour of the engine room and pilothouse. Many theme cruises. Usually 3-14 night cruises start at $500.00 / person.

EAST FORK STATE PARK

Amelia - (4 miles Southeast of Amelia off SR-125), 45106. *Activity:* Outdoors. (513) 734-4323. **www.dnr.state.oh.us/odnr/ parks/directory/eastfork.htm**. Bridle trails. 10,580 acres of camping, hiking, boating, fishing, swimming and winter sports.

CAREW TOWER

Cincinnati - 441 Vine Street (5th and Vine), Downtown, 45202. *Activity:* Outdoors. (513) 241-3888. *Hours:* Monday - Friday, 9:30 am - 5:30 pm. Saturday, 10:00 am - 9:00 pm. Sunday, 11:00 am - 4:45 pm. *Admission:* $2.00 Adult, $1.00 Children (under 12). A 1930's Art Deco building that is the tallest building downtown. Observation deck.

CINCINNATI ART MUSEUM

Cincinnati - 953 Eden Park Drive, 45202. *Activity:* The Arts. (513) 639-2995. **www.cincinnatiartmuseum.org**. Art collection presents 5000 years of visual arts. Favorites include medieval armor and arms, old musical instruments, Andy Warhol's Pete Rose and the futuristic robot. *Family Fun Tour:* Saturday, 1:00 – 3:00 pm – Free.

CINCINNATI BENGALS

Cincinnati - Paul Brown Stadium, 45202. *Activity:* Sports. (513) 621-3550. **www.nfl.com/bengals**. Professional football at the new Paul Brown Stadium. Average ticket price $36.00. (August – January).

CINCINNATI CITY HALL

Cincinnati - 801 Plum Street, 45202. *Activity:* Ohio History. (513) 352-3636. *Tours:* 2nd Grade and Older. By reservation only. One hour. If interested, ask to go on tour during Council Meeting. See a beautiful depiction of the history of the Queen City with stained glass windows.

CINCINNATI FIRE MUSEUM

315 West Court Street, Downtown, **Cincinnati** 45202

- ❑   Activity: Museums
- ❑   Telephone (513) 621-5571, **www.cincinnatifiremuseum.com**
- ❑   Hours: Tuesday – Friday, 10:00 am – 4:00 pm.
     Weekends, Noon – 4:00 pm.
- ❑   Admission: $3.00 Adult, $2.50 Senior (55+), $2.00 Children (2-12)

From the minute you walk in the restored fire station, the kids will be intrigued by the nation's first professional fire department exhibits. Displays chronicle fire fighting history from antique equipment to the cab of a newer fire truck where you can actually pull levers, push buttons, operate the siren and flash emergency lights. The museum has an emphasis on fire safety with "Safe House" models and a video about fire fighting dangers. Before you leave be sure your guide has let you slide down the 5-foot fire pole or push the hand pump engine.

CINCINNATI PLAYHOUSE IN THE PARK

Cincinnati - 962 Mount Adams Circle, 45202. *Activity:* The Arts. (513) 421-3888. **www.cincyplay.com**. Professional resident theatre offers dramas, comedies and musicals.

CINCINNATI REDS

Cincinnati - 100 Cinergy Field, 45202. *Activity:* Sports. (513) 421-REDS. **www.cincinnatireds.com**. Professional Major League baseball at Riverfront Stadium. First professional baseball team. Autographs during batting practice. *Tours:* Available by appointment (513) 421-4510. ($5.00 - $21.00) (April – September)

CONTEMPORARY ARTS CENTER

Cincinnati - 115 East Fifth Street, 45202. *Activity:* The Arts. (513) 345-8400. **www.spiral.org**. Contemporary kids workshops and clubs.

KROHN CONSERVATORY

Cincinnati - Eden Park Drive, 45202. *Activity:* Outdoors. (513) 421-4086. **http://w3.one.net/~a_fraser/krohn/floral.html**. A rainforest full of 5000 varieties of exotic desert and tropical plants. One of the nation's largest - check out their seasonal displays. Small admission.

ROOKWOOD POTTERY

Cincinnati - 1077 Celestial Street, 45202. *Activity:* Theme Restaurants. (513) 721-5456. An actual historic pottery shop where you dine in original pottery kilns. Casual food – voted best burgers, sundae bar.

SHOWBOAT MAJESTIC

Cincinnati - Moored at Broadway Street Landing, 45202. *Activity:* The Arts. (513) 241-6550. Live riverfront shows like musicals, comedies and dramas. The original owner, actor Thomas Jefferson Reynolds, raised eleven kids on board while moving from rivertown to town entertaining folks in the early 1900's. *Hours:* Open daily, (Summer), Weekends, (April, May, September, October)

TAFT MUSEUM

Cincinnati - 316 Pike Street, 45202. *Activity:* The Arts. (513) 241-0343. **www.taftmuseum.org**. See works of European and American painters, Chinese porcelains, Limoges enamels displayed in a federal period mansion. Kidstuff family programs.

CINCINNATI HISTORY MUSEUM

1301 Western Avenue, Cincinnati Museum Center
(I-75 North to Exit 1), **Cincinnati** 45203

❑ Activity: Museums
❑ Telephone: (800) 733-2077, **www.cincymuseum.org**
❑ Hours: Monday - Saturday (& Holidays), 10:00 am - 5:00 pm.
    Sunday, 11:00 am - 6:00 pm. (Closed Thanksgiving and
    Christmas)
❑ Admission: $6.50 Adult, $4.50 Children (1-12). Combo prices
    with other museums in the Center. Parking fee.
❑ Miscellaneous: Gift Shops - Worth a good look!

Walk through re-created streets of Cincinnati. Visit the Fifth
Street Market and Millcreek Millery - try on hats of the
early 1900's and then shop next door at the pretend open air
market. Next, walk through a life-like forest with shadows and
birds wrestling and singing. The kids can play on a miniature
cabin and flat boat. You'll visit with The Flynns Family (*ring the
doorbell first*) talking about life at home during World War II.
Hop on board a streetcar with the conductor telling news of the
war. Pre-schoolers can play in the "Garden for Victory" where
they pretend to plant and harvest a garden (in a sandbox with
plastic vegetables and utensils). The produce from Victory
Gardens was canned for soldiers. Moms and grandmothers will
have to check out the "Leg Makeup Bar" (clue: there was a
stocking shortage during the war). Very authentically presented,
clever displays throughout the whole museum. Cincinnati folks
should be proud.

CINCINNATI MUSEUM OF NATURAL HISTORY AND SCIENCE

1301 Western Avenue, Cincinnati Museum Center
(I-75 North to Exit 1), **Cincinnati** 45203

❑ Activity: Museums
❑ Telephone: (800) 733-2077, **www.cincymuseum.org**

❑   Hours: Monday - Saturday, 10:00 am - 5:00 pm.
    Sunday, 11:00 am - 6:00 pm
❑   Admission: $6.50 Adult, $4.50 Children (1-12). Combo prices
    with other Center museums. Parking fee.
❑   Miscellaneous: Gift shops. All are worth a visit. Many science
    projects to do at home.

Want to know a lot about the Ohio Valley's Natural and Geological history? Start at the Ice Age of fossils and re-created walk-through glaciers. (There are two routes - one that is challenging and involves much climbing and navigating, and the other that is wheelchair or stroller accessible). On to the simulated Limestone Cavern with underground waterfalls and a live bat colony (behind glass!). You can pretend you're an archeologist digging up dinosaur bones in a sandbox with tools and brushes in Dinosaur Hall. In the recycling center, take a look at the garbage used by an average family and ways to reduce it. When you see a pile of garbage bags stacked on end and towering to the ceiling, your family will want to consider ways to sort recyclables and reduce unnecessary waste. Find out "All About You" as you explore inside, outside and beneath your great body. Brush a huge tooth, see under the skin of your hand, pretend in the office of doctors and dentists, or maybe play pinball as your "food ball" goes through the digestive system. Plan a day at this extremely well done exhibit!

CINERGY CHILDREN'S MUSEUM

Cincinnati Museum Center, 1301 Western Avenue (I-71 south to I-275 west; I-75 south exit 2A; I-75 north exit 1), **Cincinnati** 45203

❑   Activity: Museums
❑   (800) 733-2077 or (513) 287-7000, **www.cincymuseum.org**
❑   Hours: Monday – Saturday, 10:00 am – 5:00 pm.
    Sunday, 11:00 am – 6:00 pm. Closed Thanksgiving & Christmas.
❑   Admission: $5.50 Adults, $3.50 Children (1-12). Combo discount
    prices for other museums.

❑   Miscellaneous: Museums stores. Skyline Chili and Snack Bar.

Start in the Woods, kiddies. The dim lighting adds mystery to the slides, tunnels, rope climbing mazes and walls, and treehouses. The Energy Zone has kids move plastic balls along a conveyor to a gigantic dump bucket. It's actually a gigantic physics experiment in this Zone - lots of machines and tubes to move balls. Kids At Work lets them make real-life and pretend structures from blocks, pebbles and Legos. They can even use a 12 foot crane to move and lift blocks. Other highlights are the Little Sprouts Farm (age 4 and under), Water Works, Kids Town (pretend town), Animal Spot or Children Just Like Us (life-size color cutouts let kids see how African, Australian, Russian and Eskimos live. Don't you wish Moms and Dads that we had this kind of fun place to go when we were kids?

OMNIMAX THEATER

Cincinnati Museum Center (I-71/I-75 to Ezzard Charles Drive),
Cincinnati 45203

❑   Activity: Amusements
❑   Telephone: (513) 287-7000, **www.cincymuseum.org**
❑   Hours: Sunday, 11:00 am – 6:00 pm, Monday, 1:00, 2:00, 3:00 pm, Tuesday – Thursday, 1:00, 2:00, 3:00, 7:00 & 8:00 pm. Friday, 1:00, 2:00, 3:00, 7:00, 8:00 & 9:00 pm. Saturday, 11:00 am – 9:00 pm, hourly. Extended holiday hours.
❑   Admission: $6.50 Adult, $5.50 Senior, $4.50 Children (3-12)
❑   Miscellaneous: Shows viewed on a 5 story, 72-foot wide domed screen.

FRISCH'S COMMISSARY

3011 Stanton Ave. (I-71 to Taft Road West Exit), **Cincinnati** 45206

❑   Activity: Tours
❑   Telephone: (513) 559-5288
❑   Tours: Wednesday and Thursday, 9:00 am. Ages 8 and above. Maximum 15 people. One hour. Reservations required

This commissary supplies 85 Big Boy Restaurants in Ohio, Indiana, and Kentucky (and they're still family owned). They prepare cooked soups, salad dressings, raw meats, vegetables, and baked goods. Children will marvel at large-scale production, especially when the tour guide describes the quantities of ingredients used for each product. For example, two people peel 600 pounds of carrots by hand each day. The bakery ovens can hold 24 pies at one time. They save the restaurants time by pre-slicing or shredding vegetables and bagging them. We understand they use an air compressor to blow the skins off onions!

CINCINNATI OPERA

Cincinnati - 1241 Elm Street, 45210. *Activity:* The Arts. (513) 621-1919. **www.cincinnatiopera.com**. Second oldest opera group in the US produces grand opera in Music Hall.

CINCINNATI SYMPHONY ORCHESTRA

Cincinnati - 1241 Elm Street, 45210. *Activity:* The Arts. (513) 381-3300. The CSO presents soloists, pops concerts and an artist series in Music Hall. CSO RiverBend Music Center hosts Symphony/Pops Orchestra, plus contemporary artists (May-September). Lollipop Concerts for kids.

ENSEMBLE THEATRE OF CINCINNATI

Cincinnati - 1127 Vine Street, 45210. *Activity:* The Arts. (513) 421-3555. **www.cincyetc.com**. Professional resident theatre develops and produces new works with an emphasis on Ohio and Cincinnati artists. (September – June)

FOREST VIEW GARDENS

Cincinnati - 4508 North Bend Road (1 mile South off I-71, exit 14), 45211. *Activity:* Theme Restaurants. (513) 661-6434. *Hours:* Thursday – Sunday. Bavarian styled restaurant with singing servers.

CINCINNATI MIGHTY DUCKS

Cincinnati - 2250 Seymour Avenue, 45212. *Activity:* Sports. (513) 351-3999. **www.ticketmaster.com**. Semi-Professional hockey and soccer teams. Home games at Cincinnati Gardens. ($5.00 - $14.00 range) (October – March). Join the Mighty Ducklings Kids Club.

U.S. PLAYING CARD COLLECTION MUSEUM

Cincinnati - 4590 Beech Street (Norwood), 45212. *Activity:* Museums. (513) 396-5731. *Hours:* Tuesday and Thursday, Noon – 4:00 pm. Factory Gift Shop and Museum. Watch a video explaining the history of card games or view playing cards dating back to the 16th century.

UNITED DAIRY FARMERS

3955 Montgomery Road, Cincinnati 45212

☐   Activity: Tours
☐   Telephone: (513) 396-8700 - Ask for Consumer Relations.
☐   Admission: Free
☐   Tours: Mondays and Fridays, 9:30 am. (1 ½ hours, Ages 6 and up). Maximum 25 persons.

See milk being filled in containers (and the large vats where they store raw and treated milk). The plastic bottles are also made on the premises from blown pellets of plastics. As a group, weigh yourselves on their giant truck scale! Best of all, watch ice cream packed and frozen (you even get to step inside the deep-freeze room). Get a free ice cream sundae (flavor of the day - right off the production line!) as a souvenir.

HARRIET BEECHER STOWE HOUSE

Cincinnati - 2950 Gilbert Avenue (SR-3 and US-22), 45214. *Activity:* Ohio History. (513) 632-5120. **www.ohiohistory.org/ places/stowe**. *Hours:* Tuesday - Thursday, 10:00 am - 4:00 pm. *Admission.* Donations. The home of the author of "Uncle Tom's Cabin" novel that brought attention to the evils of slavery.

Displays describe the Beecher family, the abolitionist movement and the history of African-Americans. Request the video about the story of the book. Mrs. Stowe's journal is available for viewing.

WILLIAM HOWARD TAFT NATIONAL HISTORIC SITE

2038 Auburn Ave. (I-71 to exit 2, Mt. Auburn), **Cincinnati** 45219

- ❑ Activity: Ohio History
- ❑ Telephone: (513) 684-3262, **www.nps.gov/wiho**
- ❑ Hours: Daily, 10:00 am – 4:00 pm
- ❑ Admission: Donations

V isit the birthplace and boyhood home of a US President and Chief Justice. Four of the rooms are furnished to reflect Taft's family life 1857-77. Other exhibits depict his public service career. See actual family portraits. Children's group tours give kids the opportunity to dress up from a trunk of period hats and over-garments and play with old fashioned toys. This really helps the children understand life for a young person in the mid-1800's.

CINCINNATI ZOO & BOTANICAL GARDENS

3400 Vine Street (I-75 to Exit 6), **Cincinnati** 45220

- ❑ Activity: Animals & Farms
- ❑ Telephone: (800) 94-HIPPO, **www.cincyzoo.org**
- ❑ Hours: Daily, 9:00 am – 8:00 pm (Summer). 9:00 am - 5:00 pm (Winter). 9:00 am – 7:00 pm (Rest of the Year).
  Children's Zoo – 10:00 am - 4:00 pm
- ❑ Admission: $11.00 Adult, $8.50 Senior (62+), $5.50 Children (2-12). Children's Zoo, Camel rides, Train rides are $1-2 additional. Parking Fee.
- ❑ Miscellaneous: Safari Restaurant. Concessions. Camel, elephant and train rides. Stroller rentals.

R anked one of the top 5 zoos in the United States, its highlights are the Bengal tigers and Kemodo dragons (10 feet long and 300 lbs!). Their landscaped gardens duplicate the animals' world and the Jungle Trails exhibit even has a tropical rainforest. The first Insectarium (you guessed it!) in the nation is also here.

UNIVERSITY OF CINCINNATI – DEPT. OF ATHLETICS

Cincinnati – 45221. *Activity:* Sports. **www.ucbearcats.com**. (513) 556-CATS. 18 sports. Fall, Winter, Spring.

CONEY ISLAND

6201 Kellogg Avenue (Off I-275), **Cincinnati** 45228

❑ Activity: Amusements
❑ Telephone Number (513) 232-8230, **www.coneyislandpark.com**
❑ Hours: Daily, (Memorial Weekend – Labor Day). Pool, 10:00 am – 8:00 pm. Rides, 11:00 am – 9:00 pm
❑ Admission: $9.00- $15.00, Ages 4+. Half price after 4:00 pm. Free Parking

S unlite, the world's largest re-circulating pool with a huge slide and 7 diving boards, is one of the many fun attractions. Also, Zoom Flume water toboggan, Pipeline Plunge tube water slide, kiddie rides, miniature golf, bumper boats, pedal boats and picnic areas.

RIVERCITY DUCKS

Cincinnati – 45231. *Activity:* Tours. (513) 761-6688 or (888) 567-4386. **www.rivercityducks.com**. Ride the duck! It's a boat - it's a bus and it's great fun! A 50 minute narrated cruise about town. Call for a cruise schedule.

PARKY'S FARM

Cincinnati - 10245 Winton Road (Winton Woods Park), 45240. **http://hamiltoncountyparks.org/farmwwrc.htm**. (513) 521-PARK. *Activity:* Animals & Farms. Explore orchards and crops plus farm animals. Pony rides and PlayBarn (farm theme play pits with plastic apples and eggs to jump in).

SURF CINCINNATI

11460 Sebring Dr. (Off I-275, 5 miles West of I-75), **Cincinnati** 45240

- ❑   Activity: Amusements
- ❑   Telephone: (513) 742-0620
- ❑   Hours: Daily, 10:30 am – 8:30 pm. (Memorial Day - Labor Day)
- ❑   Admission: $11.00 and up (ages 3+). Reduced rates after 3:30 pm

Waterpark with a ½ acre wave pool, kid's pool, waterslides, inner tube rides, sundeck, beach, miniature golf, go carts, and concessions.

CINCINNATI BALLET

Cincinnati – 45250. *Activity:* The Arts. (513) 621-5219. Classically based professional ballet company performs classic and contemporary works. Pirouette Club - meet with dancers backstage, Adopt-a-Dancer - have meals together, Sugar Plum Parties. **www.cincinnatiballet.com**. (September – May)

QUEEN CITY RIVERBOAT TOURS

Cincinnati Area - 303 Dodd Drive (located in Dayton, KY), *Activity:* Tours. (606) 292-8687. Spirit of Cincinnati" and "Queen City Clipper.

BB RIVERBOATS

Covington Crossing (just over the bridge)
Cincinnati Area (Covington, KY)

- ❑   Activity: Tours
- ❑   Telephone: (800) 261-8586, **www.bbriverboats.com**
- ❑   Admission: $10.00 Adult, $9.00 Senior (60+) and $5.00 Children (4-12)
- ❑   Tours: 1 ½ hour sightseeing cruises on the Ohio River. Several times daily. Reservations Required. (May – October)

Docked at the foot of Madison Street see the Modern "Funliner", "Mark Twain" sternwheeler or steamboat "Becky Thatcher", Also theme cruises like mini-vacation, holiday or "Skyline Chili". Many cruises offer additional lunch, brunch and dinner cruise options.

LITTLE MIAMI STATE PARK

Corwin - (North of Corwin), 45068. *Activity:* Outdoors. (513) 897-3055. **www.dnr.state.oh.us/odnr/parks/directory/lilmiami. htm**. Bridle trails. 452 acres of hiking, fishing, and winter sports.

STONELICK STATE PARK

Edenton - (1 mile South of Edenton off SR-727), 45162. *Activity:* Outdoors. (513) 625-7544. **www.dnr.state.oh.us/odnr/parks/ directory/stonelck.htm**. 1,258 acres of camping, hiking trails, boating, fishing, swimming and winter sports.

JUNGLE JIM'S INTERNATIONAL FARMERS MARKET

Fairfield - 5440 Dixie Highway, 45014. *Activity:* Amusements. (513) 829-1919. **www.junglejims.com**. *Hours:* Open daily 8:00 am - 10:00 pm. A grocery store is an adventure? This store, selling exotic and even normal foods, is! Plastic animals and giant fruits greet you. Once inside, the store is divided into theme areas. Visit Amish Country, The Ocean, Europe, South America, India and the Middle East. Try some new food like medallions of alligator.

BUTLER COUNTY HISTORICAL SOCIETY MUSEUM

Hamilton - 327 North 2nd Street, 45011. *Activity:* Ohio History. (513) 893-7111. **http://home.fuse.net/butlercountymuseum**. *Hours:* Tuesday – Sunday, 1:00 – 4:00 pm. Small admission (ages 12+). Benninghofen House, a 19th Century Victorian mansion. Period furnishings.

LANE-HOOVEN HOUSE

Hamilton - 319 North Third Street, 45011. *Activity:* Ohio History. (513) 863-1389. *Hours:* Monday – Friday, 9:00 am – 4:00 pm. Octagonal home with spiral staircase. Donations.

PYRAMID HILL SCULPTURE PARK

Hamilton - 1763 Hamilton-Cleves Road (I-275 to SR-27 to SR-128), 45011. *Activity:* Outdoors. **www.pyramidhill.org**. (513) 868-8336. This park currently has 10 titled sculptures. Especially noticeable is "Abracadabra" by internationally famous sculptor, Alexander Liberman. Many passengers flying into Cincinnati can see the 2 ½ story high, bright red contemporary walk-thru sculpture from above.

SHADY – NOOK

Hamilton - 879 Millville – Oxford Road (US-27), 45013. *Activity:* Theme Restaurants. (513) 863-4343. Bring your grandparents who remember the famous Moon River radio program. As you eat you're treated to a theater organ, tapes of 1930's and 1940's radio shows or a sing along.

PAINT CREEK STATE PARK

Hillsboro - (17 miles East of Hillsboro on US-50), 45133. *Activity:* Outdoors. (937) 365-1401. **www.dnr.state.oh.us/odnr/parks/directory/paintcrk.htm**. Nature programs. Pioneer farm. 10,200 acres of camping, hiking, boating and rentals, fishing, swimming and winter sports.

ROCKY FORK STATE PARK

Hillsboro - 9800 North Shore Drive (6 miles SE of Hillsboro off SR-124), 45133. *Activity:* Outdoors. (937) 393-4284. **www.dnr.state.oh.us/odnr/parks/directory/rockyfrk.htm**. 3,464 acres of hiking, camping, boating and rentals, fishing, swimming.

PARAMOUNT'S KINGS ISLAND

I-71 to Exit 25A or 24, (24 miles N. of Cincinnati), **Kings Mills** 45034

- ❏ Activity: Amusements
- ❏ Telephone: (800) 288-0808, **www.pki.com**
- ❏ Hours: Daily, 9:00 am – Dark (Memorial Day – Late August) Weekends only, (April, May, September, October)

❑ Admission: Approximately $40.00, Child (3-6) and Seniors (60+) Approximately $20.00. Parking Fee

❑ Miscellaneous: 3 restaurants plus 60 fast food areas. Shows and entertainment.

Some of the featured attractions at King's Island are:

WATERWORKS – heated wave pool, children's play area, lazy river, plus 16 water slides and rides.

ACTION ZONE – The Beast (longest wooden coaster), The Outer Limits (1ˢᵗ indoor coaster to catapult in the dark at high velocity), Days of Thunder (racing car simulator of high speed stock car racing).

DROP ZONE - pulse pounding height.

FACE OFF - 5 G's inverted face to face coaster.

HANNA BARBERA LAND – Scooby Doo's Magic-To-Do, Cartoon characters.

NICKELODEON SPLAT CITY – Green Slime Zone (water spray, pipe work maze, Mess-A-Mania). Most popular with school age kids.

IRONS FRUIT FARM

Lebanon - 1640 Stubbs Mills Road, 45036. *Activity:* Animals & Farms. (513) 932-2853. Pick strawberries, cherries, red raspberries, blackberries, and blueberries. Corn, squash, apples, etc. are also sold. Petting zoo.

TURTLE CREEK VALLEY RAILWAY

198 South Broadway (US-42), **Lebanon** 45036

❑ Activity: Tours

❑ Telephone: (513) 398-8584

www.angelfire.com/biz/TurtleCreekValley/newindex.html

❑ Departures: Late Morning, Noon, Early Afternoon. Wednesday, Friday, Saturday, Sunday (May – October). Saturday, Sunday (April, November, December)

❑ Admission: $10.00 Adult, $9.00 Senior (60+), $6.00 Children (3-12)

❑   Miscellaneous: Station Depot with Gift Shop. Discount Days –
Holidays (Summer). The passenger cars do not have restrooms
and are not heated or air-conditioned.

A one-hour ride in a refurbished train car reminiscent of
yesteryear in the old Indiana and Ohio Railroad through rural
countryside (fields and farmlands). Turtle Creek was named for
the famous Indian Chief "Little Turtle".

WARREN COUNTY HISTORICAL SOCIETY MUSEUM

Lebanon - 105 South Broadway, 45036. *Activity:* Ohio History.
(937) 932-1817. *Hours:* Tuesday   Saturday, 9:00 am – 4:00 pm,
Sunday, Noon – 4:00 pm. Village Green with shops. Collection of
Shaker furniture.

"LOVELAND CASTLE" - CHATEAU LAROCHE

12025 Shore Dr. (2 miles South of Kings Island), **Loveland** 45140

❑   Activity: Tours
❑   Telephone: (513) 683-4686
      www.clermontcvb-ohio.com/05attchateau.html
❑   Hours: Daily, 11:00 am – 5:00 pm (April to mid-September)
      Weekends, 11:00 am – 5:00 pm (October – March)
❑   Admission: $1.00 per person. Self-guided tour.
❑   Miscellaneous: Only medieval castle in the US. Call for
      directions or follow signs from downtown Loveland.

This is a real hidden castle! Chateau LaRoche was the vision of
Harry D. Andrews and construction spanned some 50 years
beginning in 1929. He actually did 99% of the work himself! The
castle is authentic in its rugged structure with battlement towers, a
princess chamber, a dungeon, narrow passageways, tower
staircases, a "king's" dining room, and tower bedrooms. Over
32,000 hand-made (cast in milk cartons donated by neighbors)
bricks were used to build the structure. Learn a lot about castle
building and why the front door has over 2500 nails in it. Don't
miss this real adventure that your children and you will love!

CINCINNATI POLO CLUB

Mason – 45040. *Activity:* Sports. (513) 398-0278. Sundays at 2:00 pm. (Summer)

THE BEACH

2590 Waterpark Drive (I-71 Exit 25B - 20 miles
North of Cincinnati) **Mason** 45040

- ❑ Activity: Amusements
- ❑ Telephone: (800) 886-SWIM, **www.thebeachwaterpark.com**
- ❑ Hours: Daily, opens 10:00 am, Closing varies. (Memorial Weekend to mid-September)
- ❑ Admission: $6.00 - 20.00 (Children – Senior – Adult)
- ❑ Miscellaneous: Food Service. Parking fee.

Over 40,000 square feet of beach and two million gallons of water and waves await you!   Favorites include the Pearl leisure pool, Aztec Adventure watercoaster, Thunder Beach Wave Pool and the Lazy Miami River inner tube ride.   The young children's water area has Splash Mountain with warm water!

SORG OPERA HOUSE

Middletown - 57 South Main Street (Opera House), 45042. *Activity:* The Arts. (513) 425-0180. **www.sorgopera.com**. Historic 1891 theatre presents opera productions. (October – April)

GOVERNOR BEBB PRESERVE

Morgan Township - 1979 Bebb Park Lane (Rt. 126), *Activity:* Ohio History. (877) PARK-FUN. **http://members.xoom.com/ bebbvillage**. *Hours:* Saturday and Sunday, 1:00 - 5:00 pm. (May – September). Visit the small 1812 village with the restored log cabin (birthplace of William Bebb - born in 1802). He was the governor of Ohio from 1846 - 48 and a trial lawyer noted for his emotional zeal.

THE DUDE RANCH

Morrow - 3205 Waynesville Road (I-71 to SR-123 southeast), 45152. *Activity:* Outdoors. **www.theduderanch.com**. (513) 899-DUDE. Horseback riding thru woods and meadows, authentic cattle drives, hayrides, pony rides and party/picnic facilities.

FORT ANCIENT STATE MEMORIAL

6123 SR-350 and Middleboro Road (I-71 to Rt. 123 to SR-350)
Oregonia 45054

☐   Activity: Ohio History
☐   Telephone: (513) 932-4421
      www.ohiohistory.org/places/ftancien
☐   Hours: Wednesday - Sunday, 10:00 - 8:00 pm. (Memorial Weekend - Labor Day). Museum closes at 7:00 pm. Daily, 10:00 am – 5:00 pm (Spring and Fall)
☐   Admission: $5.00 Adults, $1.25 Children (6-12).

The newly renovated Ohio Historical Society museum has Ohio's entire Indian heritage displayed from prehistoric to modern times. The 100 acre field is where graves and artifacts were found and is also home to the second largest earthwork in the nation (constructed by Hopewell Indians between 300 BC - 600 AD).

HUESTON WOODS STATE PARK

Oxford - Route 1 (5 miles North of Oxford off SR-732), 45003. *Activity:* Outdoors. (513) 523-6347. **www.dnr.state.oh.us/odnr/ parks/directory/huestonw.htm**. Nature Programs. Bike rental. 3596 acres of camping, hiking trails, boating and rentals, fishing, swimming and winter sports. Family cabins, Lodge rooms with golf, indoor/outdoor pools, sauna and fitness available.

MCGUFFEY MUSEUM

Oxford - Spring and Oak Streets, 45056. *Activity:* Museums. **http:// www.muohio.edu/campusmap/campusmap/sw/mcguffey_ museum.html**. (513) 529-2232. *Hours:* Weekends, 2:00 - 4:00 pm (Except August and Holidays). *Admission:* Free. See an original collection of McGuffey Reader (lesson books on the three R's and morality, i.e. brotherly love, honesty and hard work). The home, *(built in the early 1830's)* is where William Holmes McGuffey wrote his readers while preparing classwork for children. Check out the eight-sided desk!

MIAMI UNIVERSITY

Oxford – 45056. *Activity:* Tours. (513) 529-1809. **www.muohio. edu/visitors**. Points of interest include formal gardens, Anthropology Museum, Zoology Museum, Geology Museum, Art Museum, Library and Chapel.

GRANT BIRTHPLACE MUSEUM

Point Pleasant - 219 East Grant Avenue (off US-52), 45157. *Activity:* Ohio History. **www.ohiohistory.org/places/grantbir**. (513) 553-4911. *Admission:* $1.00 Adult, $.75 Senior, $.50 Children (6-12). *Tours:* Tuesday – Saturday, 9:30 am – 5:00 pm. Sunday Noon – 5:00 pm (April - October). 5th grade and above. Civil War General and 18th Presidents birthplace cottage with period furniture. The small white home has no heat and is sparsely lit – daytime in comfortable weather is best.

RANKIN HOUSE STATE MEMORIAL

Rankin Hill (NE off US-52, Race St. or Rankin Rd.), **Ripley** 45167

- ❑   Activity: Ohio History
- ❑   Telephone: (937) 392-1627
     www.ohiohistory.org/places/rankin
- ❑   Hours: Wednesday – Sunday, 10:00 am – 5:00 pm (Summer)
     Weekends Only (September and October)
- ❑   Admission: $2.00 Adult, $0.50 Children (5-12)

This restored home of Reverend John Rankin (early Ohio abolitionist) was part of the Underground Railroad and home to Eliza, a character in "Uncle Tom's Cabin", who found refuge off the Ohio River. Winding roads lead to the remote cabin hidden in a clearing in the woods.

HERITAGE VILLAGE MUSEUM

Sharonville - 11450 Lebanon Pike, Sharon Woods Park (US-42, 1 mile south of I-275, exit 46), 45241. *Activity:* Ohio History. (513) 563-9484. *Hours:* Wednesday – Sunday, Noon - 4:00 pm. (May – October) *Admission:* $5.00 Adult, $3.00 Senior (62+), $2.00 Youth (6-11). See 18th Century Ohio. Nine actual buildings of Southwest Ohio including a farmhouse, train station, homes, icehouse, smokehouse, and medical office (see Civil War medical and pharmaceutical equipment). Dressed interpreters. Bicycle rental, hiking trails.

FAYETTE COUNTY HISTORICAL MUSEUM

Washington Court House - 517 Columbus Avenue (eastern junction of US Routes 62 and 22), 43160. *Activity:* Ohio History. (740) 335-2953. *Hours:* The Museum is open weekend afternoons from May through October. Admission is free. Morris Sharp built this 1875 Victorian Itallanate home with the stated purpose to erect "A Showplace for The City of Washington." 14 rooms that contain fine pieces depicting the County's history. See a Wonder Stove (made in The City of Washington in 1906) that sold for $37.50 and operated on artificial gas, a collection of unusual tools, a 1850's piano forte and a 1870 pump organ. A trip to the museum's tower offers an interesting panorama of the city.

CAESAR CREEK STATE PARK

Waynesville - 8570 East SR-73 (SR-73, 6 miles West of I-71, near Waynesville), 45068. *Activity:* Outdoors. (513) 897-3055. **www.dnr.state.oh.us/odnr/parks/directory/caesarck.htm** Bridle trails. 10,771 acres of camping, hiking trails, boating, fishing, swimming and winter sports. Pioneer Village is open seasonally.

SKY CREAM & DELI

Waynesville - 4925 North SR-42 (Airport), 45068. *Activity:* Theme Restaurants. (513) 897-7717. May through October watch skydivers jump while you enjoy a snack. 15-minute airplane rides available.

COWAN LAKE STATE PARK

Wilmington - (5 miles South of Wilmington off US-68), 45177. *Activity:* Outdoors. (937) 289-2105. **www.dnr.state.oh.us/odnr/ parks/directory/cowanlk.htm**. Nature programs. Bike Rental. 1,775 acres of camping, hiking trails, boating and rentals, swimming, winter sports and a lodge/cabins.

Seasonal &
Special Events

MOST LISTINGS OCCUR ON WEEKENDS UNLESS NOTED OTHERWISE

Free = Free Admission

(Listings sorted by Area and City within each month)

JANUARY

MARTIN LUTHER KING MARCH & PROGRAM

C - City Hall & Vets Memorial, **Columbus**. (614) 645-3334. Free. (January - month-long)

WINTERFEST / KIDSFEST

CE - Secrest Auditorium, **Zanesville**. (740) 454-6851. Chili cook-off, prayer breakfast, floral contest, ice carving competition and parade tribute to Dr. King. Saturday before Martin Luther King Day. (January)

WINTERFEST

NE – Alpine Valley Skiing, 10620 Mayfield Rd., **Chesterland**. www.alpinevalleyohio.com. Enjoy volleyball in the snow, snowshoe obstacle race course, bikini slalom and a children's obstacle slalom. Lift ticket fee. (January - Saturday only)

FEBRUARY

ICE CARVING FESTIVAL

CE - Roscoe Village. **Coshocton**. (800) 877-1930 or (740) 622-9310. Carving contests, tours, kids games. (Saturday in mid-February)

ICE FESTIVAL

NE - Public Square, **Medina**. (800) 463-3462. Cash prizes and medals for an ice carving competition. Free. (Saturday in mid-February)

MARCH

BUZZARD DAY

NE - Cleveland Metroparks, **Hinckley** Reservation, (440) 351-6300. Annual migration of the buzzard with breakfast watch. Admission. (March)

MAPLE SYRUP FESTIVALS

Syrup making demos. Pancake dinners/breakfasts. Sugarbush tours by foot or by wagon.

- ❏ **C** - *Camp Lazarus* – Delaware. (740) 548-5502
- ❏ **C** - *Dawes Arboretum*. (740) 323-2355.
- ❏ **CW** - *Bellbrook Park*, Bellbrook. (937) 848-7050.
- ❏ **CW** - Indian Lake. (888) LOGANCO
- ❏ **CW**- *Brukner Nature Center*. Troy. (937) 698-6493
- ❏ **NC** - *Feindel's Sugar Bush*. Bascom. (419) 447-5866
- ❏ **NC** - *Malabar Farm*. Mansfield. (419) 892-2784
- ❏ **NE** - *Township Park*, Boardman, (330) 726-8105. Admission.
- ❏ **NE** - *Holden Arboretum*, (440) 946-4400. Kirtland. Daily except Monday. Admission.
- ❏ **NW** - *Johnny Appleseed Metro Parks*, Lima, (419) 221-1232
- ❏ **SC** - *Hocking Hills*. (740) 385-9706
- ❏ **SC** - *Mapleberry Farms*. Waverly. (740) 947-2331

ST. PATRICK'S DAY PARADES & CELEBRATIONS

Cincinnati, Cleveland, Dublin (Columbus), and Toledo.Downtown.

APRIL

EASTER EGG HUNTS

Easter Bunny appearance, treat stations, egg hunts, and kid's entertainment and crafts.

- ❑   **C** - Columbus Recreation & Parks, (614) 645-3300.
- ❑   **C** - *Great Eggspectation. Columbus Zoo*, (614) 645-3550, ages 2-12. Admission.
- ❑   **C** - *Slate Run Farm*, Egg decorating & egg rolling contests. Admission.
- ❑   **CW** - *Zane Shawnee Caverns*. Bellefontaine. (937) 592-9592
- ❑   **CW** – *Young's Dairy*, Yellow Springs, Over 4000 colored Easter eggs. Free. (937) 325-0629
- ❑   **NC** - Oak Harbor. Post office.
- ❑   **SW** - *Great Easter Egg Scramble*, Cincinnati Zoo, (513) 281-4700.
- ❑   **SW** - *Easter Eggstravaganza*, Hamilton County Park, (513) 521-PARK.

GEAUGA COUNTY MAPLE FESTIVAL

NE - Chardon.   (440) 286-3007. Sap Run contest, midway, parades, bathtub races and maple syrup production and sales. Weekend after Easter. (April)

I-X CENTER INDOOR AMUSEMENT PARK

NE - Cleveland, (Brookpark) - 6200 Riverside Drive, 44142. (216) 676-6000. *Hours:* Only open in April, Hours vary daily. (Call for details), *Admission:* $12.00 General, $7.00 Senior. Food service. After riding the World's Tallest Indoor Ferris Wheel (10 stories high) you can SCREAM through 150 rides! Also features a video arcade, miniature golf, laser kareoke, kiddie area and live entertainment. (April)

MAY

MEMORIAL GOLF TOURNAMENT

C - Dublin - Muirfield Village Golf Course), 43017. (614) 889-6700. PGA Tour. Course designed by Jack Nicklaus. TV coverage. Monday – Wednesday, Practice rounds. Thursday – Sunday, Tournament. (Late May for one week).

ICE CREAM FESTIVAL

C - Ye Olde Mill, **Utica.** (800) 589-5000. **www.velvet-icecream.com.** Velvet Ice Cream hosts a tribute to our national dessert, ice cream, with family entertainment and lots of food made from ice cream. Kids can feel like they're in the movie, Babe, as they watch sheep herding with border collies. You must catch the kiddie tractor pull. Admission. (Memorial Day Weekend)

HOPALONG CASSIDY FESTIVAL

CE - Downtown **Cambridge.** (740) 439-6688. William Boyd, better known as "Hop-a-long Cassidy" was originally from Cambridge. This celebration includes western entertainment, a cowpoke dinner and visiting Hollywood stars. (1st weekend in May)

RAILROAD FESTIVAL

CE - Dennison. (800) 527-3387. Enjoy the heritage and history of the famous World War II Dennison Depot with food, games, contests, rides and parade. Train rides. (Week in the middle of May)

A WORLD A'FAIR

CW - Convention Center, 22 East Fifth Street, **Dayton.** (937) 427-3355. 35 countries present their dances, foods, customs and culture. Admission. (3rd weekend in May)

STRAWBERRY FEST

NC - Huron County Fairgrounds. **Norwalk**. (419) 663-4062. A Strawberry theme street fair with crafts and foods. Bake-off, pie eating contest, parade. Free. (Memorial Day Weekend)

HOT ROD SUPER NATIONALS

NE - **Canfield** 44406. (317) 236-6522. Show-N-Shine, Pro vehicles, Burnout. (Late May)

FEAST OF THE FLOWERING MOON

SC - **Chillicothe** 45601. (800) 413-4118. This three-day themed event features Native-American dancing, crafts and village as well as a mountainman encampment depicting pioneer life in the early 1800's. Extensive quality arts and crafts displays, food, entertainment, and a variety of activities to see and do. Yoctangee City Park. Admission is free. (Memorial Day Weekend – Friday thru Sunday)

VINTON COUNTY WILD TURKEY FESTIVAL

SC - **McArthur**. (740) 596-5033. Turkey calling contests, street fair and parade during the wild turkey hunting season. Free. (May)

INTERNATIONAL STREET FAIR

SE - Court Street, **Athens**. (740) 593-4330. Dance, music, food, arts and cultural displays by 40 international student and community organizations. Free. (mid-May - Saturday only)

JUNE

CRANBERRY BOG ANNUAL OPEN HOUSE

C - Cranberry Bog State Nature Preserve, **Buckeye Lake**. (614) 265-6453. Take a tour of the island's rare and fascinating plants by pontoon boat. Admission. (Held the last Saturday in June)

FESTIVAL LATINO

C - **Columbus** Downtown Riverfront. (614) 645-7995. www.musicintheair.org. Celebrate Latin culture, food (contemporary and traditional) and music (Mambo, Salsa, Conjunto, Flamenco). Free. (June)

STRAWBERRY FESTIVAL

CE - B & O Depot, 300 East Church Street, **Barnesville**. (740) 425-4300. A day beginning with strawberry shortcake and maybe ending with strawberry sundaes. Also crafts and entertainment. Free. (2nd Saturday in June)

STRAWBERRY FESTIVAL

CE - Village Park, **Canal Fulton**. (800) 435-3623. Strawberry cake and ice cream, a vintage baseball game and canal boat rides. Admission. (1st Saturday in June)

ITALIAN AMERICAN FESTIVAL

CE - Stark County Fairgrounds, 305 Wertz Avenue, **Canton**. (330) 494-0886. Italy in Ohio with entertainment, foods, dancing, exhibits, rides and a bocci tournament. Thursday - Sunday. Admission. (Last weekend in June)

HOT AIR BALLOON FESTIVAL

CE - Coshocton County Fairgrounds, 707 Kenilworth Avenue, **Coshocton**. (740) 622-5411. Balloon launches at dawn and dusk, Nightglow (Saturday), entertainment and rides. Free. (2nd weekend in June)

TRI-STATE POTTERY FESTIVAL

CE - **East Liverpool**, 43920. (330) 385-0845. Celebration of pottery heritage featuring pottery olympics, industry displays, potters at work, ceramic museum, international doorknob tossing championships, factory tours (local companies like Hall China or Pioneer Pottery), art show, rose show, window displays, amusement rides and daily entertainment. (June)

ORRVILLE DEPOT DAYS

CE - Orrville. Orrville Depot Museum. 145 South Depot Street. (330) 683-2426. Mostly railroad-related festival, with both model trains and real trains. Tour 3 Orrville Museums. Most activities by donations. (June)

FORT STEUBEN FESTIVAL

CE - Old Fort Steuben Site, Steubenville. (740) 283-4935. www.oldfortsteuben.com. This first American Regiment was built to protect government surveyors from hostile Indians. Next to the fort site is the first Federal Land Office built in the U.S. in 1801. Watch mountain men reenactment groups, storytellers and craftspeople. Admission. (2nd weekend in June)

CITYFOLK FESTIVAL

CW - Downtown Dayton. (937) 223-3655. Hundreds of the country's best folk performers and artists entertain you with shows, activities, games, crafts and food. (June)

FIESTA LATINO-AMERICANA

CW - Fraze Pavilion, 695 Lincoln Park Blvd., Kettering. (937) 297-3720. Enjoy hot Latin music, exciting dance, authentic foods, crafts and children's activities. Fee for concerts. (2nd Saturday in June)

KIDS FEST

CW - Lincoln Park Commons, 675 Lincoln Park Blvd., Kettering. (937) 296-2587. Designed for young children and their parents to participate in activities ranging from hands-on crafts to face painting. Free. (3rd Saturday in June)

STRAWBERRY FESTIVAL

CW - Troy, the Strawberry Capital of the Midwest. (937) 339-7714. The first full weekend in June the fountain on Town Square runs pink water! Loads of fresh-picked berries and strawberry foods are sold. Parade, entertainment and hot-air balloons. Free. (June)

KEEPING THE TRADITIONS NATIVE AMERICAN POWWOW

CW - Blue Jacket grounds. **Xenia**. (937) 376-4318. Native American dancing, singing, foods. One of the largest powwows in Ohio. Admission. (Last weekend in June)

PRAIRIE PEDDLER

NC - Bunker Hill Woods, State Route 97, 3 miles east of **Butler**. (419) 663-1818. **www.prairietown.com**. Almost 200 costumed craftspeople offer their items made with frontier style tools, foods cooked over open fires and bluegrass music. Stop by the Medicine Show and buy a bottle of elixir. Fee. Also held in first 2 weekends of October. (Last 2 weekends of June)

INTERNATIONAL FESTIVAL

NC - Downtown Veterans Park, **Lorain**. Dance, music and authentically prepared foods from many different countries throughout the world. **www.loraininternational.com**. Free. (Last full weekend in June)

OHIO SCOTTISH GAMES

NC - Oberlin. (440) 775-7003.High School and College grounds. A weekend of Scottish traditions from the parade of tartans to the drumming and piping competition. Admission. (Last weekend in June)

FESTIVAL OF FISH

NC - Victory Park, **Vermilion**. (440) 967-4477. Walleye and perch sandwiches, "crazy" craft race, entertainment, crafts and a lighted boat parade. Free. (June)

GRAND PRIX OF CLEVELAND

NE - Burke Lakefront Airport, Downtown **Cleveland**. (216) 781-3500 or (800) 498-RACE. The world's top Indy Car drivers compete on the 213 miles of racing. Also a Grand Prix Parade on Friday. Admission. (Last weekend in June)

GREAT LAKES MEDIEVAL FAIRE

NE - 3033 State Route 534, 15 miles south of **Geneva.** (888) 633-4382. The recreation of a 13ᵗʰ century English village with jugglers, jesters, musicians, crafts, full-armored knights and sumptuous foods. Admission. (Weekends late June to early August)

OHIO IRISH FESTIVAL

NE - West Side Irish-American Club, 8559 Jennings Road, **Olmsted Falls.** (440) 779-6065. Celebrating the best of Ireland with lively Irish dance reels and lots of Irish food like tasty scones. Admission. (Last weekend in June)

TRAINS, PLANES & AUTOMOBILES FEST

NW - Bluffton Airport, 1080 Navajo Drive, **Bluffton.** (419) 358-5675. Airplane rides, tandem skydiving, antique cars and model trains. Free. Saturday only. Fees for air rides. (June)

PORK RIND HERITAGE FESTIVAL

NW - **Harrod.** (419) 648-3427. Fresh popped pork rinds, hog roast, parade, crafts and live entertainment. Free. (June)

CIVIL WAR REENACTMENT

NW - **Lima** - Ottawa Metro Park. (419) 221-1232. Professional re-enactors portray life as it was during the Civil War. Members from the cavalry, infantry and artillery reenact one battle on Saturday and one on Sunday. Sutlers selling wares from Civil War times can be found on the grounds. (last weekend in June)

OHIO NATIONAL CHAMPIONSHIP AMA MOTORCYCLE RACES

NW - **Lima** - (419) 478-1836. (Last Saturday in June)

NATIONAL THRESHERS ANNUAL REUNION

NW - Fulton County Fairgrounds, State Route 108, **Wauseon**. (419) 335-6006. Working gas tractors and over 30 operating steam engines on the sawmill, threshing wheat and plowing machines. Admission. (June)

KIDS FEST

SW - Sawyer Point, **Cincinnati**. (513) 621-9326. Three stages of entertainment, boat rides and 130+ activities. (Sometimes in early June)

BANANA SPLIT FESTIVAL

SW- **Wilmington** Courthouse. (877) 428-4748. Celebrate the birthplace of the banana split (first made at Hazzard's Drug Store in 1907). (2nd weekend in June)

JULY

CRUISIN' ON THE RIVERFRONT

C – **Columbus**, Riverfront. (614) 258-1983. Hundreds of classic cars and motorcycles. 50's style diner food, oldies bands, Elvis Extravaganza Impersonator Contest, Canine scavenger hunt, kid's corner, rides, climbing wall, arts & crafts. (Last weekend in July)

FOLKLIFE CELEBRATION

C - **Columbus**, Village Green, (Worthington). (614) 431-0329. A celebration of living traditions in crafts, performances and foods. Includes the cultures of Africa, Asia, Germany, India, Europe and Appalachia. (Last Saturday in July)

U. S. AIR & TRADE SHOW

CW – Dayton International Airport, **Dayton**. (937) 898-5901. **www.usats.org**. This is the leading event of its kind highlighted by the outstanding civilian and military air show performances. The event includes ground flight simulators, aerobatics, barnstormers, air races, pyrotechnics and sky divers. Admission. (3rd weekend in July)

JULY 4TH CELEBRATIONS

All cities listed (by area, alphabetically) include parades, entertainment and fireworks.

C - _Ashville_ (740) 983-4797

C - _Columbus_ (614) 891-2666. Red, White & Boom! July 3rd. Largest fireworks display synchronized to music and lights in the Midwest.

C - _Columbus_ (614) 298-2901. Independence Day at Ohio Village. Old fashioned activities in a re-created Civil War-era town.

C - _Dublin_ (614) 761-6500

C - _Marysville_

CE - _Deersville_, Tappan Lake Park (740) 922-3649

CE - _Martins Ferry_ Sky show.

CE - _Massillon_ Picnic in the Park, Stadium Park.

CE - _Zanesville_ (740) 452-7571. Stars & Stripes on the River.

CW -_Beavercreek_

CW - _Centerville_ (937) 433-5898. Americana Festival

CW - _Dayton_ (937) 225-4674 Jefferson Township Days. July 3-6.

CW - _Huber Heights_ (937) 233-5700 Soar to New Heights. July 2-5.

CW - _Lakeview_, Indian Lake (937) 843-5392 Decorated boat parade.

NC-_Mansfield_ Beach Party & Fireworks.

NC - _Mansfield_ (419) 756-6839 Freedom Festival. Airport air show.

NC - _Perrysville_ Fourth of July Beach Party, Plsnt Hill.

SC - _Waverly_ (740) 947-4349. Boat Parade.

NC - _Port Clinton_ (419) 734-5522

NC - _Put-in-Bay_ (419) 285-2804 Perry's Victory Memorial. 3 days.

NE - _Austintown_

NE - _Brunswick_

NE - _Cleveland_ (216) 623-1105. Festival of Freedom

NE - _Eastlake_ (440) 951-1416 Freedom Festival. July 3-6. Boat races.

NE - _Fairport Harbor_ (440) 357-6209 Mardi Gras. July 2-6.

NE - _Garfield Heights_ Home Days Festival. July 2-6.

NE - _Ravenna_ Balloon A-Fair Fourth of July

SE -_Marietta_ (740) 376-0055 Red, White & Blues

SW - _Cincinnati_ All American Birthday Party

NW - _Lima_. (419) 223-1010. Star Spangled Spectacular.

SW - _Hillsboro_ (937) 393-9957. Festival of the Bells. July 3-5.

SW - _Jeffersonville_ (740) 426-6331 Community Days.

INDIAN POW WOW

CW - Peddler's Market. **Springfield**. (937) 663-4345. (July)

ASHLAND BALLOONFEST

NC - Main Street, **Ashland**. (419) 281-4584. Hot air balloon races and twilight balloon glow. Ashland is a top balloon manufacturer – factory tours available. (Long weekend before 4th of July)

LORAIN COUNTY AIR SHOW

NC – Lorain County Airport, 44050 Russia Rd, **Elyria**. (440) 323-4063. Military & civilian aircraft, land and air. WWII to present. (4th weekend in July)

GREAT MOHICAN INDIAN POW-WOW

NC - Mohican State Park, SR-3, 1 mile south of **Loudenville**. (419)994-4987. **www.mohicanreservation.com/powwow**. Nine different tribes gather to a pow-wow featuring foods, music, crafts, hoop dancers and storytellers. Learn the proper throwing of a tomahawk or a new Native American custom. Admission. (2nd weekend in July and 3rd weekend in September)

IRISH FESTIVAL

NE - Cuyahoga County Fairgrounds, 164 Eastland Blvd., **Berea**. (440) 251-1711. Irish culture at its best with dancing , music, arts & crafts, storytelling and workshops. Admission. (3rd weekend in July)

GREATER YOUNGSTOWN ITALIAN FEST

NE - Canfield Fairgrounds, **Canfield**. (330) 549-0130. Celebrate Italy with food, music, crafts, contests, rides and games. Admission. (July)

KIDSFEST

NE – Nautica Entertainment Complex, **Cleveland**. (216) 247-2722. Playground World Pavilion, Treasure Island, sand castle building, Edible Art, Thomas the Train and great kid's entertainment. Admission. (2nd weekend in July)

ZOO BLOOMS

NE - Cleveland Metroparks Zoo, 3900 Brookside Park Drive, **Cleveland**. (216) 661-6500. Tours of the zoo's specialty gardens, a children's garden activity area and a ladybug release (100,000 ladybugs). Admission. (July – Saturday only)

ALL AMERICAN SOAP BOX DERBY

NE – Derby Downs, 1-77 & State Route 244 East, **Akron**. (330) 733-8723. The annual gravity "grand prix" of soap box derby racing is still run the same way since 1934. Youths from over 100 local competitions participate and learn workmanship, completing a project and competing. Parade at 10:00 a.m. Admission. (One of the last weekends in July or first weekends in August)

LAGRANGE STREET POLISH FESTIVAL

NW - Lagrange Street between Central & Mettler Sts., **Toledo**. (419) 255-8406. All kinds of Polish foods, polish bands, dancers, a polka contest, rides and craft area. Free. (1st full weekend in July)

AUGUST

OHIO'S AGRICULTURAL FAIRS

(614) 728-6200. Schedules available through the Ohio Department of Agriculture.

CIVIL WAR ENCAMPMENT

C - Ohio Statehouse. **Columbus**. (800) 345-4FUN. Union infantry, encampment, magic lantern show, 19th century games, cooking demos. (2nd weekend in August)

OHIO STATE FAIR

C – Ohio Expo Center, I-71 & 17th Avenue, **Columbus**. (614) 644-4000. **www.ohiostatefair.com**. Includes the largest junior fair in the nation, small circus, laser light shows, petting zoo, rodeo, tractor pulls, horse shows, fishing and lumberjack shows, exhibitors from agriculture to the arts, rides and big name entertainment. Admission. Family Value Days. (17 days beginning the end of the 1st week of August)

KIDS ZOOFARI

C - **Columbus** Zoo (Powell). (614) 645-3581. Fun food, magicians, clowns, storytellers, performances. Admission. (August - Saturday evening only)

IRISH FESTIVAL

C – Coffman Park, 6665 Coffman Road, **Dublin**. (614) 761-5400. A weekend of all things Irish, from entertainment, dance competitions and sports demos to the very best in Irish foods. Admission. (1st weekend each August)

ALL OHIO BALLOON FESTIVAL

C – Union County Fairgrounds, **Marysville**. (800) 642-0087. Unique hot-air balloons from all over the country in colorful ascensions and a balloon glow. Balloon rides, entertainment and crafts. Admission. (August)

SWEET CORN FESTIVAL

C – Lions Park, Chautauqua Blvd., **Millersport**. (740) 467-3943. Hot buttered corn on the cob, entertainment, large midway, nightly square dancing, parade and the Nashville Show on Saturday. Fee for parking. (Usually in August, occasionally held in September)

ZUCCHINI FESTIVAL

C – Lancaster Park, **Obetz**. (614) 497-2518. Try some yummy zucchini fudge or burgers while seeing a parade, riding amusement rides, listening to music or looking over crafts. Free. (August)

PROFESSIONAL FOOTBALL HALL OF FAME FESTIVAL

CE - Canton. (800) 533-4302. Check out the 9 days of celebrating football greats including a parade, enshrinement ceremony and a televised professional game. Some fees. (1st week of August)

CANAL FESTIVAL

CE - Coshocton. (800) 877-1830. Historic Roscoe Village canal boat rides highlight the celebration of the canal boat era. Parade and crafts show, entertainment and fiddle contests. Admission. (3rd weekend in August)

PIONEER DAYS

CE – Gnadenhutten Historical Park & Museum, 352 Cherry Street, **Gnadenhutten**. (330) 254-4143. An 1840's pioneer encampment, entertainment, parade, arts and crafts. Free. (1st weekend in August)

TUSCARAWAS COUNTY ITALIAN-AMERICAN FESTIVAL

CE– Downtown, **New Philadelphia**. (330) 339-6405. Italian foods, pizza eating contests, bocci and morri tournaments, music and dance. Free. (August)

GRECIAN FESTIVAL

CE – Civic Center, 1101 Market Avenue, **North Canton**. (330) 494-8770. Live music, crafts shows, Greek imports gifts and delicious Greek foods and pastries. Admission. (August)

INDIAN FESTIVAL

CE – **Powhatan Point**. (740) 795-4440. An authentic Native American event including crafts, dancing, an historic reenactment, storytelling, archery and more. Free. (Last weekend in August)

MOCH SERIES HYDROPLANE RACING

CE - Steubenville - (800) 510-4442 or (740) 283-4935. Rated the #1 M.O.C.H. Hydroplane Racing Event in the United States. www.steubenvilleoh.com. (August)

MOUNTAIN DAYS

CW - Eastwood Park. Dayton. (937) 235-0701. Appalachian region heritage with music, arts and crafts, square dancing, children's activities, mountainmen, American Indians and authentic Appalachian food. (August)

SWEET CORN FESTIVAL

CW – Community Park East, Dayton-Yellow Springs Road, Fairborn. (937) 879-3238. Steamed corn-on-the-cob, crafts, entertainment, and a corn eating contest. Free. (August)

ANNIE OAKLEY DAYS

CW - Darke County Fairgrounds, 752 Sweitzer Road, Greenville. (800) 504-2995. Annie Oakley's hometown celebrates with a parade, live entertainment, a sharpshooter's contest and a contest to name Miss Annie Oakley. (3rd weekend in August)

THE WAR OF 1812 ENCAMPMENT

CW - Johnston Farm. Hardin Road. Piqua. (937) 773-2522. Re-enactors gather where General Harrison's army camped. Ohio frontier and military life, drills and skirmishes. (August)

BUCYRUS BRATWURST FESTIVAL

NC - Sandusky Avenue, Bucyrus. (419) 562-2728. German foods, live entertainment, rides, kid's activities during the day. (August)

CORN FESTIVAL

NC – North Ridgeville. (440) 327-3737. Sweet corn prepared Amish-style, parade, midway, crafts and live bands every night. Free. (August)

ANNUAL KITE FLY

NC - Perry's Memorial, **Put-in-Bay**. (419) 285-2804. Pro flyers or bring your own. (August - Saturday only)

GREAT LAKES WOODEN SAILBOAT REGATTA

NC – Battery Park Marina, **Sandusky**. (419) 871-8174. Wooden sailboats large and small are raced for special awards in many categories. Free. (August)

IRISH FEST

NE – Yellow Duck Park, State Route 46, **Canfield**. (330) 533-3773. Irish entertainment, traditional foods, border collies and more. Admission. (August)

TWINS DAYS FESTIVAL

NE – I-80/90 to SR-91, follow signs. **Twinsburg**. (330) 425-3652. The largest gathering of twins in the world (*usually over 2500*) includes twins contests, entertainment, fireworks and the nationally televised "Double Take" parade. Small fee for non-twins. Twinsburg was originally named by the Wilcox twins in the early 1800s. (1st weekend in August)

ITALIAN AMERICAN HERITAGE FESTIVAL

NE – Courthouse Square, **Warren**. (330) 393-3444. Celebrate Italian heritage with cultural exhibits, entertainment, foods, parade, competitions, games and rides. Admission. (mid-August)

RED HAWK AMERICAN INDIAN POWWOW

NE – Willow Ranch, off US-422 on South Hubbard Road, East of **Youngstown**. (330) 534-0424. Native American traditions shown through dance, song, art and food. Admission. (2nd weekend in August)

NATIONAL TRACTOR PULL CHAMPIONSHIPS

NW - Bowling Green. (888) FULPULL. **www.pulltown.com**. (3rd weekend in August).

GERMAN-AMERICAN FESTIVAL

NW – Oak Shade Grove, 3524 Seaman Street, **Oregon**. (419) 691-4116. Continuous live German music, foods and entertainment. Admission. (Last weekend in August)

FIESTA MEXICANA

NW – Broadway & Segur Avenue, **Toledo**. (419) 242-7071. Folkloric dancing, ethnic foods, mariachi bands, arts and crafts and gifts . Admission. (2nd weekend in August)

ALL ABOUT KIDS EXPO

SW – Convention Center, 525 Elm Street, **Cincinnati**. (513) 684-0501. Event for kids ages 2 to 12 including interactive play, nature and entertainment. Admission. (August)

OHIO HONEY FESTIVAL

SW – Courthouse Square, **Oxford**. **www.ohiohoneyfest.org** or (888) 53-HONEY. Celebrate the "Ohio Bee & Honey Week" by enjoying honey in jars, ice cream, candy and other desserts. Parades, entertainment and the world famous "Living Bee Beard". Free. (August)

OHIO RENAISSANCE FESTIVAL

SW – 5 miles East of Waynesville on SR-73 at **Harveysburg**. (513) 897-7000 or **www.renfestival.com**. The recreation of a 16th century English Village complete with costumed performers, strolling minstrels, may pole dances, full-armored jousting, sword play or feast on giant turkey legs and hearty bread bowl meals. This event is often named as one of the "Top 100 Events in North America" by the American Bus Association. Admission. (Begins end of August through mid-October)

SEPTEMBER

GERMAN VILLAGE OKTOBERFEST

C – Columbus Public School Grounds, South Grant & E. Livingston. **Columbus**. (614) 224-4300. Polka bands from local and distant towns, German foods and artists, Kinderplatz area for kids (rides, playground, youth performers, hands-on crafts and science). Admission. (1ˢᵗ full weekend after Labor Day)

GREEK FESTIVAL

C – Greek Orthodox Cathedral, Short North Area, **Columbus**. (614) 224-9020. Gyros, baklava, music, dance, tours of the church, cooking demos and videos about Greece. Admission. (Labor Day Weekend)

KIDSPEAK KIDSFEST

C – Franklin Park, 1777 East Broad Street, **Columbus**. (614) 645-3343. Hayrides, roving performers, games & prizes, hands-on crafts, rides, youth agencies and lots of freebies to take home. Free. (3ʳᵈ Sunday of September)

LITTLE BROWN JUG

C – Delaware County Fairgrounds, 236 Pennsylvania Avenue, **Delaware**. (800) 335-3247. The most coveted horse race for three-year old pacers held on the fastest half-mile track in the world. Kick off parade with the largest all-horse, mule and donkey parade east of the Mississippi. Admission. (mid-September - Saturday only)

NATIVE AMERICAN POWWOW

C – Helmat Haus, 4555 Jackson Pike, **Grove City**. (614) 443-6120. Authentic Native American dancing, arts, crafts and singing. (Labor Day weekend)

POPCORN FESTIVAL

C – **Marion**. (740) 387-FEST or **www.popcornfestival.com**. Highlights include a parade, tours of the Popcorn Museum, popcorn sculptures and nationally known entertainment nightly. Free. (Weekend after Labor Day)

BUCKEYE FLINT FESTIVAL

C – Courthouse Square, **Newark**. (740) 345-1282. Ohio's gemstone is flint rock and you'll learn everything you could want to know about flint through displays, entertainment, crafts and food preparation. Free. (Last weekend in September)

TOMATO FESTIVAL

C – Civic Park, 6800 Daugherty Drive, **Reynoldsburg**. (614) 866-2861. Ohio's tomato harvest is celebrated with things like free tomato juice, fried green tomatoes, tomato pies, tomato fudge, tomato cakes & cookies, Tiny Tim Tomatoland, crafts, parade and The Largest Tomato Contest ($100 per pound). Fee for parking. (September - Wednesday through Sunday)

BUCKEYE TREE FESTIVAL

C - **Utica** - Ye Olde Mill, 11324 SR-13. (740) 892-3921 or 800-589-5000. Celebrate Ohio's heritage and state tree. Step from a time machine into the 1800s to see Ohio artisans and craftsmen dressed in the clothing of the era to demonstrate life on the Ohio frontier. These men and women will carve, quilt, and weave with the machinery of time. The official Buckeye Tree Lady will take the stage to tell of the history of the Buckeye Tree in Ohio. Children can enjoy crafts, pony rides, zoo animals, and horse-drawn wagons. A Boy Scout group, dressed in Native American costume, will perform authentic Indian dances. Free. (2nd Sunday in September)

OHIO PUMPKIN FESTIVAL

CE – Barnesville. (740) 695-4359. All kinds of pumpkin contests (largest pumpkin, pumpkin rolling and pie eating), parade, foods, fiddle contest, rides, crafts and entertainment. Free. (Thursday – Sunday - last full weekend of September)

INTERNATIONAL MINING AND MANUFACTURING FESTIVAL

CE – Cadiz. Parades, labor force bands, a coal house, coal products and crafts, ethnic foods and a coal shoveling contest. Free. (September - Thursday thru Sunday)

OHIO SWISS FESTIVAL

CE – Sugarcreek. (330) 852-4113. Experience the best of Switzerland from Polka bands, dancing, tons of Swiss cheese, Steinstossen (stone throwing) and Schwingfest (Swiss wrestling). Free. (Last Friday & Saturday of September)

POPCORN FESTIVAL

CW – Beavercreek. (937) 427-5514. A balloon rally, live entertainment and most of all, "popcorn showers". Free. (September)

KITE FESTIVAL

CW – U.S. Air Force Museum, Wright-Patterson AFB, **Dayton.** (937) 255-4704. Kite making, safety and flying workshops. Fee for workshops. Free. (Labor Day Weekend)

PREBLE COUNTY PORK FESTIVAL

CW – Preble County Fairgrounds, 722 South Franklin Street, **Eaton.** (937) 456-7273. Start your day feasting on sausage & pancakes, and then later try some hot off the grill barbecued pork chops. Enjoy crafts, entertainment, a parade and contests. Free. (mid-September weekend)

PRETZEL FESTIVAL

CW – Veteran's Memorial Park, **Germantown**. (937) 855-7521. Food, games, rides and live music/shows. Free. (September)

RASPBERRY FESTIVAL

CW - Rothschild Berry Farm, 3143 East SR-36. **Urbana**. (800) 356-8933. Celebrate the raspberry harvest with entertainment, foods and children's activities. (September)

MELON FESTIVAL

NC – **Milan**. (419) 499-2766. **www.accnorwalk.com**. Melons in baskets, by the slice, muskmelon ice cream and watermelon sherbet. Melon eating contests. Parade, rides, crafts and a kiddie pedal tractor pull. Free. (Labor Day Weekend)

CHICKENFEST!

NE – Lake Anna, Park & Sixth Streets, **Barberton**. (330) 753-8471. "Chick-o-lympics", great chicken dishes to eat and entertainment. Free. (September)

CANFIELD FAIR

NE - **Canfield** Fairgrounds. **www.canfieldfair.com** or (330) 533-4107. Grandstand headliners, the World's Largest Demolition Derby, Truck and Tractor Pull, agricultural displays, milk a cow, pet pigs, Elephant Encounter. Admission. (September – Wednesday thru Sunday)

CLEVELAND NATIONAL AIR SHOW

NE – Burke Lakefront Airport, downtown **Cleveland**. (216) 781-0747. **www.clevelandairshow.com**. One of the nation's top air shows featuring the best in military jet demonstrations and civilian aerobatics performers. Thunderbirds and Blue Angels Flybys. Labor Day Weekend. Admission. (September)

GRAPE JAMBOREE

NE – **Geneva**. (440) 466-5262. The local grape harvest is celebrated with parades, fresh-picked grapes, grape stomping contests, grape products, rides and entertainment. Free. (September)

POTATO FESTIVAL

NE – Buchert Park, **Mantua**. (330) 274-8093. Potato foods, potato cook-off, potato stomp race, mashed potato eating contest, entertainment, rides and a parade. Fee for parking. (Saturday after Labor Day)

BALLOON A-FAIR

NE – **Ravenna**. (330) 296-3247. Downtown street festival with a parade, hot air balloon flights, fireworks and more. Fee for some events at Sun Beau Valley Farm. (3rd weekend in September)

RIVERFEST

NW – Promenade Park, downtown **Toledo**. (419) 243-8024. Festival and parade. Free. (Labor Day Weekend)

RIVER DAYS

SC – **Portsmouth**. (740) 354-6419. Parade, rides, crafts, entertainment and children's events. Free. (Labor Day Weekend)

OHIO RIVER STERNWHEEL FESTIVAL

SE – **Marietta**. (800) 288-2577. Twenty plus sternwheelers dock for the weekend, some for commercial and some for residential use. Continuous musical entertainment, fireworks and grand finale sternwheel races. Free. (Weekend after Labor Day)

OKTOBERFEST-ZINZINNATI

SW – Fifth Street, downtown **Cincinnati**. (513) 579-3191. The nation's largest authentic Oktoberfest featuring seven areas of live entertainment, food and a children's area. (3rd weekend in September)

RIVERFEST U.S.A.

SW – Sawyer Point, **Cincinnati**. (513) 621-9326. A kids carnival, entertainment, a sand volleyball open and spectacular fireworks draw hundreds of thousands of parents and children. (Labor Day - Sunday only)

THUNDER IN THE HILLS HYDROPLANE RACE

SW - Hillsboro - Rocky Fork Lake State Park. (937) 393-4883. Hydroplane boat racing, 3rd largest race in the country. Free. (September)

SCARECROW FESTIVAL

SW – **Washington Court House**. (740) 636-2340. A street fair, parade, live entertainment and a living scarecrow contest. Free. (mid-September)

CARAMEL FESTIVAL

SW – **Winchester**. (513) 695-0950. Caramel foods, live Nashville entertainment, rides and crafts, parade (Saturday), and children's show. Free. (Labor Day weekend)

APPLE FESTIVALS

Apples & cider. Apple pie eating contests. Apple peeling contests. Apple butter. Candy apples. Wagon/hayrides. Apple Dumplings. Parades. Pioneer crafts. (September / October)

❏ *Participating Areas:* Jackson, Smithfield, Lebanon, Piqua Historical Area, Aullwood Audubon Farm, Delta, Mapleside Farms (330) 225-5577, Gnadenhutten, Clinton, Groveport, Van Buren, Forest, Oak Harbor, Historic Century Village, Enon, Grand Rapids, Roscoe Village, Zoar Village, and Sauder Farm Village, Franklin County Northwest Village (at fairgrounds), The Apple Cabin (Lodi, 330/ 948-1476), Apple Hill Orchards (Mansfield, 419/884-1500), Johnny Appleseed MetroParks (Lima, (419) 221-1232), Rockwell Orchards (Barnesville, (740) 425-2710).

PIONEER / PEDDLER FESTIVALS

Early 1800's frontier life. Re-enactors, craft demonstrations, authentic open fire, wood cooked food and folk entertainment.

❑   Historic Lyme Village, Gnadenhutten Historical Park, Ye Olde Mill, and Hale Farm and Village, Clays Park Resort (800/535-5634), Governor Bebb Preserve.

HARVEST FESTIVALS

Press cider. Apple butter making. Veggie harvest. Living history demos. Lumberjacks. Butter churning. Grainthreshing.

❑   September / October
❑   Participating Areas: Lake Farmpark, Atwood Lake, Cincinnati Zoo, Bloomington, Hale Farm, Granville Strongsville, Carriage Hill Metropark Farm, Heritage Reserve Park, Wolcott Museum Complex, Lakeside, Marblehead, Burr Oak State Park, Monroe County.

OCTOBER

OKTOBERFEST

German music, dancing, food (potato salad, brats), crafts, games and rides.

❑   *Participating Areas*: Cambridge, Beaver, Conneaut, Cuyahoga Falls, Galion, Minster, Harmar Village, Boardman, Wooster, Zanesville, Urbana, Bremen, Vandalia and Portage Lakes, Stark County.

PUMPKIN PATCHES/ HAYRIDES/ CORN MAZES/ FALL PLAYLANDS

- ❑   **C** - *Buckeye Country Corn Maze*. Waldo. (740) 389-3696.
- ❑   **C** - *Lynd Fruit Farm*. Pataskala. (740) 927-7013.
       www.lyndfruitfarm.com
- ❑   **C** - *Circle S Farms*. Grove City. (614) 878-7980.
- ❑   **CE** - *Catalpa Grove Farm*. Columbiana. (330) 482-4064.
- ❑   **CE** - *Detwiler Farm*. Columbiana. (330) 482-2276
- ❑   **CE** - *Less & Less Farm*. Salem. (330) 533-6387.
- ❑   **CW** - *Fulton Farms*. Troy. (937) 335-6983.
- ❑   **CW** - *Young's Jersey Dairy*. Yellow Springs. (937) 325-0629.
- ❑   **NC** - *Apple Hill Orchards*. Mansfield. (419) 884-1500.
- ❑   **NE** - *Hillside Orchard*. Hinckley. (330) 225-4748.
- ❑   **NE** - *Mapleside Farms*. Brunswick. (330) 225-5576.
- ❑   **NE** - *Richardson Farms*. Medina. (330) 722-4029.
- ❑   **NE** - *Countryside Farm*. Lowellville. (330) 536-2178.
- ❑   **NE** - *Haus Cider Mill*. Canfield. (330) 533-5305.
- ❑   **NE** - *Patterson Farms*. Chesterland. (440) 729-9809.
- ❑   **SW** - *Minges Farm*. Harrison. (513) 367-2035.
- ❑   **SW** - *Shaw Farm*. Milford. (513) 575-2022.
- ❑   **SW** - *Windmill Farm Market*. Springboro. (513) 885-3965.

PUMPKIN FESTIVALS

Largest Pumpkin Contest.   Old fashioned games.   Rides.   Pie eating contests.

- ❑   *Participating Areas*: Hudson, Huntsburg, Huber Heights, Wellsville

PUMPKIN FESTIVAL

C – Circleville. (740) 474-7000. Ohio's largest and oldest harvest celebration has seven parades, lots of pumpkin, squash and gourds, pumpkin foods (cotton candy, burgers, chips and ice cream), rides and entertainment.   See some of the largest pumpkins and the world's largest pumpkin pie (approx. 350 lbs. and 5 feet in diameter).   Contests galore like hog calling, egg toss, pie eating and carved pumpkins. Free. (October - Wednesday thru Saturday)

ALL AMERICAN QUARTER HORSE CONGRESS

C – Ohio Expo Center, I-71 & 17th Avenue, **Columbus**. (614) 943-2346 before October, (614) 294-7469 (during show). The world's largest single breed horse show with seven acres of commercial exhibits and demos. Fee per vehicle. (Two weeks long during mid-to-late October)

WORLD'S LARGEST GOURD SHOW

C – Morrow County Fairgrounds, U.S. 42 & State Route 61 South, **Mount Gilead**. (419) 362-6446. Gourd crafts, fresh gourds, gourd cleaning and carving demos, and the gourd show parade. Even make music from a gourd! Admission. (1st full weekend – Friday thru Sunday in October)

ENCHANTED FOREST

CW – Aullwood Audubon Farm, 9101 Frederick Road, **Dayton**. (937) 890-7360. A non-scary family Halloween event including a guided walk in the woods to meet costumed animal characters and stories around a campfire. Admission. (October - last full weekend nights)

GREAT OUTDOOR UNDERWEAR FESTIVAL

CW – **Piqua**. (937) 773-1625. A fun festival celebrating Piqua's history as the "Underwear Capital of the World" (they used to have ten underwear factories, now there are none). Have fun as you enjoy a Long John parade, the Undy 500, Drop Seat Trot, Boxer Ball, Bed Races and Celebrity Underwear Auction. Free. (2nd weekend in October)

WOOLLYBEAR FESTIVAL

NC – **Vermilion**. (440) 967-4477. An annual tribute to the weather "forecasting" woollybear caterpillar with a huge parade, caterpillar races, woollybear contests for kids, crafts and entertainment. Free. (1st Sunday in October)

ASHTABULA COUNTY COVERED BRIDGE FESTIVAL

NE – Ashtabula County Fairgrounds, **Jefferson**. (440) 576-3769. Ashtabula is known as the working covered bridge capital of the Western Reserve. Enjoy a tour of 15 covered bridges during the beautiful fall season, plus entertainment, crafts, draft horse contests and a scarecrow contest. Admission. (2nd weekend in October)

JOHNNY APPLESEED FESTIVAL

NW – AuGlaize Village, off US-24, 3 miles West of **Defiance**. (419) 393-2662. The historic village is busy with crafts, apple butter, cider and molasses making, and harvest demonstrations. Admission. (October)

HOCKING FALL COLOR TOUR

SC – Hocking State Forest, **Rockbridge**. (740) 385-4402. Enjoy a guided tour at Cedar Falls and a hayride through the fall colors, along with a bean dinner. Free. (October)

PAUL BUNYAN SHOW

SE – Hocking College Campus, **Nelsonville**. (740) 753-3591. Ohio's largest forestry exposition features lumberjack competitions, forestry displays, guitar pickers championship and chainsaw sculpting. Admission. (October)

FARM FESTIVAL

SE – Bob Evans Farm, State Route 588, **Rio Grande**. (800) 994-3276. Down on the farm feeling with over 100 craftspeople, country music, square dancers, homestyle foods and contests such as apple peeling, cornshelling, cow chip throwing and hog calling. Admission. (mid-October)

HARVEST HOEDOWN FESTIVAL

SW - Bloomingburg - (740) 437-7531. A Ma & Pa look-a-like contest, antique tractor show, dog show, tobacco spitting contest, kiddie tractor pulls, old-fashioned bonnet making contest, pie baking contest, hayride, pony rides, and more! Parade (Saturday at 10:00 am). Free. (1st weekend in October)

OHIO SAUERKRAUT FESTIVAL

SW – Waynesville. (937) 897-8855. All kinds of sauerkraut foods like cabbage rolls, sauerkraut candy, pizza, and desserts, fair food, crafts and live entertainment. Fee for parking. (2nd weekend in October)

NOVEMBER

COLUMBUS INTERNATIONAL FESTIVAL

C – Veterans Memorial, 300 West Broad Street, **Columbus**. (614) 228-4010. More than 60 nationalities and cultures will participate in a mix of dance, music, foods and crafts. Educational interactive activities for kids. Admission. (1st weekend in November)

FESTIVAL OF TREES

C – **Columbus**. (614) 273-6134. More than 100 decorated trees, each with different themes, Kwanza and Hanukkah displays, music, visits with Santa and children's hands-on activities. Admission. (Late November week-long.)

DAYTON HOLIDAY FESTIVAL

CW – Downtown **Dayton**. (937) 224-1518. Dayton kicks off the holiday season with live entertainment, a large children's parade, a street fair with rides and the tree lighting. Free. (Weekend after Thanksgiving)

SUGARPLUM FESTIVAL OF TREES

CW – Convention Center, 22 East Fifth Street, **Dayton**. (937) 226-8405. Beautifully decorated trees on display along with lots of crafts of the season. Admission. (November)

THANKSGIVING DAY PARADES

Downtown Cleveland, downtown Columbus, downtown Cincinnati, downtown Hamilton and downtown Toledo.

DECEMBER

CHRISTMAS DECORATIONS/OPEN HOUSES

Buildings decorated for holidays, Santa visit, entertainment.

- ❑ Wolcott Museum Complex, Orrville Depot Museum, Allen County Museum, Paulding Museum, Shawnee State Park, Milan Museum Complex, Stan Hywet Hall & Gardens, Aullwood Audubon Center, Hanby House, Mac-O-Cheek Castle, Logan County Historical, Zoar, Belmont County Museum, Glendower State Memorial, Malabar Farm, Quail Hollow State Park, Lyme Village, City of Tiffin and Jefferson Depot, Lanterman's Mill, Oak Hill Cottage (800) 642-8282.

CHRISTMAS TREE FARMS

Travel by wagon to the tree patch where you pick and hand cut your family tree. Check out your local Parent or Family Magazine in November/December for participating farms.

FESTIVALS OF LIGHTS

All include hundreds of thousands of lights and holiday
/storybook characters. Daily, evenings (unless noted). Admission.
(Thanksgiving - January 1)

❑   **C** – *Griggs Reservoir.* Columbus. (614) 461-6285. Drive thru.

❑   **C** – *Wildlight Wonderland.* Columbus Zoo. (614) 645-3550. Ice
     skating, carolers, delicious treats and wagon/train rides. Begins
     Thanksgiving weekend.

❑   **CE** – *Christian Indian Christmas.* Gnadenhutten Historical Park.
     (740) 254-4143. Drive through display depicting Christian
     Indians celebrating Christmas. Open daily every evening in
     December.

❑   **NC** - *Firelands Festival of Lights.* The Lodge at Sawmill Creek.
     Huron. (800) SAWMILL. By car or carriage.

❑   **NW** – *Bluffton Blaze of Lights.* (419) 358-5675. Begins
     Thanksgiving weekend. Santa parade, wagon rides.

❑   **CW** – *Clifton Mill Legendary Light Display.* (937) 767-5501.
     Miniature village, Santa' s workshop and 1802 log cabin. Closed
     Tuesdays.

❑   **CW** – *The Lights at Ludlow Falls.* (937) 698-3318.

❑   **NE** – *Festival of Lights.* Yellow Duck Park. Mahoning Valley.
     Ohio's largest display. Drive Thru. Begins 3rd week of
     November.

❑   **NE** – *Country Lights.* Lake Farmpark. (800) 366-3276. Wagon
     rides, holiday shopping & music or make wooden toys at Santa's
     workshop.

❑   **NE** – *Holiday Lights.* Cleveland Metroparks Zoo. (216) 661-
     6500. Caroling, entertainment, model train display, Santa visits
     and Wolf Wilderness cabin. Weekends only.

❑   **NE** – *Holiday Lights Celebration.* Akron Zoological Park. (330)
     375-2550. Santa and delicious food.

❑   **NW** – *Lights Before Christmas.* Toledo Zoo. (419) 385-5721.
     Begins the 3rd weekend of November.

- ❑ **SC** - _Rudd's Christmas Light Display_. Blue Creek. (937) 544-
  3500. More than 250,000 lights decorate hills and valleys of 40
  acre farm. Walking tour, free.
- ❑ **SW** – _Cincinnati Zoo_. (513) 281-4700. Ice skating, decorated
  villages, and Santa. Begins Thanksgiving weekend.
- ❑ **SW** - _Holiday Lights on the Hill_. Pyramid Hill Sculpture Park.
  Hamilton. (513) 868-8336.
- ❑ **SW** – _Holiday in Lights_. Sharon Woods. (513) 381-2397.
  Begins the third of November.

TRAIN RIDES WITH SANTA

Train trip in decorated coaches with Santa. Songs and treats along
the way. Weekends only.

- ❑ **C** – _Buckeye Central Scenic Railroad_. (740) 366-2029. Dress
  warmly.
- ❑ **NC** – _Trolleyville USA_. (440) 235-4725. Heated.
- ❑ **SW** – _Turtle Creek Valley Railway_. (513) 933-8012.
- ❑ **SE** - _Hocking Valley Scenic Railroad_. (800) HOCKING.

KWANZAA FESTIVALS

A celebration of African-American people, their culture and unity.

- ❑ **NC** – _Elyria_. (440) 366-5656. Free.
- ❑ **NE** – _Tri – C_. (216) 987-4801.

CAPITAL HOLIDAY LIGHTS

C – Ohio Statehouse, downtown **Columbus**. (800) 345-4386. A
traditional candlelighting ceremony , family activities inside and a
nightly outdoor stage show with high-tech lighting effects. Free.
(All December weekends)

HOLIDAYS AT OHIO VILLAGE

C– Ohio Village & Ohio Historical Center, I-71 & 17th Avenue, **Columbus**. (800) 653-6446. Celebrate a traditional 19th century holiday complete with old-fashioned music, games, foods and shopping. Admission. (Daily for two weeks in mid-December)

LIVING CHRISTMAS TREE CONCERTS

C – Grace Brethren Church, 8225 Worthington-Galena Road, **Columbus**. (614) 431-8223. 150 voice choir fills the branches of two large trees as they sing along with a themed story and live animals. Admission. (December)

CHRISTMAS CANDLELIGHTINGS

CE – Historic Roscoe Village, State Route 16/83, **Coshocton**. (800) 877-1830. Shop all day for holiday gifts in a 19th century holiday setting and then stay for the candlelighting ceremony each night at 6:00 pm. Fee for parking. (December - Saturdays only)

HOLIDAYS AT LONGABERGER HOMESTEAD

CE - **Dresden** Area. (740) 322-5588. Holiday Light Tour, Gingerbread Classics, Snow Friends Breakfast, Holiday Parade, shopping and food. (1st - 3rd weekend in December)

CHRISTMAS MUSIC SPECTACULAR

CW – Palace Theatre, 605 North Market Avenue, **Canton**. (330) 454-8172. 85,000 lights along with toy soldiers, Victorian costumes and sing-alongs. Admission. (mid-December - Thursday thru Sunday)

HOLIDAY LANTERN TOURS

NE - Hale Farm and Village. **Bath**. (330) 666-3711. Guided by lantern light only, learn about holiday customs and legends of mid-1800 Northeast Ohio. (2nd long weekend in December thru December 23rd)

BLACK NATIVITY

NE – Karamu House, **Cleveland**. (216) 795-7070. (December)

WINTERFEST

NE – I-X Center, 6200 Riverside Drive, **Cleveland** (Brookpark). (800) 897-3942. A holiday extravaganza including games, rides, entertainment and ice skating. Begins the day after Christmas through the following weekend. Admission. (December)

TOBOGGAN RUN

NE – Cleveland Metroparks Chalet in Mill Stream Run Reservation, **Strongsville**. (440) 572-9990. Toboggan chutes 1000 feet long and 42 feet tall. Admission. Thursday – Sunday. (Month-long beginning December thru February)

WINTERFEST

NE - Eastwood Expo Center, **Niles**. (330) 534-8467. Holiday indoor amusement park with kiddie rides, carnival games, Santa Choo Choo, Frosty, Rudolph. Admission. (mid-December to late December weekends)

CAROLFEST

SW – Music Hall, **Cincinnati**. (513) 621-1919. Holiday music and caroling sing-alongs. Admission. (1st Sunday of December)

KROHN CONSERVATORY

SW – **Cincinnati**. (513) 421-4086. Huge lit evergreens, live nativity and a poinsettia Christmas tree. Admission. (December)

CHRISTMAS FESTIVAL

SW – **Lebanon**. (513) 932-1100. Holiday characters, musicians strolling the streets, a candlelit parade of sixty horse-drawn carriages, a train display and warm food. Free. (1st Sunday of December)

CHRISTMAS IN THE VILLAGE

SW – Waynesville. (513) 897-8855. Carriage rides, Victorian street strollers, carolers and a live nativity depict a traditional Dickens holiday. Free. (Two weekends in early December)

NEW YEARS EVE CELEBRATIONS

A family oriented non-alcoholic event with indoor and outdoor activities such as kid's/parent's food, entertainment and crafts, and a countdown to midnight.

- ❑ **C** – *First Night Columbus*, Ohio Statehouse Square, downtown Columbus. (614) 481-0020. **www.firstnightcols.com**. Admission.
- ❑ **NC** – *First Night*, State Routes 20 & 83, North Ridgeville. (440) 327-3737. Admission.
- ❑ **NE** - *First Night*, Downtown Akron. (330) 762-8555
- ❑ **NE** – *Opening Night*, Courthouse Square, Warren or Canfield. (330) 399-1212. Admission.
- ❑ **NW** – *First Night Lima*, Downtown. (419) 222-1096
- ❑ **NW** – *First Night*, Downtown Toledo. (419) 241-3777

NOTES

NOTES

NOTES

GROUP DISCOUNTS & FUNDRAISING OPPORTUNITIES!

Dear Coordinator:

We're excited to introduce our books to your group! These guides for parents, grandparents, teachers and visitors are great tools to help you discover hundreds of fun places to visit. KIDS ♥ PUBLICATIONS titles are great resources for all the wonderful places to travel either locally or across the region.

We are two parents who have researched, written and published these books. We have spent thousands of hours collecting information and *personally traveled over 10,000 miles* visiting all of the most unique places listed in our guides. The books are kid-tested and the descriptions include great hints on what kids like best!

Please consider the following Group Purchase options: *For the latest information, visit our website:* **www.kidslovepublications.com**

- ❑ **Group Discount/Fundraising** – Purchase books at the price of $10.00 each and offer the (~25%) savings off the suggested retail price to members/friends. <u>Minimum order is ten books</u>. You may mix titles to reach the minimum order. Greater discounts (~35%) are available for fundraisers. Call for details.

- ❑ **Available for Interview/Speaking** – The authors have a treasure bag full of souvenirs from favorite places. We'd love to share ideas on planning fun trips to take children while exploring your home state. The authors are available, by appointment, at (614) 792-6451. The minimum guaranteed order is: 30 books in Ohio, 50 books for other states. There is no additional fee involved.

<u>**Call us soon at (614) 792-6451 to make arrangements!**</u>
Happy Exploring!

Attention Parents:

All titles are "Kid Tested". *The authors and kids personally visited all of the most unique places* and wrote the books with warmth and excitement from a parent's perspective. Find tried and true places that children will enjoy. No more boring trips! Listings provide: Names, addresses, telephone numbers, websites (*except Kids Love Indiana*), directions, and descriptions. All books include a bonus chapter listing state-wide kid-friendly Seasonal & Special Events!

KIDS LOVE INDIANA ™

❖ **Discover places where you can "co-star" in a cartoon or climb a giant sand dune.** Almost 600 listings in one book about Indiana travel. 10 geographical zones, 193 pages.

KIDS LOVE KENTUCKY ™

❖ **Discover places from Boone to Burgoo, from Caves to Corvettes, and from Lincoln to the Lands of Horses.** Over 500 listings in one book about Kentucky travel. 6 geographic zones. 224 pages.

KIDS LOVE MICHIGAN ™

❖ **Discover places where you can "race" over giant sand dunes, climb aboard a lighthouse "ship", eat at the world's largest breakfast table, or watch yummy foods being made.** Almost 600 listings in one book about Michigan travel. 8 geographical zones, 237 pages.

KIDS LOVE OHIO ™

❖ **Discover places like hidden castles and whistle factories.** Almost 1000 listings in one book about Ohio travel. 9 geographical zones, 257 pages.

KIDS LOVE PENNSYLVANIA ™

❖ **Explore places where you can "discover" oil and coal, meet Ben Franklin, or watch you favorite toys and delicious, fresh snacks being made.** Over 900 listings in one book about Pennsylvania travel. 9 geographical zones, 268 pages.

ORDER FORM

KIDS LOVE PUBLICATIONS
7438 Sawmill Road, PMB 500
Columbus, OH 43235
(614) 792-6451
Visit our website: **www.kidslovepublications.com**

#	Title		Price	Total
	Kids Love Indiana		$12.95	
	Kids Love Michigan		$12.95	
	Kids Love Pennsylvania		$12.95	
	Kids Love Ohio		$13.95	
	Kids Love Kentucky		$13.95	
COMBO PRICING – INDICATE TITLES ABOVE				
	Combo #2 - Any 2 Titles		$21.95	
	Combo #3 - Any 3 Titles		$29.95	
	Combo #4 - Any 4 Titles		$36.95	
	Combo #5 - All 5 Titles		$43.95	
			Subtotal	
		(Ohio Residents Only) $1.00 per book	Sales Tax	
			Shipping	
			TOTAL	

Note: All combo pricing is for different titles only . For multiple copies (10+) <u>of one</u> title, please call or visit our website for volume discounts.

[] Master Card   [] Visa
Account Number _ _ _ _ - _ _ _ _ - _ _ _ _ - _ _ _ _
Exp Date: _ _ / _ _ (Month/Year)
Cardholder's Name _____
Signature *(required)* _____

(Please make check or money order payable to: KIDS LOVE PUBLICATIONS)

Name: _____
Address:_____
City:_____State:_____
Zip:_____Telephone:_____

All orders are shipped within 2 business days of receipt by US Mail or Fed-X Ground. Your satisfaction is 100% guaranteed or simply return your order for a prompt refund. Thanks for your order!